THE PRESENT REIGN
OF JESUS CHRIST

A HISTORICAL INTERPRETATION
OF THE BOOK OF REVELATION

D1726268

The Present Reign of Jesus Christ
By Robert Caringola

Truth in History

© Copyright 1995-2017 Robert Caringola

ISBN-10 0-9649189-0-0
ISBN-13 978-0-9649189-0-0

THE PRESENT REIGN OF JESUS CHRIST

ROBERT CARINGOLA

TRUTH IN HISTORY

OWASSO, OKLAHOMA

Contents

PART I

PART II
THE OTHER SIDE OF THE SCROLL
BEGINNING AGAIN THE CHRISTIAN ERA

DEDICATION

This book, *The Present Reign of Jesus Christ,* is written to those who at all costs have received the love of the truth. May this dissertation on the *Book of Revelation* impart to you an understanding of your destiny in Christ's growing kingdom. With this capstone of Scripture, our Lord completed His testimony using the language of the prophets, and with the spirit of prophecy, He gloriously asserted the credibility of His Word.

"NO GREATER MISCHIEF CAN HAPPEN TO A CHRISTIAN PEOPLE THAN TO HAVE GOD'S WORD TAKEN FROM THEM, OR FALSIFIED, SO THAT THEY NO LONGER HAVE IT PURE AND CLEAR. GOD GRANT WE AND OUR DESCENDANTS BE NOT WITNESSES OF SUCH A CALAMITY."

—Martin Luther
Table Talk

Foreword

Fools rush in where angels fear to tread. Many fools have been exposed by their writings. This is especially true in the area of eschatology, or end times of Bible prophecy. The apostle Paul boasted about being a fool for Christ's sake in his inspired writings of the Holy Scriptures. Robert Caringola's hard work in historical research has enabled him to understand the language of the prophets and their symbolism in Scripture. He would be classified as a "fool for Christ's sake."

Today, God is sovereignly calling out men and women to reveal His secrets of Scripture. Caringola is one of those God has chosen to reveal those secrets. The Book of Revelation is still a mystery to many Bible scholars and saints who sit in the pews of local churches. Only those who are willing to be taught by the Spirit will understand this Bible prophecy. To the rest, it will remain a mystery. Revealed truth puts faith in the reader's heart to give a future and a hope.

One of the greatest proofs of the validity and truthfulness of the Bible is fulfilled prophecy. Prophecy speaks of future events. History verifies fulfilled Bible prophecy. For this reason, history is an **essential** part of God's plan and purpose in the Revelation of Jesus Christ, the last book of the Holy Writ. Caringola has been guided by the greatest Teacher alive on planet earth in his historical interpretation of that book; the teacher is the Holy Spirit. His divine providential leading has brought forth this very timely book.

With divine wisdom, Caringola has dispelled the misinterpretation of very godly people from the past concerning this book. He does not attempt to go beyond the present hour of this prophecy, but leaves the reader with a bright hope for the future. He leaves room for the Spirit of Truth to guide us to the future triumphant return of our Lord and Savior.

For the earth shall be filled with the (revealed) knowledge of the Lord, as the waters cover the sea.

In the trials that Caringola has encountered in historical writings, he has emerged by the comfort and strength of the Holy Spirit. May the same Comforter comfort and guide you through your journey into biblical truth.

The late Wilson Phillips,
Senior Pastor
Abundant Life Ministries
Springfield, Missouri

Introduction

The Present Reign of Jesus Christ is the story of the Christian Church, a story told through the spirit of prophecy. Jesus Christ, being that very selfsame Spirit, gave to John a pre-written history of His Kingdom-just as He had given to the prophet Daniel more than six centuries before. It revealed how the Church was destined to grow from a *"stone"* to a *"great mountain and fill the whole earth"* (Daniel 2:35). This history is the very capstone of the Bible-the Book of Revelation.

There is a marked difference between the Revelation and all other New Testament writings. It does not resemble history as written in the Gospels or Acts, nor the reality of the epistles. Instead we immediately entertain the atmosphere of prophets like Daniel and Ezekiel. Jesus revealed to us the struggle of His Church seen through His eyes, veiled from the world and written in the *symbolic language* of the prophets.

The Christian church grew like a forest of understanding in its ability to interpret and apply the apocalyptic language to individual lives, changing seasons and circumstances. As the centuries passed, the picture became clearer. Christians saw not only themselves, but also the fierce anti-Christian forces which were to arise and cause much bloodshed. To be forewarned was to be forearmed. Violent storms were destined to beat against the true Church, but when the terrible tempests blew, she stood fast *"in the kingdom and patience of Jesus Christ"* (Revelation 1:9).

Before we examine John Fox's essay covering the scope of the Revelation, a startling fact must be mentioned concerning the damaging storms wrought against its true interpretation. Principles of interpretation, keys of knowledge, true prophetic understanding and sanctified common sense have been blown to the wind. When one opens the pages of this book, he will immediately notice that it is not a fanciful speculation of futuristic events. This writing is the documented fulfillment of the prophecies of the *Book of Revelation* as they have been unfolding throughout the entire Church Age. This is the Great Protestant Historical Interpretation (**Historicism**). To counter it with interpretations which teach the apocalyptic prophecies as having been fulfilled before-and encompassing the fall of Jerusalem in A.D. 70 (**Preterism**)—or to teach that the seals, trumpets and vials are reserved for yet future events (**Futurism/ Dispensationalism**)—is to strike a blow at the very heart of the Protestant faith and its blood-bought heritage. This book will vindicate that statement and clearly define those terms and their origins. Be courageous! Read on. Resist the urge to show disdain prior to thoughtful and prayerful investigation. Dr. Paley stated the issue well:

> There is a principle which is a bar against all information, which is proof against all argument, and which cannot fail to keep a man in everlasting ignorance. This principle is contempt prior to investigation.

Solomon stated the issue in more forceful language: "He who answers a matter before he hears it, is a folly and a shame unto him" (Proverbs 18:13).

The Book of Revelation is the most feared and misunderstood of all Holy Writ. The preceding paragraph gave you a clue as to why that is. We are faced with a seemingly impossible task of understanding it. What a paradox! Jesus Christ claimed this prophecy to be His revealing, "The Revelation of Jesus Christ," but in current dispensationalist teachings Christ is far from revealed. Actually, the reality of His present kingdom (Daniel 7:14; Luke 22:29; Matthew 21:43); the understanding of His rule in the midst of His enemies (Psalms 110:2) until they are all put under His feet (Psalms 110:1; Acts 3:21; Hebrews 10:12,13); and who those enemies really were and are presently are concealed now more than ever. We, the Body of Christ, have been deceived by one of the most calculated and patient deceptions in all of Christian history. This book will unmask that deception and present the true alternative which began to be taken from the Protestants in 1826. We have gone from men who lectured kings and rulers on Bible prophecy to a march in folly which has ripped destiny out of our hearts.

An example of the power of true apocalyptic interpretation is seen in the works of Robert Flemming who was invited before the English court of William of Orange, King William III, to lecture on Bible prophecy. It was approximately 1690. The king asked when the papacy would fall from its temporal power in Europe. Flemming not only instructed the king, but in 1701 also published his historicist understanding in a book called *Apocalyptic Key.* Almost a hundred years before its fulfillment, Flemming understood that the question encompassed the events of the fifth vial in the Book of Revelation and wrote the following:

> The fifth vial which is to be poured out on the seat of the beast, or the dominions which belong more immediately to, and depend upon, the Roman See; that I say this judgment will begin about A.D. 1794, and expire about 1848. B.W. Johnson, *The People's New 'Testament,* (Christian Publishing Company, 1889), page 482.

History records the French Revolution's "Reign of Terror" in the year 1794. It marked the beginning of the end of papal power in Europe, a power which she had possessed for 1,260 years. Events in 1848 further vindicate this man's remarkable insight, when the Pope was driven from

Rome. Since that date, though returned and protected by the French until 1870, the Pope's temporal power has been at an end.

Where are like teachers today? Read on and see how our magnificent Lord has asserted the credibility of His Word upon His written prophets. Read on and discover where we are in the unfolding scheme of Christ's glorious Revelation. There are still ministers who can teach with the insight of a Robert Flemming.

The challenges facing this work are formidable. The resistance will come from powerful schools of thought and entrenched paradigms, but nevertheless, outlining the ensuing destruction of the eschatological forest must be pursued. The storms have done their damage. Limbs of knowledge are scattered everywhere, and I'm going to attempt to reassemble them for you. The cliche, "You can't see the forest for the trees," applies to our situation. Turn on the television and ask yourself: "Are these teachers students of divine prophecy, or are they sensationalist speculators?" Furthermore, the most dangerous part of this book will be identifying the eye of the storm. The wreckage has left an extremely discernible trail, and I intend to follow it. Why shouldn't I? Why shouldn't you? Christ prophesied it, and according to Scripture, prophecy is a *"sure word"* (2 Peter 1:19). Be prepared for a startling revelation.

The Revelation is a book of symbolic prophecy. The credibility of the Bible stands or falls on prophetic accuracy. If the prophets prophesied inaccurately, then we have no authority to proclaim the Scriptures as "God breathed." However, history has vindicated the claims of Scripture. God has truly asserted the credibility of his Word upon the written prophets. Libraries are full of books that have recorded events which fulfilled Bible prophecy. Unfortunately, many objections are raised, by those who lack sanctified common sense, when the knowledge of history is proclaimed as *vital* in the interpretation of prophecy. They say all that is needed is the

Bible. Well, they are correct when dealing with matters like salvation but without a good understanding of history, one is crippled and infantile in his ability to interpret prophecy. Let us examine one of the prophecies of Jesus to illustrate this point.

In Matthew 23 we read of Jesus' fierce condemnation of the scribes and Pharisees. He warned them and their generation that they would be judged and destroyed for their wickedness. In Chapter 24 we read that Christ left the temple and ascended to the Mount of Olives, and the disciples followed. They were disturbed by the violent verbal exchange, but the fury wasn't over yet. From the Mount of Olives, Jesus pointed down to the temple and said, *"There shall not be left here one stone upon another, that shall not be thrown down"* (Matthew 24:2b). In other words, He prophesied the destruction of the temple. He went on to prophesy the events which would precede and encompass this cataclysmic event. He made sure they understood that His words would be fulfilled in *their generation* (Matthew 24:34).

Now a question for every student and teacher of Bible prophecy. Where in the Scriptures do we read of the fulfillment of this prophecy? Give up? Good, because its fulfillment is not recorded in Holy Writ. Where must you go to obtain the information? The history books. Thank God for Flavius Josephus and his work, *The Jewish War.* Josephus and others recorded the exact fulfillment of our Lord's prophetic utterance. In A.D. 70 the prophecy was fulfilled in every detail. God used a secular historian to glorify His word. A myriad of examples could be presented to drive home this point.

The Book of Revelation requires much the same vindication. Its object was to reveal the future. This is stated in its opening sentence, *"God gave to him [John] to show unto his servants the things which should shortly come to pass"* (Revelation 1:1). Its aim was not just limited to immediate events, but rather to show *the things* which must come to pass. In other words, it was written to reveal the outlines of coming history as far as that history would affect the destiny of the Church. The great historicist interpretation reveals *the things* (historical events) as they unfolded during the New Covenant Age. Like Josephus, God has raised up many historians to record the events as they transpired. Many did not realize they were being used of God for that purpose. The American editor of *Lang on Revelation* stated:

> The writer must acknowledge that, after a careful consideration of the principle views that had been presented, he has been constrained to the conclusion that the scheme of interpretation advocated by Elliott and Barns [historicism] is in most parts correct. The points of resemblance between the symbols and the events of history, especially as portrayed by the infidel Gibbon, are too many, too striking, and too exact, to allow the thought that they are merely fortuitous. It would seem as though God had raised up the great historian just mentioned to perform a work for the Bible and the Church, which could not have been so effectively performed by a friend. At times it seems as though he was writing history expressly to elucidate prophecy *(Lang on Revelation,* page 213).

The Revelation engulfs one in the world and language of the prophets. Their language was *symbolic.* Even a superficial reading of the Apocalypse reveals this. Nevertheless, you have been bombarded by teachers who demand literal interpretation. One example wreaks havoc upon that type of carnal thinking. For example, the first prophecy in the Bible, Genesis 3:15: *"And I will put enmity between thee and the woman, and between thy seed and her seed: it shall bruise thy head, and thou shalt bruise his heel."* A literal interpretation envisions a struggle between a man and a snake. However, interpreted in the symbolic language of the prophets, one understands that this is a prophecy about the future conflict between Jesus and Satan.

The storms of *futurism, dispensationalism* and *preterism* have left severe breaches in the foundation of prophetic truth. They must be repaired and restored. For all those who understand the compulsion to *"root out, and to pull down, and to destroy, and to throw down, to build, and to plant"* (Jeremiah 1:10), Isaiah 58:12 should be a great encouragement to you.

> And they that shall be of thee shall build the old waste places: thou shalt raise up the foundations of many generations; and thou shalt be called, The repairer of the breach, The restorer of paths to dwell in.

H. Grattan Guinness, England's great historicist teacher of Bible prophecy, wrote words of analysis and rebuke to those who dare to teach what they know not. With these words I close this preface for I am tempted to further rebuke those who have created the breach in the interpretation of the holy prophets, but I reserve for the text, the triumph of truth.

> A wide distinction exists and should be recognized between students and expositors of the Word and works of God who humbly, soberly and reverently search into the facts of nature and Scripture, of providence and prophecy, reach conclusions which sanctified common sense can approve, and speculators,

who, running away with isolated and mysterious expressions, indulge in imaginations of their own and become prophets, instead of students of divine prophecy.[1]

---

1 H. Grattan Guinness, *The Approaching End of the Age,* p. xiii.

FOX'S OVERVIEW

Every writer is tempted to strive to create something new, to enter into forms of revisionism so as to make people think that the revelation or wisdom being imparted is a new creation. A march in folly it truly is, for Solomon wrote the divine understanding long ago: *"The thing that hath been, it is that which shall be; and that which is done is that which shall be done: and there is no new thing under the sun"* (Ecclesiastes 1:9).

The overview which I have chosen to insert at this point is extracted from the late John S. Fox's book, A *Flood of Light Upon the Book of Revelation.* I pray that it will create an outline in your heart and prepare you to digest the vital information presented in this dissertation. He entitled this essay an "Essential Key Chapter"; that it truly is. The systematic teachings in this book will verify all points alluded to by Fox. Fox states:

"The Book of Revelation is deemed by many to be one of the most difficult books in the Bible; but, when properly handled, starting on the right road, with a clear understanding of the essential truths … the whole story can be understood quite easily. It is a book of symbols, written thus by our wise and loving God, who, while leaving mankind with free will or free choice, and foreseeing the moves of men and nations from beginning to end, is all the while silently overruling, and steering the barque onwards, from the fruitless ways of self-will and false religion into the haven of a world-wide kingdom for His Son in which His Will shall eventually be done on earth, even as in heaven. Through this Book of Revelation, He displays once again that He alone is God, with power to fulfill His Will; doing also what no others have been able to do: *'Declaring the end from the Beginning.'*

"Imagine the history of the world being pre-written in a language unknown to mankind! Its truth would remain hidden until such time as the words of that language could be deciphered and understood; or until events themselves interpreted the meaning. Just so with the Book of Revelation, written in symbolic language, speaking of Seals, Trumpets, Vials; of suns, moons and stars; of beasts, scorpions, dragons and colored horses; of thunders, lightnings and great woes; of earthquakes, fires, olive trees and candlesticks. It speaks, with rich contrast, of the true and the false; of the true Woman chased by a Serpent or Dragon; and of a false Woman gorgeously clothed, deceiving multitudes in the earth into believing that She alone is the one to follow. It speaks of a 'Great City' full of evil, and of a 'Beloved City' which one day will be full of glory. In Chapter 19 it speaks of great rejoicing when all that has deceived the earth is destroyed, with great multitudes saying 'Alleluia' when salvation, glory, honor, power and Truth are revealed. A 'Lamb' has appeared, bringing light into the darkness, and a precious city is built up, fashioned (symbolically) of *pure gold like unto clear glass' whose foundations are 'garnished with all manner of precious stones.'* Finally, there is a wonderful 'Bride' revealed, which, partnered by the Spirit of God, says to whosoever will: *'Come... And let him that is athirst, come. And whosoever will, let him take of the water of life freely.'*

"All these things certainly sound very wonderful: but what do they really mean? Can we unravel the story? Can we decipher the strange symbols, or find a key to unlock the hidden treasures of this Book?

SHORTLY TO COME TO PASS

"John, the apostle of Jesus Christ, described as 'The disciple whom Jesus loved,' experienced very hard times in his old age, for when he was ninety years of age he was taken to the prison-island of Patmos. There, however, in that very place, his precious Master, the risen Christ, met him face to face, passing on the whole story of the Book of Revelation.

"The opening verse of the first chapter tells us that God, who alone knows all things, had 'given' this Revelation to his beloved Son, .Jesus Christ. Jesus, when passing it on to John, told him plainly that it was a story of the things 'which must shortly come to pass.' It was a pre-written history, foretelling events from that time (A.D. 96) onwards ...

"In addition to presenting this pre-written history concerning the true Church ... , this Book of Revelation also foretold approaching developments in the great and powerful Empire of Rome, ruling the then-known prophetical 'earth.' The Empire of Rome was destined within two centuries to crack in half, and within three centuries to fall completely, making way for an entirely new System, a religious System (Papal Rome) which would succeed it and hold temporal power in Europe for a period of 1,260 years ... The latter edifice built upon self-power and religious pride, would oppose, and for a time overcome the true humble followers of the Lord Jesus Christ ... It would continue to strive for power and for world domination until the only righteous Ruler, God's Son, Jesus Christ, should come with. full authority and power from His Father, and reign over the now enlarged Israel, until finally all nations, kindreds, tongues and languages should 'serve and obey Him.'

"The story of the Book of Revelation opens triumphantly first and foremost with a glorious vision or portrait of the Lord Jesus Christ Himself as He appeared in all His resurrection fullness to His faithful servant John. May God grant that in our lives, and in the lives of the coming generation also, we all may turn our eyes upon Jesus from the beginning, and then keep Him in view always, even unto the end.

"In that prison Isle of Patmos the Lord Jesus began the story of the Book of Revelation by giving John seven individual messages to seven existing Churches ... These messages reflected also a panorama of the history of Christendom from John's day until the end of this present age.

"The actual book or scroll, as seen by John in his vision, had no pages as books have today. It was the old type of book, a Scroll, which, while being gradually unrolled, revealed the sequence of events step by step between the first and second Advents of the Lord Jesus. If we do not understand and abide by the simplicity of the sequence of the prophecies, nothing but muddled nonsense will be the outcome of our study. There is a danger, in fact, a great temptation, amongst multitudes of Bible expositors, to take an attractive-looking verse, placing it perhaps a thousand years too soon or too late, and weaving around it pure fantasy, with no backing of truth whatsoever. Such rough handling, unfortunately, has been frequently employed by many interpreters, turning men away from the Book's beauty, making it indeed a 'Mystery,' whereas God gave all Scripture for our edification to be clearly read and understood, thus unfolding and revealing His power and glory.

PAST, PRESENT OR FUTURE

"In this Book of Revelation, and elsewhere in the Bible, God foretold, exposed and denounced the works and doctrines of a great apostate Church System which would rise out of and succeed the wreckage of the pagan-Roman Empire. This System, as we shall see clearly further on, was Papal Rome. The Roman world had been ruled by paganism until the fourth and fifth century A.D.: but now a change was destined to come to pass, this new-found Power being clearly symbolized in the Book of Revelation as a *religious* Power by saying that it would be seen sitting '*in the temple of God';* that is to say, in the Church itself, swaying the lives of men and nations and ruling with great power from a self-appointed pinnacle which it had set up.

"As the darkness of the middle ages thereafter began to be illuminated by the hard-won labors of the Reformation, all the Reformers *without exception* had it revealed to them by the Spirit of God that Papal Rome had fulfilled exactly every detail foretold concerning this new religious edifice, and was therefore, this apostate or Anti-Christ Power, which, while purporting to be the only true Church of Christ, was actually fighting against Him and His.

"When this devastating exposure became revealed from the Scriptures themselves, the first reaction of Papal Rome (as also foretold in the Word of God) was to try to destroy the Bible. They thus gathered all the early-English Bibles they could lay their hands on, and had public burnings of them. One of these ceremonies was conducted by Bishop Tunstall in A.D. 1530 at Paul's Cross, when William Tyndale's English translation of the New Testament was burnt publicly. However, when this endeavor eventually proved fruitless, they began to massacre and burn at the stake the living witnesses of the Truth, two of the most notable of whom were Bishops Ridley and Latimer who were burnt alive at Oxford in A.D. 1555 during Catholic Mary's reign.

"When it was seen that both these drastic measures failed to stem the incoming tide of truth and of the kingdom of God on earth, the only procedure remaining to the Papal Church was to endeavor to misinterpret all such verses of Scripture which foretold and condemned its System, making the condemnation contained in these verses appear to fall, if possible, on some other party instead of upon themselves. This endeavor, however, soon produced two opposing schools of thought even within their own ranks.

These constituted the two categories numbered 1 and 2 below:

1. PRETERISTS. The school known as the *Praetorists* declared that the anti-Christ Power of Scripture had already come and gone, being fulfilled in the Roman Emperors Vespasian and Titus who had attacked the Jews, ransacked Jerusalem and burnt the Temple, in the year A.D. 70. [This was the work of the Spanish Jesuit, **"Alcazar."**]

2. FUTURISTS. The school known as the *Futurists* said that this great power must be future, even suggesting that it would not appear until after the Second Advent of Jesus Christ. The originator of this second erroneous thesis was a Jesuit called **'Ribera.'** [It was this Jesuit who first *"broke"* the divine time measure of the seventy weeks of Daniel 9. He extended the final week (seven years) into the future, yet to be fulfilled.]

3. HISTORICISTS. Quite distinct from the two foregoing schools of thought were the Reformers, who were <u>all without exception</u> *Historicists;* that is to say, those who believed that the Book of Revelation (accompanied by the prophecies of Daniel and others) foretold a perfect sequence of the history of Christendom throughout this present evil age from beginning to end; and that it also exposed with paramount certainty the complete failure of both pagan and Papal Rome to bring in Christ's kingdom.

"Since the Book of Revelation is a pre-written history of Christendom, then obviously a knowledge of history is essential for its correct interpretation. It is God's Word in which He most wonderfully foretold (A.) The history of the true Church; (B.) The rise and fall of pagan Rome, with its useless military pagan rule of force; (C.) The rise and fall of Papal Rome, with its useless apostate System of false religious rule; (D.) The preparation for, the rise of, and unshakable endurance of God's rapidly-approaching kingdom of righteousness and truth, reigned over by His beloved Son, our Lord Jesus Christ, aided by the tested and proven members of His faithful elect or Church, who will reign with Him *"over the House of Jacob"* (Luke 1:32-33), to perfect the latter first; and then finally lead *'all nations of the earth'* into God's way of peace, happiness and life, until His kingdom fully comes, and His will is *'done on earth, even as it is done in heaven.'* "

THE DATE

It is important that a brief consideration of the date of the Revelation's authorship be addressed at this point. A literature war between the *Futurists/Dispensationalists* (Ribera's theologians) and the *Preterists* (Alcazar's theologians), concerning this issue is currently going on.

Remarkably, the futurists and the historicists both agree, and rightly so, that the true dating of the Book of Revelation occurred near the end of Domitian's reign, which would put the date at approximately A.D. 96. However, it is the contention of preterist writers that the Apocalypse must have been written sometime before the fall of Jerusalem, A.D. 70. I believe their most consistent date is A.D. 68. It basically amounts to two false interpretations jockeying for position against one another. Futurists and preterists (remember, these are Catholic counter-Reformation teachings) find themselves caught in the same contradiction when it comes to the *most vital* of the interpretative issues: **the year-for-a-day principles!** Are the prophetical days in the books of Daniel and the Revelation interpreted as literal days, or does the prophetic code of Ezekiel 4:6 apply, which states: *"I have appointed thee each day for a year?"*

I addressed this immense contradiction in my book *Seventy Weeks: The Historical Alternative.* My point here is to simply equip you with a basic understanding of this quagmire, by presenting an outstanding excerpt from B. W. Johnson's *The People's New Testament.* His is not the only essay on this issue. Other commentators of even greater historical and scholastic weight could be presented here, but I believe Johnson's version is extremely reader-friendly. If you consider this issue irrelevant, then please go on to the next chapter. It won't affect your understanding of this book. Johnson's argument:[2]

"Only two dates for the composition are named, (1.) that always assigned to it by the ancient church, near the end of the reign of the Emperor Domitian, which extended from A.D. 81 to A.D. 96, and (2.) that which has been urged by certain modern critics, the latter part of the reign of Nero, about A.D. 65-68. The first date is supported by the historical testimony. *It is urged in behalf of the second that there are internal evidences in its favor, but when these are examined they are found to resolve themselves into certain theories of interpretation* [Alcazar's] *and were it not for the necessity of these, this date would never have been proposed* [italics mine]. Before stating the grounds for assigning the date to the latter part of the reign of Domitian, about A.D. 95, 96, I will briefly consider the reasons urged in favor of the date in the reign of Nero. It is held (1.) that the work must have been written while the temple was still standing (Rev. 11:1) and that chap. 11:2 and chap. 20:9 prove that the City of Jerusalem was still standing but in a state of siege. It seems strange to me that a Bible student could use this argument. Every New Testament student knows that both the temple and Jerusalem are used elsewhere as symbols of the church, and how much more likely that the terms would be used as symbols in a book which is largely composed of symbols from beginning to end! It seems strange that in a vision composed of symbols any one should insist that John on Patmos, a thousand miles distant, literally saw the temple or Jerusalem. Besides, when John in chap. 11:8 speaks of the city as spiritually called Sodom and Egypt, he shows that he cannot mean the literal Jerusalem. A holy city is the symbol of the church; a wicked city symbolizes an apostate church; a city trodden down by the Gentiles,

---

2   Should you desire to examine a much weightier argument, I recommend that you study the points debated by the great E. B. Elliott. In the fourth volume of his yet-to-be-matched dissertation on the Apocalypse entitled *Horae Apocalypticae,* he wrote in the appendix a "CRITICAL EXAMINATION AND REFUTATION OF THE THREE CHIEF COUNTER-SCHEMES OF APOCALYPTIC INTERPRETA-TION..." page 529.

is a church overcome by worldly influence. The language of chap. 20:9 utterly excludes the Jewish capital in the reign of Nero.[3] (2.) It is held that chap. 17:11 refers to Nero, and hence as will be shown in the text, a forced interpretation is made the basis for determining the date. The theory itself is skeptical in that it convicts John of holding and sanctioning a popular error. (3.) It is also urged that there are certain solecisms in the Greek original which are wanting in John's gospel, and from this it is argued that the Revelation must have been written much earlier than the gospel, before John had fully mastered the language. Upon this point I quote from Prof. Wm. Milligan, of the University of Aberdeen, Scotland, a thorough scholar in New Testament Greek: 'The solecisms [grammatical errors; deviation from correct idiom] are not such as proceed from an ignorance of the Greek language, and they would not have been removed by greater familiarity with it. However we attempt to account for them, they are obviously designed, and imply a more accurate knowledge of the grammatical forms from which they are intentional departures. At the same time, in the book are passages (for example chap. 18) which, in their unsurpassable eloquence, exhibit a familiarity of the Greek tongue, on the part of the writer, were explanation necessary.'[4] (4.) It is said that the Jewish imagery belongs to John's earlier rather than his later years. To this it may be replied that no New Testament writer shows a stronger Jewish feeling than is found in John's gospel. It is John who states, "Salvation is of the Jews" (John 4:22); that Jesus is "the King of Israel" (John

---

3   The exegetical assumption of modern critics that this passage (Rev. 11:1) proves the temple at Jerusalem to have been still standing at the time when the Apocalypse was written affords another sign of the deep fall of these critics into a false literalism. *Lang on Revelation,* page 26.

4   Winer *(Grammar of the Greek Testament),* discussing the solecisms of the Apocalypse, says, "In some instances they are the result of design; in other they are to be referred to carelessness on the part of the writer ... In this light they should always be considered, and not ascribed to the ignorance of the writer, or regarded Hebraisms ... But, with all the simplicity and the oriental tone of his language, the author knows well and observes well the rules of the Greek syntax" (page 672). It also should always be kept in mind that Revelation is written, not as a calm, sedate, elaborate composition, like John's gospel, but with the fire and ecstasy of a prophet. This accounts for the differences of style.

1:49), and Old Testament thoughts and figures constantly appear in the fourth gospel.

THE REAL DATE

"It is thus seen that the argument in favor of the early date [A.D. 68] is easily answered. On the other hand the *historical* argument in favor of the later date [A.D. 96] is convincing to the mind which can be swayed by historical evidence. Commencing with the positive and definite statement of Irenaeus there is unbroken agreement for nearly four centuries that the date of the work belongs to the persecution of the reign of Domitian. 'To properly weigh the statement of Irenaeus, born in the first quarter of the second century, and elected Bishop of Lyons in A.D. 178, it is necessary to keep in mind he was a disciple of Polycarp, who suffered martyrdom in A.D. 155. In one of his letters Irenaeus speaks to a fellow disciple of how intimate they had been with Polycarp and how often they had heard the aged saint tell of John the apostle. Hence it is apparent that Irenaeus must have known from Polycarp the leading facts of John's history, and especially the circumstances connected with his exile to Patmos. This witness, whose opportunity for knowing the facts is unquestioned, declares, *"Revelation was seen no long time since, but almost in our generation, towards the end of the reign of Domitian"* (A.D. 96). With this plain statement agree all the church fathers who speak of the subject, not only of the second century, but for three centuries. There is no variation in the historical accounts. All statements support the conclusion that St. John was banished to Patmos by Domitian (A.D. 81-96). Some writers place the exile in the fourteenth [year] of his reign, and all agree that the Visions of which Revelation is the record were received in Patmos.[5]

---

5 *The Bible* (Speaker's) *Commentary.* New Testament, Vol. IV, page 432.

"One writer in the fourth century makes the blunder of assigning the banishment to the reign of Claudius Caesar, a blunder which finds no endorsers, a blunder which is supposed to have been a verbal mistake, *but it is not until the sixth century that we find the opinion expressed that the banishment belonged to the persecution of the reign of Nero* [italics mine], and up to the twelfth century there are only two writers who endorse this date. They cannot be called witnesses, since the earliest of them was separated from the death of John by a period greater than that which separates us from the discovery of America by Christopher Columbus. Hence, it is no misstatement of the facts to say that the historical proof, in favor of the later date, is uniform, clear and convincing.

INTERNAL TESTIMONY

"The historical conclusion is corroborated by convincing internal testimony. I condense from Godet's *Bible Studies,* second series, certain points which bear upon the question of Date: (1.) 'The condition of the churches indicated' in the second and third chapters renders the early date improbable. These churches were not founded before A.D. 55-58. Paul wrote to two of these churches, Ephesus and Colosse, in A.D. 62 or 63; Peter wrote to all the churches of that region several years later still; Paul wrote his second letter to Timothy, at Ephesus, probably as late as A.D. 67; in these letters there is no hint of John being in that section of the world, or of the spiritual decay revealed in the letters to the angels of the churches of Ephesus, Sardis and Laodicea; yet this theory requires us to believe that no later than A.D. 68 or 69, John found these churches spiritually dead. There is no reasonable doubt, but that the second and third chapters of Revelation describe a condition which could only have arisen a generation later than the date of Paul's last contact with these churches. (2.) Godet notes the fact that an ecclesiastical organization reveals itself in the seven churches about the close of the first century. In each church there is one man, 'the angel of the church,' through whom the whole church is addressed. There is no hint of any individual enjoying a distinction like this until about the beginning of the second century. (3.) The expression, 'the Lords-day,' does not occur in the earlier apostolical writings. They always speak of the "First Day of the week" instead. The term used in A.D. 68 was "the First Day of the week," but the writers of the second century from the beginning use "the Lord's-day." This term, then, points to a period near the beginning of the second century as the date of Revelation. (4.) The expressions in chap. 2:9 and 3:9 point to a complete separation between the church and the synagogue. This complete separation did not take place until the epoch of the destruction of Jerusalem. Such language as we find in these two places can only be accounted for by a fact so momentous as the overthrow of the Jewish states and hence belongs to a later date.

"This discussion might be continued, and it is of importance to any correct interpretation that the date should be clearly settled, but I believe that enough has been said to show that all the facts point to 'near the end of the reign of Domitian, or about the year A.D. 96.' It might be of service to add that the persecution of Nero, as far as it is known, *was* local and confined to Rome; that death, instead of banishment, was the favorite method of punishment with him; that it is not probable that he would have *put to death* Paul and Peter and *banished* John; and that there is no evidence that John, as early as A.D. 68, had ever visited the region of the seven churches. On the other hand, the persecution of Domitian was not local; we know also that he sent other Christians into exile; we know also that the later years of John's life were passed at Ephesus and in the region of which it was the center."

Thus ends Johnson's arguments. I pray that you have examined them. If you still have your doubts, that's OK. It is the systematic unfolding of the Revelation which will establish the truth of its historical interpretation. Remember what the preterists aren't telling you (most don't know themselves) is that their historical argument is necessitated to propagate Jesuit theology-Alcazar's deception-an interpretation of the prophecies which were designed to crush the Protestant Reformation!

FALSE TEACHERS

Second Peter 2:1-2:

> *But there were false prophets also among the people, even as there shall be false teachers among you, who privily shall bring in damnable heresies …*

> *And many shall follow their pernicious ways; by reason of whom the way of truth shall be evil spoken of.*

For one to proclaim at this point in history that "God has flawlessly asserted the credibility of His Word upon His prophets," is truly a daring move, considering all the prophecy books which have been written in the last few decades. What nonsense most have been! Christians are just about fed up with prophetic speculators. I wish we could laugh, but we can't. The results have been tragic. Many ministers are scared and confused. They don't know what to believe anymore. Teachers who study Church history are continually faced with *startling contradictions* between their beliefs in eschatology and what the historic positions of the Church have been- positions which were well thought out and experienced by some of the greatest minds and martyrs Christianity has produced, beginning with the apostles. On the Day of Pentecost, Peter arose, not just in boldness, but likewise with knowledge and divine revelation. Notice very carefully his words and his quote from Psalm 110:1. This volley alone destroys dispensationalism's entire prophetic scheme. Acts 2:32-35 says:

> *32 This Jesus hath God raised up, whereof we all are witnesses.*
> *33 Therefore being by the right hand of God exalted, and having*

received of the Father the promise of the Holy Ghost, he hath
shed forth this, which ye now see and hear.
34 For David is not ascended into the heavens: but he saith
himself, The Lord said unto my Lord, Sit thou on my right hand,
35 Until I make thy foes thy footstool.

Peter proclaimed that Christ will remain enthroned in the heavenly, *"ruling in the midst of his enemies"* (Psalm 110:2b), until all his enemies are defeated. This testimony is further emphasized by Peter's proclamation that the heavens must *"receive"* and *"retain"* Christ until the restoration promised by *"all his holy prophets since the world began"* (Acts 3:20,21). This truth is further expounded by the writer of Hebrews 10:12-13:

> *But this man, after he had offered one sacrifice for sins for ever,*
> ***sat down*** *on the right hand of God;*
> *From henceforth expecting* ***[waiting]*** *till his enemies be made*
> *his footstool.*

Friends, do you see what is consistently being proclaimed by the Scriptures? *All the enemies of Christ* and His Church must fall before He can be released from the heavenly. For example: Islam must fall; Hinduism must fall; Catholicism likewise must fall first. Are you getting the picture? Similarly, Paul proclaimed this truth about the end without contradiction to the teachings of Peter or David. He stated:

> ***Then cometh the end ...*** *when he shall have put down all*
> *rule and all authority and power. For he must reign [from his*
> *heavenly throne; through his body], till he hath put all enemies*
> ***under his feet*** *(1 Corinthians 15:24,25).*

Who are Christ's feet? Paul recorded this revelation for us. When writing to the Ephesian church, the apostle used the example of marriage to teach a symbolic principle of the Church. He stated, *"For the husband is the head of the wife, even as Christ is the head of the church: and He is the savior of the body"* (Ephesians 5:23). He also stated that Christ is *"far above all principality, and power, and might, and dominion … and hath put all things under His feet, and gave Him to be the **head over all things to the church, which is His body…***" (Ephesians 1:21-23). In Colossians 1:18, Paul wrote, *"And He is the Head of the body, the church…"* These verses of Scripture clearly reveal that Christ is the Head of His Body, the Church. If Christ is our Head, and we are His Body, it appears logical to **assume** that we have feet. Have you ever seen feet connected directly to a head? Of course not! Feet are attached to a body. This simple truth has profound implications for eschatological interpretation. Our eschatology cannot contradict this truth which is taught many times in the Scriptures.

Now here is my point: Paul ended his letter to the Roman church with this powerful and encouraging admonition, *"And the God of peace shall bruise Satan under your feet shortly"* (Romans 16:20). We are the body and the possessors of feet. The day will come when all enemies are put under our feet. And what will happen when that occurs? Christ will return.

Now where do we have the authority to teach that Christ's greatest earthly enemy, the Antichrist, will appear *after* Christ has left his heavenly throne and raptured His church? Isn't that what the futurists are trying to tell us? Do you know where this teaching came from? Do you know why it was birthed, and who birthed it? Let's open Pandora's box and discover more about Ribera and Alcazar, fathers of two damnable heresies.[6]

---

6   I intend to deal with *Futurism, Preterism,* and several other *"isms,"* contrary to the Bible, in the language of Scripture. You've been warned. As you will see, when Jesus calls a religious system a *"harlot,"* I intend to attach identical terminology.

In 1585, a Jesuit priest named Francisco Ribera (1537-91) started to work independently. He looked deeply into Bible prophecy. The result of his work was a twisting and maligning of prophetic truth. Ribera's futuristic interpretation of Daniel 9 was furthered by the work of another Jesuit, Cardinal Robert Bellarmine (1542-1621). These two were swiftly followed by a third, the Jesuit Luis de Alcazar (1554-1613).

In exposing these Latin apocalyptic expositors of the Counter Reformation era, the historicist Elliott summarized their prophetic positions:

> So at length, as the 16th century was advancing to a close, two stout Jesuits took up the gauntlet and published their respective, but quite counter opinions on the Apocalyptic subject: the one **Ribera,** a Jesuit Priest of Salamanca, who about A.D. 1585 published an Apocalyptic Commentary, which was on the grand points of Babylon and Antichrist that we now call the **futurist** scheme; the other, **Alcazar,** also a Spanish Jesuit, but of Seville, whose scheme was on main points we now designate as that of the **preterists.**[7]

In fairness to the futurist/dispensationalist position, I would like to insert the following abridged excerpt from Clarence Larkin's work *Dispensational Truth.* This book was first copyrighted in 1918. It emerged on the scene shortly after the *Scofield Reference Bible,* which is hailed by the dispensationalists as an "accurate" interpretation of Scripture. The shocking point of this writing by Larkin is that he informed the reader that *he knew* why Ribera wrote, which was "…to rid the Papacy of the stigma

---

7   E.B. Elliot, *Horae Apocalypticae*, "History of Apocalyptic Interpretation," page 465.

of being called the Antichrist." And remarkably, Larkin terms Ribera's theology as having been "wonderfully revived."[8] He stated:

> The "Preterist School" originated with the Jesuit Alcazar. His view was first put forth as a complete scheme in his work on the Apocalypse, published in AD. 1614. It limits the scope of the Apocalypse to the events of the Apostle John's life, and affirms that the whole prophecy was fulfilled in the destruction of Jerusalem by Titus, and the subsequent fall of the persecuting Roman Empire, thus making the Emperor Nero the "Antichrist." The purpose of the scheme was transparent; it was to relieve the Papal Church from the stigma of being called the "Harlot Church" and the Pope from being called the "Antichrist." It is a view that is now but little advocated.[9]

> The "Historical School," … interprets the Apocalypse as a series of prophecies predicting the events that were to happen in the world and in the Church from John's day to the end of time. The advocates of this School interpret the symbols of the Book of Revelation as referring to certain historical events that have and are happening in the world. They claim that "Anti-

---

8   Clarence Larkin's charts are the basis for most of the futurist's eschatological visual teaching aids. They have been programmed in our minds. They must be washed out by *"the water of the word."* These charts not only destroy the purpose of divine time measures, they likewise pervert the true teachings of the Kingdom of God. And to make matters worse, you come away from Larkin's work thinking that God has dealt with mankind in dispensations instead of covenants-seven of them if you care to count. There is no new Jewish dispensation yet to come; it has **all** been fulfilled in the New Covenant.

9   Well Clarence, this view is picking up steam. Mainly due to the efforts of the Reconstructionists. This is a tragedy. They are some of the most brilliant biblical thinkers alive, and they seek to vindicate their teachings with preterism. They often boast that their prophetic interpretations (Chilton's/Alcazar's) are unchallengeable! Nonsense! They are easily dismantled with truth. Even Larkin could see that preterism was transparent. If they will scramble and read the great historicist writers, I believe they'll see a marvelous influx of historicism intertwined with certain relevant truths (**those addressing the Kingdom's** "growth principle") of Reconstructionism.

christ" is a "System" rather than a "Person" [not exactly true-a "dynasty" of men is the teaching], and is represented by the Harlot Church of Rome. They interpret the "Time Element" in the Book on the "Year-Day Scale."

This School has had some very able and ingenious advocates. This view, like the preceding, was unknown, to the early church. It appeared about the middle of the twelfth century, and was systematized in the beginning of the thirteenth century by the Abbot Joachim. Subsequently, it was adopted and applied to the Pope by the forerunners and leaders of the Reformation, and may be said to have reached its zenith in Mr. Elliott's "Horae Apocalypticae." It is frequently called the Protestant interpretation because it regards Popery as exhausting all that has been predicted of the Antichristian power. It was a powerful and formidable weapon in the hands of the leaders of the Reformation and the conviction of its truthfulness nerved them to "love not their lives unto the death." It was the secret of the martyr heroism of the sixteenth century. IT WAS THE UNIFYING DOCTRINE OF THE REFORMATION!

The "Futurist School" interprets the language of the Apocalypse "literally" except such symbols as are named as such [now that's consistency!] and holds that the entire Book, from the end of the third chapter, is yet "future" and unfulfilled, and that the greater part of the Book, from the beginning of chapter six to the end of chapter nineteen, describes what shall come to pass during the last week of "Daniel's Seventy Weeks."[10] This

---

10   This is the root of the rotten tree of dispensationalism, the issue of the Seventy Weeks. It was Ribera who first broke the time measure and put 3½ years of the final week into the future, hence "futurism." YOU CANNOT FIND ONE PROTESTANT WHO BELIEVED THAT LIE BEFORE 1826. More about this later. This was the central issue in my book *Seventy Weeks: The Historical Alternative*. The Seventy Weeks were fulfilled ir their entirety (B.C. 457 - A.D. 34). Get a copy of the book. I have challenged an empire of superstition with it.

view, while it dates in modern times only from the close of the sixteenth century, is really the most ancient of the three [that's a lie]... And has been restored to the Church in these last times. In its present form it may be said to have originated at the end of the sixteenth century, with the Jesuit Ribera, who, actuated by the same motive as the Jesuit Alcazar, sought to rid the Papacy of the stigma of being called the "Antichrist," and so referred the prophecies of the Apocalypse to the distant future [again, "futurism"]. This view was accepted by the Roman Catholic Church and was for a long time confined to it, but strange to say, it has wonderfully revived **since** the beginning of the nineteenth century, and that among Protestants ... [we can thank S. R. Maitland for that wonderful revival which has caused the Church to lose its destiny.][11]

John summarized the true joy of the apostles in his third epistle. He stated, *"I have no greater joy than to hear that my children walk in truth"* (3 John 4). Truth is a relevant issue with our God, as it has been with ministers all throughout history. The truth of the Book of Revelation has literally been assaulted by a flood of futuristic and preterist surges in this century. We have foolishly rejected the "old paths" (Jeremiah 6:16) in pursuit of simplified, sensationalistic speculation. Ribera and Alcazar could never have imagined that the "Protestants" would be their main propagators and apologists in the twenty first century.

Regardless of the writings or of the influence of those who teach counter schemes, the Scriptures assure us that truth will ultimately triumph. David proclaimed, *"This truth endureth to all generations"* (Psalm 100:5). And Solomon warned us, *"Buy the truth, and sell it not"* (Proverbs 23:23). Though the Body of Christ is presently drowning in dispensation-

---

11   Clarence Larkin, *Dispensational Truth*, page 5.

alism, Isaiah promised that *"like a flood, the spirit of the Lord shall lift up a standard against him"* (Isaiah 59:19), "him" being the spirit behind this deception. Dispensationalism is not just an interpretation; it's a spirit!

The leader of the Reformation, Martin Luther, declared, "Peace if possible, but truth at any rate." I feel that we have no option but to be like-minded. These issues are not the trivial pursuit of heady irrelevant theological issues. Rather, the very truth of the gospel of the Kingdom is threatened. Ministers today are faced with the same challenges presented to the Reformation fathers. Antichrist must again be identified and put behind us, or may I say, put under our feet, and the business of Kingdom growth and destiny again be proclaimed from the pulpits. The Reformation father Philip Melanchthon stated the case plainly. He argued, "**We cannot yield, nor can we desert the truth.**"[12]

And, thank God, Luther himself remained determined in the arena of unfolding truth. "I am vexed not a little," he said, "by this talk of compromise, which is a scandal to God." These two men, embracing the truths which the historicist interpretation revealed, believed that these truths were worth fighting and dying for. Let's now begin to equip our fundamental understanding, outline, and systematically examine the great Protestant Historical Interpretation of the Book of Revelation. In doing so we will discover what Ribera and Alcazar removed from the Body of Christ—the true knowledge of Antichrist.

---

12   R.Tudor .Tones, *The Great Reformation,* page 141. Melanchthon made this stand at the Diet of Augsburg, 1530.

PROPHETIC PERIODS

The beauty and genius of the symbolic language in the Revelation is enhanced by several prophetic periods which I will refer to as *divine time measures*. You will recall that the English historicist Robert Flemming was able to calculate the year, or the approximate *era*, in which the papacy's temporal dominion of Europe was destined to fall. How did he do this? He called upon his knowledge of the Revelation's *year-for-a-day* principle to correctly interpret the prophetic times.

In Washington, D.C. at a theological summit. A friend arranged a lunch engagement with the late David Chilton, author of several books on the subject of preterism. He is hailed by some in the Reconstructionist camp as beyond challenge in his prophetic teachings. As we broke bread and entered into debate, I turned our conversation to the subject of the year-for-a-day application when interpreting divine time measures of the Bible. Of course, the context dictates the interpretative scale. I said, "David, by what authority do you interpret the divine time measure of Daniel's seventy weeks a year-for-a-day, but when it comes to the rest of the prophetic periods, both in Daniel and the Revelation, you interpret (as the dispensationalists do) each day on the literal scale (day-day theory)? Would you please explain that to me? And by what *authority* do you teach this?" I went on to remind him that it was on Alcazar's authority, not Christ's. I continued to share with him historical examples of men who understood this code and applied it with staggering accuracy. He had no comment.[13]

---

13   I reference the reader to my chapter entitled, "Thomas Newton's Year-Day Principle," in my book, *Seventy Weeks: The Historical Alternative*. I show how both Newton and Adam Clarke were able to predict an event (to the year) centuries before it transpired.

This is a vital issue in prophetic study. Without knowledge of the year-for-a-day interpretation, you have no insight as to the staggering accuracy of the Book of Revelation, specifically as it covers several important periods of Church history. It is a history written in advance, a history written in the symbolic language of the prophets. Only the God of the Bible has been able to encapsulate history within the confines of His foretold will. Thus in written form, He establishes His power and authority over all.

There are eight divine time measures in the Book of Revelation. I will not address the Millennium at this point. They are:

1. The ten days' tribulation of the church at Smyrna   Rev. 2:10
2. The duration of the scorpion torment   Rev. 9:5
3. The career of the Euphratean horsemen   Rev. 9:15
4. The time of the down-treading of the Holy City   Rev. 11:2
5. The prophesying of the two witnesses   Rev. 11:3
6. The time they lay unburied   Rev. 11:9
7. The sojourn of the woman in the wilderness   Rev. 12:6
8. The period of the domination of the beast   Rev. 13:6

I don't intend to present a vast and comprehensive study on the measurement of prophetic periods. There are several outstanding works written on this issue.[14] However, I do want to outline the concept. As you read through the historical interpretation of the Revelation it will become apparent that what I am now presenting is truth. I will begin with the contemplations of the prophet Daniel. The prophetic books of Daniel and Revelation are a double witness to the sovereign growth, struggle and

---

14   The following works will equip any serious student with a good knowledge of prophetic measures. It is a biblical study long forgotten and feared by dispensationalists. The works are: Dr. H. Grattan Guinness' *Light for the Last Days* and *The Approaching End of the Age*. Rev. E.P. Cachemaille's *The Visions of Daniel and of the Revelation Explained*, and Uriah Smith's *Daniel and the Revelation*.

triumph of the kingdom of God on this earth. They are inseparable. It is to E. P. Cachemaille's *The Visions of Daniel and of the Revelation Explained,*[15] that this brief discourse is very largely indebted.

Great revelation has of the last several centuries been shed upon the measurement and understanding of the Bible's prophetic periods or divine time measures. We can see the importance of this knowledge in the life and struggles of the prophet Daniel. Now relative to the divine time measures that he was given it is understood that *"the words were shut up and sealed till the time of the end"* (Daniel. 12:9). It is logical to assume that as the time of the end draws near, the meaning of those prophetic times must become clearer. Not only are the meanings relevant, but also the application of them when revealing the destiny of the Church.

The purpose of this chapter is to acquaint you with some principles whereby the divine time measures are applied and interpreted.

When Daniel studied the prophecies of his predecessor Jeremiah (Daniel 9:1-2), who wrote a record of tragic events which transpired while Daniel was yet a child, the prophet perceived that the Babylonian captivity of the Jews had not been a single catastrophe, but rather a gradual process; and that it was accomplished in stages during a period of about twenty years. The margin of decay was widely relative to the seventy year period of captivity. Somewhere in this period, the initial date of the captivity needed to be found; but it was not an easy task. The Jewish monarchy had tottered and collapsed in several successive disasters. Which one defined the historic beginning? This question was complicated by the fact that the events were near his own time.

Moreover, what type of year was the captivity to be measured by? Dear reader, don't panic; there are three kinds of years used in the calcu-

---

15   E.P. Cachemaille, *The Visions of Daniel and of the Revelation Explained,* "The Measurements of Prophetic Periods," pages 109-132.

lation of divine time measures in Scripture. This knowledge was critical for Daniel, because the actual time of the captivity could vary up to two years depending on the measurement used.

While contemplating this scenario, Daniel must have concluded that the restoration might be as gradual as the captivity had been. Therefore, these events might occupy *"eras"* rather than specific events. This is an important point to keep in mind. However, as we go through the Book of Revelation, we will see many identifiable specific dates signaling the beginning and ending of several prophetic periods. Where there is justifiable historic variation, I will rely on the most credible scholars and sanctified common sense.

The position of historicist students on prophecy at present is very similar to that of Daniel. The Book of Revelation reveals to us that we are on the verge of a great transition. Many call it a Restoration. I prefer Reformation. (The dispensationalists don't know what to call it. I believe their favorite term is "Escape.") I hope we will rival the Protestant Reformation of the sixteenth century, both in revelation knowledge and in the glorious struggle it will dictate. True students of Bible prophecy are presently comparing the facts of history with the remaining forecasts of prophecy.

Scholars such as Grattan Guinness received immense help in their studies of prophetic periods from the knowledge of astronomy, which taught them that God measures years in different lengths; one is measured by the sun (365 days; the seasons),[16] one by the moon (354 days; twelve lunations), and one by the conjoint movement of both (360 days; prophetic)-the *solar, lunar* and *calendar* years. Bible prophecy employs each of these astronomical measures. I am confident you can entertain more than most preachers think you can. If some of you only knew what most ministers think of your learning capacity when it comes to the

---

16   These periods are given in round numbers only.

Bible! The apostle Paul said, *"Prove all things."* If you were not capable, he wouldn't have commanded this.

I will quote from Cachemaille some concluding points to be made in this chapter relative to "eras, not dates only." He observed that the fundamental principle of measurement is the following:

> The years of crisis in the fall of the people of God spread over an era, including several dates for commencement. From this whole era, and from each of these included dates, the great prophetic periods are to be measured; and we then reach a corresponding era of close, including several critical closing dates.
>
> Thus there is an era, and not one single date only, for commencement; and a like era, not a solitary date only, for close …
>
> All three measures of time are employed; lunar years of 354 days are employed; calendar or symbolic years of 360 days; solar years of 365 days. Hence these visions direct our attention to no one date alone, to no one year only, as marking the end of a prophetic period; but rather to an *era,* in which, measured from the various commencing dates by the various scales, the period is found to run out again and again. Each of these closings are marked by events that have a terminal character, and that are distinct steps or stages in a great historical movement … [17]

Much criticism has been wrought against the historicist interpretation because of this very issue. I want to present to you an excerpt of

---

[17]   E.P. Cachemaille, *The Visions of Daniel and of the Revelation Explained,* pages 112-113.

uninformed presumptuous erroneous criticism from the sensational futurist, Grant Jeffrey:

> Almost all previous commentators on prophecy have ignored the true length of the biblical year (360 days) which the prophets used and have thus miscalculated the time periods involved in many of the prophecies. In addition, the "Historical" school of interpretation has unfortunately insisted that the prophecies of Daniel and Revelation, which refer clearly to 1,260 literal days of the reign of Antichrist, must be interpreted as a period of 1,260 years (on the Day-Year Theory-the idea that whenever a prophecy says a day, it automatically must mean a year).[18]

> Some great scholars, including Rev. John Cummings, Dr. Grattan Guinness in his *Approaching End of the Age,* and Bishop Newton's *Dissertations on the Prophecies* have tried in vain to force this interpretation to somehow indicate the period of the Roman Catholic Papacy, and have set dozens of commencement and termination points for such a 1,260 day-year period; all without success.[19]

Luther stated, "I contend with no man's person, but only that which concerns words of truth." I likewise follow the same philosophy. When I address authors and their works, I mean no harm to their Christian

---

18   This is a blatant misrepresentation of the historicist position. Jeffrey himself must admit that the year-for-a-day scale is used in the calculation of the seventy weeks. But like Cardinal Bellarmine, he declares war on its application to the rest of the prophecies in Daniel and Revelation. Jeffrey furthers the cause of the Catholic Counter-Reformation, and the scary thing is that he most likely doesn't know it! *"Art thou a teacher in Israel, and knowest not these things?"* (John 3:10).

19   Again, it is evident that Jeffrey is regurgitating the same old futurist line. It is evident that he has never studied Guinness or Newton. If he had, he would have found out that in 1754, Bishop Newton predicted the exact year that the temple site would be regained by the Jews-1967. Reference: *Seventy Weeks: The Historical Alternative,* "Thomas Newton's Year-Day Principle," pages 67-71.

stature. Nevertheless, our bookstores are filled with some of the most horrific teachings when it comes to Bible prophecy. And these horrific teachers have the audacity to discredit the Protestant Historicist School without even having a working knowledge of it. I assure you that future debates will be extremely revealing. I have wrestled within myself as to how much preparatory information to present before opening the Book of Revelation. I believe I have said enough. It is time to open the revealing of Jesus Christ. It is a revelation, not a mystery. And I hope that the format which I have chosen will aid you in following the systematic teaching and likewise equip you to teach this material yourselves. When futurism and preterism are exposed for what they really are, there will be a cry sounded around the world for courageous teachers who can present these glorious truths.

"NOW I HAVE TOLD YOU BEFORE IT
COME TO PASS, THAT, WHEN IT IS COME
TO PASS, YE MIGHT BELIEVE."

—John 14:29

PART 1

REVELATION CHAPTER 1
THE VISION OF THE SON OF MAN

1 The Revelation of Jesus Christ, which God gave unto Him, to show unto His servants things which must shortly come to pass; and He sent and signified it by His angel unto His servant John: 2 Who bare record of the word of God, and of the testimony of Jesus Christ, and of all things that he saw. 3 Blessed is he that readeth, and they that hear the words of this prophecy, and keep those things which are written therein: for the time is at hand.

The Revelation, *Apocalypse,* or the uncovering, so the Greek word means, opens the veil of our past, present and future. Christ himself gives us the knowledge.[20]

The series of events were soon to begin unfolding. Lange interprets the word *"shortly"* by the phrase "in quick succession," which is to imply successive order. We read that Christ *"signified it,"* which literally means that this prophecy was given in signs and symbols. These signs and symbols are properly called *metaphors.*[21] John is bearing witness to us that all he saw and heard is God's Word. It is interesting to note that both the reader and the hearer were blessed. This, no doubt, refers to the custom of reading the apostolic writings publicly in the churches, a custom well stablished by the first century. This prophecy is a matter of considerable urgency.

The phrase *"for the time is at hand"* leaves no room for dispensational-

---

20   See Chapter 5. The Son was given a sealed book of the future.

21   Metaphor: A figure of speech founded on resemblance. For example, Jesus called Herod a "fox" (Luke 13:32). For an outstanding essay on the figurative style of the prophets-ie., *allegory, parable* and *metaphor*-see Adam Clarke, *Clarke's Commentary,* "Introduction to the Book of Isaiah," pages 3-16.

ism's two millennia of delay!

> *4 John to the seven churches which are in Asia: Grace be unto*
> *you, and peace, from Him which is, and which was, and which is*
> *to come: and from the seven Spirits which are before His throne.*

The seven churches are named in verse 11. They are all from the historic region called Asia. In the first century, Asia referred to a Roman province of which Ephesus was the capital. All seven churches reside in that province. Why Christ chose seven churches is not absolutely defined. Many suppose that these seven were to symbolize the whole Church of Christ. It is understood that seven is a perfect and sacred number. However, we know that there were more than seven churches in this region. We have Colosse, Miletus (Acts 20:17) and Hierapolis (Colossians 4:13) being named in the New Testament. Why weren't these churches addressed? If our Lord only intended these letters to be applicable to the immediate time, why then did He forget to mention the great churches at Rome and Jerusalem? As we will see, God had a great purpose for these letters. These churches and their cities have long since passed away. These seven churches represent seven successive church ages in the history of the Lord's New Testament church.

From The Seven Spirits: We must remember that the number seven is denoting sacred perfection, not an inward plurality, and revealing to us the fullness and perfection of the Holy Spirit's gifts and operations. We will see these "sevens" continually repeated through the prophecy.[22]

> *5 And from Jesus Christ, who is the faithful witness, and the*

---

22   Isaiah 11:2 seems to reveal the concept of the seven spirits: *"And the Spirit of the Lord shall rest upon Him, the Spirit of wisdom and understanding, the Spirit of counsel and might, the Spirit of knowledge and of the fear of the Lord."*

first-begotten of the dead, and the Prince of the kings of the earth. Unto Him that loved us, and washed us from our sins in His own blood,

6 And hath made us kings and priests unto God and His Father; to Him be glory and dominion for ever and ever. Amen.

These verses complete the apostolic benediction, and like that in the apostolic epistles, they reveal that the Revelation is an epistle also. These proclamations of first-begotten of the dead, redemption by His blood, priesthood and dominion are all weighty systematic studies in themselves.

The First-Begotten Of The Dead: This expression is parallel to 1 Cor. 15:20,23; Heb. 1:6; Rom. 8:29; and Col. 1:15,18. These verses reveal that Christ wasn't literally the first raised from the dead; for many others were raised before Him. Paul reminded us that God calls things that be not as though they were (Rom. 4: 17), therefore vindicating the release from the dead of many before Christ's resurrection by virtue of the fact that in due time it would be accomplished. However, it is in His redemptive resurrection that we have our hope of eternal life.

And Hath Made Us Kings And Priests: All his disciples constitute a kingdom; a kingdom that will grow until it fills this earth (Daniel 2:35,44).[23] The apostle Peter likewise proclaimed the truth of our priesthood. See 1 Peter 2:9. No disciple needs a priest to offer sacrifice for him. You can go directly to the throne through your mediator, the only mediator, Jesus Christ. Paul told Timothy, *"For there is one God, and one mediator between God and men, the man Christ Jesus"* (1 Timothy 2:5).

And Washed Us From Our Sins In His Own Blood: Thank God that the great reformer, Martin Luther, understood this truth. Satan confronted him in a dream. He laid before him a scroll containing a list of his sins.

---

23   B. W. Johnson insists that a revision is necessary. He stated: "He made us 'to be a kingdom; to be priests unto his God.'" *The People's New Testament,* page 416.

Luther agreed that he had committed them. Then Luther looked Satan in the eye and quoted him the following: *"The blood of Jesus Christ... cleanseth us from all sin"* (1 John 1:7). Satan vanished.

To *Him Be Glory And Dominion For Ever And Ever:* The prophet Daniel understood both Christ's dominion and the dominion which belonged to His Church. Daniel prophesied, *"And there was given Him dominion, and glory, and a kingdom ... His dominion is an everlasting dominion, which shall not pass away, and His kingdom that which shall not be destroyed ...But the saints of the Most High shall take the kingdom, and possess the kingdom for ever, even for ever and ever"* (Daniel 7:14,18).[24]

> *7 Behold, He cometh with clouds; and every eye shall see Him, and they also which pierced Him: and all kindreds of the earth shall wail because of Him. Even so, Amen.*

This verse warns the reader about one of the prophecy's major themes—judgment.

Behold, He Cometh With Clouds: This is a very familiar biblical metaphor for judgment.[25] This cloud is a heavenly presence of authority by which the judgment is made known. It is designed to protect his people and bring judgment to the enemies of Israel. One of the most revealing figurative narratives about (God coming in the clouds is seen in Nahum's prophecy about the destruction of Nineveh which fell in B.C. 612 (Nah. 1:2-7):

> *2 God is jealous, and the Lord revengeth; the Lord revengeth,*

---

[24]   Try to apply these verses to rapture-oriented dispensationalist theology. They don't fit. You must understand the growth principle of the Kingdom to grasp this teaching.

[25]   cf. Gen. 15:17; Ex. 13:21-22; 14:19-20,24; 19:9,16-19; Ps. 18:8-14; 104:3; Isa.19:1; Ezek. 32:7-8; Matt. 24:30; Mark 14:62; Acts 2:19.

and is furious; the Lord will take vengeance on His adversaries, and He reserveth wrath for His enemies.

3 The Lord is slow to anger, and great in power, and will not at all acquit the wicked: the Lord hath His way in the whirlwind and in the storm, and the clouds are the dust of His feet.

4 He rebuketh the sea, and maketh it dry, and drieth up all the rivers …

5 The mountains quake at Him, and the hills melt, and the earth is burned at His presence, yea, the world, and all that dwell therein.

6 Who can stand before His indignation? …

7 The Lord is good, a stronghold in the day of trouble; and He knoweth them that trust in Him.

Oh, who can utter strong words against the fire in the prophet's mouth? Even in the fire of judgment, verse 7 reveals mercy and hope for the servants of God.

This terminology is the same that Jesus used when He warned His generation that judgment was pending upon them. *"Ye shall see the Son of Man sitting at the right hand of Power, and coming on the clouds of heaven"* (Matthew 26:62). In A.D. 64-70, He did come in judgment. The executioners of this judgment were the Roman legions under the command of Prince Titus (*"The prince that shall come and destroy the city and the sanctuary"* Dan. 9:26b) who destroyed their Temple and their civilization. Truly there was *"weeping and gnashing of teeth"* (Matthew 24:51).

8 I am Alpha and Omega, the beginning and the ending, saith the Lord, which is, and which was, and which is to come, the Almighty.

By this proclamation, Jesus claims to be *"the Lord God of the holy prophets"* (Revelation 22:6), nothing more, nothing less. If your Godhead theology doesn't acknowledge this, then I encourage you to rethink your concepts. Remember, this prophecy is the *"Revelation (revealing) of Jesus Christ."* He has just told you that He is Jehovah. Can you receive that?

> *9 I John, who also am your brother, and companion in tribula-*
> *tion, and in the kingdom and patience of*
> *Jesus Christ, was in the isle that is called Patmos, for the word*
> *of God, and for the testimony of Jesus Christ.*
> *10 I was in the Spirit on the Lord's day, and heard behind me a*
> *great voice, as of a trumpet,*
> *11 Saying, I am Alpha and Omega, the first and the last: and,*
> *What thou seest, write in a book, and send it unto the seven*
> *churches which are in Asia; unto Ephesus, and unto Smyrna,*
> *and unto Pergamos, and unto Thyatira, and unto Sardis, and*
> *unto Philadelphia, and unto Laodicea.*

Please notice where John is, not Patmos, but the Kingdom! He claimed to be *"in the kingdom … of Jesus Christ."* It amazes me how so many lack the revelation of the present Kingdom. We again can thank dispensationalism for that. They want you to believe that the Kingdom, and its authority, is postponed until after the second coming of Christ. But the Bible teaches that Christ established the Kingdom at his first coming. He told the Jews, *"The kingdom of God shall be taken from you, and given to a nation bringing forth the fruits thereof"* (Matthew 21:43). The logical question is, "Who did He give it to?" Jesus said: *"Fear not, little flock; for it is your Father's good pleasure to give you the kingdom"* (Luke

12:32). This kingdom belongs to those who have received Christ, not to those who reject Him. Peter explained: *"But ye are a chosen generation, a royal priesthood, a <u>holy nation</u> … which in time past were not a people, but are <u>now the people of God</u>"* (1 Peter 2:9,10). And Jesus made it clear to His disciples what they were inheriting. He said: *"I appoint unto you a kingdom, as my father hath appointed unto Me"* (Luke 22:29).

And Behind Me A Great Voice, As Of A Trumpet: At Mt. Sinai, God spoke as an exceedingly loud trumpet and made a covenant with the seed of Abraham. In Exodus 19, we read that the Ten Commandments were spoken with a trumpet voice; which made the mountain and the earth shake. The trumpet was used in Israel to signal God's presence; regulate marching; call assemblies; announce a feast; gather the nation; alert against the enemy; and herald a new king. How appropriate that this capstone of the Bible, the Book of Revelation is revealed with the voice of a trumpet.

12 And I turned to see the voice that spake with me. And being turned, I saw seven golden candlesticks;

13 And in the midst of the seven candlesticks one like unto the Son of man, clothed with a garment down to the foot, and girt about the paps with a golden girdle.

14 His head and His hairs were white like wool, as white as snow; and His eyes were as a flame of fire:

15 And His feet like unto fine brass, as if they burned in a furnace; and His voice as the sound of many waters.

16 And He had in His right hand seven stars; and out of His mouth went a sharp two-edged sword; and

His countenance was as the sun shineth in His strength.

17 And when I saw Him, I fell at his feet as dead. And He laid

His right hand upon me, saying unto me, Fear not; I am the first and the last:

18 I am He that liveth, and was dead; and behold, I am alive for evermore, Amen; and have the keys of hell and of death.

I Saw Seven Golden Candlesticks: These candlesticks are the symbols or metaphors for the seven churches (verse 20). With the presentation of the candlesticks, the reader is quickly introduced to some of the **signs and symbols** used in this prophecy. **The application of the metaphorical code is being clearly demonstrated.** These candlesticks are not literal; they are symbols; they represent churches. Not only are the churches represented by metaphor, but also their *"stars"* (messengers/pastors/prophets) are introduced with symbolic language. This should be easy to understand. You must apply this rule throughout the Revelation or else you have foolish literalism.

19 Write the things which thou hast seen, and the things which are, and the things which shall be hereafter;

Uriah Smith commented on the interpretation of this command. He stated:

A more definite command is given in this verse to John to write the entire Revelation, which would relate chiefly to things which were then in the future. In some few instances, events then in the past or then transpiring were referred to, but these references were simply for the purpose of introducing events to be fulfilled after that time, and so that no link in the chain might be lacking.[26]

---

26   Uriah Smith, *Daniel and the Revelation,* page 343.

20 The mystery of the seven stars which thou sawest in My right hand, and the seven golden candlesticks. The seven stars are the angels of the seven churches: and the seven candlesticks which thou sawest are the seven churches.

Finally, it should be remembered that Christ is not limited in His sphere of authority to just seven churches. His providential care and presence are with all His people. *"Lo, I am with you always,"* said He to His disciples, *"even unto the end of the world."*

REVELATION CHAPTER 2
THE SEVEN CHURCHES

Revelation 2 and 3 differ from the other chapters in the prophecy. In them the Lord dictates seven letters to the seven churches which have been selected to represent the entire Christian church in its seven-fold historical development. The seven letters commend and rebuke, promise and warn—in a tone of address that properly introduces a prophecy which is spoken with a very specific purpose: to reveal the various phases of the Church in history. These two chapters paint a thorough picture of the Church—its blessings and rebellion, its tribulations and persecutions, and its eventual maturity and triumph. Though the seven epistles differ in details, they will follow a remarkable general plan and possess five common features: (1.) The order to address the set authority *(angels)* in each of the assemblies. (2.) A majestic title of Jesus taken from the imagery which appeared in the vision of chapter one. (3.) A revealing of the condition of the church, whether good or bad, coupled with admonitions and exhortations. (4.) A promise to those who overcome. (5.) A closing warning to *"hear what the Spirit saith to the churches."*

EPHESUS
A. D. 30-100 (APPROX.)
A RELAXATION OF EFFORT

1 Unto the angel of the church of Ephesus write; These things saith He that holdeth the seven stars in His right hand, who walketh in the midst of the seven golden candlesticks;
2 I know thy works, and thy labor, and thy patience, and how thou canst not bear them which are evil: and thou hast tried

them which say they are apostles, and are not, and hast found
them liars;
3 And hast borne, and hast patience, and for My name's sake
hast labored, and hast not fainted.

Ephesus was the capital of the Roman province of Asia and its most splendid city. This great center was sought by Paul, who labored there three years and founded its church (Acts 18). Afterwards, he addressed to it the epistle to the Ephesians. It was at Ephesus that Timothy received his two epistles from Paul. Early church tradition reveals that John made his home there from about A.D. 70 onwards.

This was a church walking in great truth. Christ commended their labor, patience, and the ability to expose false apostles. First John 4 shows us how to test them. The Ephesian church both tested and rejected those who were *"liars."*

4 Nevertheless I have somewhat against thee, because thou hast
left thy first love.
5 Remember therefore from whence thou art fallen, and repent,
and do the first works; or else I will come unto thee quickly, and
will remove thy candlestick out of his place, except thou repent.

Christ is merciful to praise before He criticizes. Truth was not the final destiny of the Church. It simply was the road the Church would take to achieve her destiny. We can walk in great truth and lose our *"first love"*; we have been warned. This is the church of John's day: suffering persecution from the Romans and the Jews. They began to relax their effort, and there was a terrible reason for this. We have fallen into the same trap with the rise of dispensationalism.

The Church of the first century incorrectly anticipated that Christ would return after the destruction of Jerusalem. Many believed this. They had misinterpreted what Jesus said to Peter about John. The following discourse from John's gospel explains what the prophetic thinking was. John 21:20-23:

> *20 Then Peter, turning about, seeth the disciple whom Jesus loved following; which also leaned on His breast at supper, and said, Lord, which is he that betrayeth Thee?*
> *21 Peter seeing him saith to Jesus, Lord, and what shall this man do?*
> *22 Jesus saith unto him, If I will that he tarry till I come, what is that to thee? Follow thou Me.*
> *23 Then went this saying abroad among the brethren, that that disciple should not die: <u>yet Jesus said not unto him, He shall not die, but, If I will that he tarry till I come, what is that to thee?</u>*

So we can see the danger of believing something that might not come to pass. If it affected the early Church, how much more can it affect us today? This same scenario plagues the twentieth century church. Dispensationalism has given rise to prophetic lies and misinterpretations, which have robbed the Church of its future and destiny. The church at Ephesus was rebuked for this. Is Christ the same? (See Hebrews 13:8.) He has warned of quick judgment upon those who relax their effort.

> *6 But this thou hast, that thou hatest the deeds of the Nicolaitans, which I also hate.*
> *7 He that hath an ear, let him hear what the Spirit saith unto the churches; To him that overcometh will I give to eat of the tree of*

life, which is in the midst of the paradise of God.

Commentator Adam Clarke summarized the deeds **of** the Nicolaitans as follows:

> The followers of Balaam were called Nicolaitans, a sect of Gnostics, Antinomians, who taught impure doctrines and followed most impure practices. They taught a community of wives, that adultery and fornication were things indifferent, that eating of meats offered to idols was quite lawful and they mixed several pagan rites with Christian ceremonies.[27]

He That Hath An Ear, Let Him Hear: The call to solemn attention is found at the close of each epistle. The Christian life is a battle. Nevertheless, it must conclude in victory.

SMYRNA

A.D. 64-313

PAGAN ROME'S PERSECUTION

8 And unto the angel of the church in Smyrna write,· These things saith the first and the last, which was dead, and is alive; 9 I know thy works, and tribulation, and poverty, (but thou art rich) and I know the blasphemy of them which say they are Jews, and are not, but are the synagogue of Satan.

The history of Smyrna's origin is not known. It is believed that the church was established there by one of Paul's evangelists. During the second century this church was very prominent.

---

27   See, Adam Clarke, *Clarke's Commentary,* pages 976-977.

Jesus described a period of martyrdom. The word Smyrna means *"anointing oil,"* symbolic of the Holy Ghost's strengthening of these martyrs. (See Acts 1:8.) These people are destined to suffer terrible persecution, imprisonment, and even death. Christ revealed Himself as the one who was dead, but now alive. If they were called upon to seal their testimony in blood, they were to remember that their Lord had shared the same fate-that His eyes and anointing would be upon them. His grace would be sufficient for the hour. Christ triumphed over death. He will raise these saints up from the martyr's grave.

Say They Are Jews, And Are Not: John denied the right of these Jewish opposer's and persecutors the use of the term "Jews" in the sense of God's chosen people. Uriah Smith expounded, That the term *Jew* is not here used in a literal sense, is very evident. It denotes some character which was approved by the gospel standard. Paul's language will make this point plain. He says (Rom. 2:28, 29): *"For he is not a Jew which is one outwardly; neither is that circumcision which is outward in the flesh; but he is a Jew [in the true Christian sense] which is one inwardly; and circumcision is that of the heart, in the spirit, and not in the letter, whose praise is not of men, but of God."* Again he says (Chapter 9:6, 7): *"For they are not all Israel which are of Israel; neither, because they are the seed of Abraham, are they all children."* In Galatians 3:28, 29, Paul further tells us that in Christ there are no such outward distinctions as Jew or Greek; but if we are Christ's, then we are Abraham's seed (in the true sense), and heirs according to the promise ... Some were hypocritically pretending to be Jews in this Christian sense, when they possessed nothing of the requisite character. Such were of the synagogue of Satan.[28]

> *10 Fear none of those things which thou shalt suffer: behold, the*
> *devil shall cast some of you into prison, that ye may be tried; and*

---

28   2 Uriah Smith, *Daniel and the Revelation, page 352.*

ye shall have tribulation ten days: be thou faithful unto death,
and I will give thee a crown of life.
11 He that hath an ear, let him hear what the Spirit saith unto
the churches; He that overcometh shall not be hurt of the second
death.

Tribulation Ten Days: This message is prophetic. The divine time measure denotes ten years.[29] Ten persecutions are named by church historians during this period (A. D. 64-A. D. 313).[30] The last and most destructive of the persecutions lasted ten years. Historically, these ten days are called, "The Era of the Martyrs," or "The Great Persecution" under Diocletian. He issued a decree for the destruction of all the Christian churches. The slaughter extended from A. D. 303 to A. D. 313. One of the results of this persecution is that we have no New Testament manuscripts earlier than the fourth century; all were burnt. The killing was halted with the victory of Constantine.

The ten days of Smyrna is one of the greatest arguments for the messages of the seven churches being applied to successive ages. This divine time measure forces the issue. It is highly unlikely that a persecution of ten days, upon a single church, would warrant insertion relative to the vast persecutions which have historically unfolded. Uriah Smith noted: "Again, apply this persecution to any of the notable persecutions of that period, and how could it be spoken of as the fate of one church alone? All the churches suffered in them; and what, then, would be the propriety of singling out one, to the exclusion of the rest, as alone involved in such a calamity?"[31]

---

29   "*... I have appointed thee each day for a year*" (Ezekiel 4:6)

30   Several great accounts have been written about the ten terrible persecutions conducted by pagan Rome. For one of the most moving and graphic accounts, I refer the reader to John Fox's, *Fox's Book of Martyrs,* "History of Christian Martyrdom," pages 13-31.

31   Uriah Smith, *Daniel and the Revelation,* page 353.

PERGAMOS
A.D. 313-606
THE IMPERIAL CHURCH (PAPAL BEGINNINGS)

12 And to the angel of the church in Pergamos write; These things saith he which hath the sharp sword with two edges.

Pergamos was the farthest north of the seven churches. It was once the capital of the kingdom of Pergamos, which was a great and prosperous city at the time John wrote.

The name Pergamos means *"married to power."* This period extends from the professed conversion of Constantine, to the rise and establishment of the papacy. In A. D. 313, the Decree of Coronation made Rome the center of Christendom. It was a period that manifested a struggle with worldly influences entering the Church. Many professed Christianity just to gain political favor. Truly the liberated Church was marrying the power of the Roman State! This fueled the mystery of iniquity which resulted in the mature development of the papal man of sin.

13 I know thy works, and where thou dwellest, even where Satan's seat is: and thou holdest fast My name, and hast not denied My faith, even in those days wherein Antipas was My faithful martyr, who was slain among you, where Satan dwelleth.

Where Satan's Seat Is: Christ recognizes the difficult situation of his people during this period. It is clear that Satan works wherever Christians reside. However, both the Scriptures and history reveal that at special times he focuses on specific territories or historical cycles. Who can doubt that he focused or dwelt in the reigns of power during the age of Pagan Rome? It was Satan who instigated the attempt to exterminate the Church during the Smyrna period. Having failed in that attempt, he sought to corrupt the true doctrines of Christ. He would need to raise a counterfeit. The Revelation reveals this counterfeit: the Roman Catholic Church. It developed [its papal beast] during the age of Pergamos. At this time in history, the church departs from strict Bible adherence. Satan was centered in Rome, laying the groundwork for the darkest period of church history, the Middle Ages, in which over 50 million people were struck down by the papal sword of bitterness. Paul warned of this transition. Pergamos fulfilled the prophecy of the "falling away," and the removal of the "hindrance" to Antichrist. This was foretold in 2 Thessalonians 2: 3-7—a prophecy which had to come to pass before the man of sin could arise. Remarkably, the dispensationalists are still waiting for this to transpire. I suggest they open their history books. Let's examine Paul's warning and discover how it was interpreted for over a millennium. Second Thessalonians 2:3 says

> *Let no man deceive you by any means: for that day shall not come, except there come a falling away first, and that man of sin be revealed, the son of perdition.*

Dear reader, history records no greater falling away from the truth than that which was seen in this imperial age of the Church. Apostolic doctrine was blatantly disregarded and the traditions of men replaced the laws of God. The Bible was closed. Rome's Babylonian mysteries became the religion of Europe.[32]

Not only is the doctrinal falling away relevant, but also the removal of Antichrist's *hindrance.* Pergamos covers the fourth through the early seventh centuries. It was during the fifth century (A.D. 476) that the last Roman Emperor in the West was removed. The fifth trumpet (Revelation 8:12) is the specific prophecy of this event and will be examined later. With this removal, the bishop of Rome was free to arise unhindered by the pagan emperors. Paul prophesied of this in 2 Thess. 2:5-7

> *5 Remember ye not, that, when I was yet with you, I told you these things?*
>
> *6 And now ye know what withholdeth that he* [the man of sin] *might be revealed in his time.*
>
> *7 ...Only he who letteth* [hinders] *will let, until he be taken out of the way.*

The word "letteth" (let) can properly be interpreted as "restrain." What was the hindrance to the emergence of the man of sin that Paul spoke of? Well, in the primary case, the apostle speaks of it in the neuter gender: *"you know WHAT withholds."* Then he uses the masculine gender: *"HE who now hinders."* The only logical conclusion is that the hindrance or restrainer will be both neuter and masculine. As long as the Roman Empire was under pagan rule, the man of sin could not take his place of authority in the seven-hilled city. Thus the hindrance in the primary

---

32   Do not have contempt for my fury concerning the doctrines and practices of Catholicism until you've read the entire book and the following works: (1.) The Bible; (2.) John Fox's, *Fox's Book of Martyrs; (3.)* Alexander Hislop's, *The Two Babylons: The Papal Worship;* (4.) Loraine Boettner's, *Roman Catholicism;* (5.) William Cathcart's, *The Papal System;* (6.) Rev. J. A. Wylie's, *The Papacy;* (7.) Peter DeRosa's, *Vicars of Christ,* just *to* name a few witnesses *to* the nightmare the Revelation reveals. Karl Keating can never correctly argue against the truths that these works revealed. All trees are to be judged by their fruit. However, if you do not possess this knowledge, you're open season for deception. Remember, there was a reason for the Reformation. It's time for the an age of correction!

neuter gender is fulfilled in the Roman Empire, and the same hindrance in the masculine gender was fulfilled in the despotic emperors. They had to be taken out of the way first. The first five trumpets (Revelation 8:6-12) will reveal this story. In A.D. 476, Pagan Rome vanished in the west, only to be replaced by apostate Papal Rome. It was like one rising from the dead, surviving a mortal head wound. (See Revelation 13:3.) This was the understanding of the historic church. In our day, the dispensationalists teach that the hindrance is the Holy Spirit. How absurd!

Let's look at some startling observations, that is, to the futurists. You won't find this in Hal Lindsey's books.

Chrysostom, Bishop of Constantinople, A.D. 390, writes, "By the 'Hindrance' Paul means the Roman Empire." This was also believed by Augustine.

Jerome, A. D. 400, declared, "If St. Paul had written openly and boldly that the man of sin would not come until the Roman Empire was destroyed, a just cause of persecution would then appear to have been afforded against the Church in her infancy."

Bishop Wodsworth wrote in 1850, "The earliest Christian writers declared ... with one voice the 'he who letteth' was the heathen Roman Empire" *(Apocalypse,* page 520).

The Amplified Bible, 1958 footnote of 2 Thessalonians 2:6 states, "Many believe this one who restrains the Antichrist to be the Holy Spirit ... A majority think it refers to the Roman Empire."

This fulfillment in the Roman emperors has been the consistent voice of the historicist school for century after century. On the other hand, it was Ribera who taught that the hindrance was the Holy Spirit. Sound familiar? If it was the Holy Spirit, Paul would have boldly said so, since he had no hesitations in other chapters when writing about this subject.[33] I will conclude this section with a few more historic quotes that present a terrible problem for the preterists. Neither Tertullian, Jerome, nor Evangrius for a minute believed that Nero was the Antichrist. They were all anticipating his arrival after the fall of Pagan Rome.

Tertullian: "We pray for the Roman emperors and empire, for we know that convulsions and calamities are threatening the whole world, and the end of the world itself, is kept back by the intervention of the Roman Empire."

Jerome: "The Roman world rushes to destruction, and we bend not our neck in humiliation … The hindrance in Antichrist's way is removing, and we heed it not … In that one city [Rome] the whole world hath fallen."

Evangrius: "The Roman Emperors are driven from their kingdoms: wars rage: all is commotion: **Antichrist must be at hand."**

In concluding this necessary understanding relative to the Pergamos period, we see that Paul had good reason for refusing to openly name the hindrance; to do so would have brought swift; and terrible destruction to the infant Church in Thessalonica. He had already caused a disturbance when he was there speaking against Caesar. *"Remember ye not, that, when I was yet with you, I told you these things ?"* (2 Thessalonians 2:5)

---

33   Hindrance information taken from Thomas Foster's *The Antichrist-Who Is He?*

Antipas: Ancient ecclesiastical history provides no information about an individual named Antipas. However, it is the position of several scholars that "Antipas" represents a class of people, not an individual. On this issue, William Miller stated:

It is supposed that Antipas was not an individual, but a class of men who opposed the power of the bishops, or popes, in that day, being a combination of two words, *anti,* opposed, and *papas,* father, or pope; and at that time many of them suffered martyrdom in Constantinople and Rome, where the bishops and popes began to exercise the power which soon after brought into subjection the kings of the earth, and trampled on the rights of the church of Christ. And for myself, I see no reason to reject this explanation of the word *Antipas* in this text, as the history of those times is perfectly silent respecting such an individual as is here named *(Miller's Lectures,* pages 138, 139).

14 But I have a few things against thee, because thou hast there them that hold the doctrine of Balaam, who taught Balak to cast a stumbling block before the children of Israel, to eat things sacrificed unto idols, and to commit fornication.

Jesus is accusing this church of imitating Baal.[34] The age was full of teachers like the prophet Balaam who seduced the true Israel into sin. Balaam instructed the Moabite king Balak on how to lead the Children of Israel astray, while they

---

34   The Hebrew noun *ba'al* means "master," and would often appear with various suffixes, e.g., Baal-peor or Baal-berith. In the original sense this specific deity was the Semitic storm-god. He was of primary importance to the Canaanites. The Baal cults challenged the worship of Yahweh throughout Israelite history. It was Baal that Elijah confronted at Mt. Carmel (1 King 18).

were attempting to enter the Promised Land.[35] Balak coaxed them (Israel) to eat that which was sacrificed to idols. They fell into sin, and God was forced to punish them.

The Pergamos church was being tempted during this time (A.D. 313 - 606) to worship idols and commit spiritual fornication. History records this as the "rise of the papacy." The carnality of the Roman Empire deceived the Church like Balak deceived Israel of old. As we have already noted, Satan couldn't destroy the Church with ten persecutions. Now he is forced to compromise with it. Christians were tempted into joining idol feasts and heathen fornication.

By the end of the fifth century, the following unscriptural doctrines and practices had become deeply rooted in the Church: prayers for the dead; a belief in *purgatory* (place in which souls are purified after death before they can enter heaven); the forty-day Lenten season; the view that the Lord's Supper is a sacrifice, and that its administrators are priests; a sharp division of the members of the church into *clergy (officers* of the church) and *laity* (ordinary church members); the *veneration* (adoration) of martyrs and saints, *and above all the adoration of Mary;* the burning of tapers or candles in their honor; veneration of the relics of martyrs and saints; the ascription of magical powers to these relics; pictures, images, and altars in the churches; gorgeous vestments for the clergy; more and more elaborate and splendid *ritual* (form of worship); less and less preaching; pilgrimages to holy places; monasticism; worldliness; and persecution of heathen and heretics.[36]

> *15 So hast thou also them that hold the doctrine of the Nicolaitans, which thing I hate.*
> *16 Repent; or else I will come unto thee quickly, and will fight against them with the sword of My mouth.*

---

35   See Numbers Chapters 22-25 and 31.

36   See B. K. Kuiper, *The Church in History,* page 44.

The doctrine of the Nicolaitans has already been revealed in the annotations pertaining to Smyrna. These are things that Christ hates and is determined to fight against. He fights with the "sword of His mouth" which is the word of God.[37] These fights and judgments are launched by His ministers. Remember Luther. Another fight is coming.

> *17 He that hath an ear, let him hear what the Spirit saith unto the churches; To him that overcometh will I give to eat of the hidden manna, and will give him a white stone, and on the stone a new name written, which no man knoweth, saving he that receiveth it.*

The overcomers receive a white stone, a reflection of glory. New Jerusalem (True Israel) will someday reflect the Lord's glory to all the world.

In ancient courts of justice, the acquittal of a criminal was declared by a majority of white stones being cast into the judicial urn. Christ will pronounce the acquittal of all those who have overcome on judgment day.

THYATIRA
A.D. 606-1517
PAPAL TRIUMPH AND PERSECUTION
(THE DARK AGES)

> *18 And unto the angel of the church in Thyatira write; These things saith the Son of God, who hath His eyes like unto a flame of fire, and His feet are like fine brass;*
> *19 I know thy works, and charity, and service, and faith, and thy patience, and thy works; and the last to be greater than the first.*

---

37   See Eph. 6:17; Heb. 4:12; and compare Rev. 19:5.

20 Notwithstanding, I have a few things against thee, because thou sufferest that woman Jezebel, which calleth herself a prophetess, to teach and to seduce my servants to commit fornication, and to eat things sacrificed to idols.

Thyatira is mentioned in Acts 16 as the home of Lydia, who was converted at Philippi. It is probable that upon returning home, they established the church in that city.

If the Pergamos period extended through the development of the papal system (fourth through the early seventh century), then we now logically enter into the next division of the successive ages. Thyatira is the time in which this blasphemous power ruled in authority. It is the middle church of the seven, and likewise covers the Middle Ages (Dark Ages/Medieval). That is no coincidence. During this age the true church suffered terribly at the hands of the counterfeit church of Rome. Any study of history will vindicate that accusation.

That Woman Jezebel: Thyatira means "to be ruled by a woman." Jezebel was Ahab's wife who killed the prophets of the Lord, deceived her husband (Israel's king) into idolatry, and fed the prophets of Baal at her own table. Uriah Smith surmised, "A more striking figure could not have been used to denote the papal abominations."[38]

As a woman in the symbolic prophecy of the Revelation, Jezebel represents a church—a false, aggressive and violent church. Jezebel's priests (false prophets) of Baal caused Israel to worship Ashtaroth, understood to be a "mother goddess." Jeremiah calls Ashtaroth the "Queen of Heaven" (see Jeremiah 44:17,18,25). Now in reference to the Dark Ages, what system of false religion at this time in history destroyed the saints of God and elevated her priests (false prophets) causing the church to worship Mary as the "Queen of Heaven"? There can only be one answer, the counterfeit

---

38   See 1 Kings 18, 19, and 21 for the acts of this wicked queen.

church of Rome. There are numerous Catholic paintings of Mary in art galleries throughout the world labeling Mary as the "Queen of Heaven."

21 And I gave her space to repent of her fornication; and she repented not.

The Revelation reveals that Christ gave this institution thirteen centuries to repent. Revelation 10, 11, 12, 13, 16, 17 and 18 reveal the essence of this struggle in Europe. It is a time when Israel in the wilderness was trodden under foot and existed in symbolic sackcloth for 1,260 years. (See Revelation 11:2,3; 12:6,14; 13:5.) She has never repented, therefore her destruction is foretold in Revelation 17 and 18.

22 Behold, I will cast her into a bed, and them that commit adultery with her into great tribulation, except they repent of their deeds.
23 And I will kill her children with death; and all the churches shall know that I am he which searcheth the reins and hearts: and I will give unto every one of you according to your works.

The history of the Dark Ages is filled with the accounts of the scourges that accompanied the papal empire. Its most horrific period came with the plague of The Black Death, beginning in A.D. 1247. Pope Clement VI at Avignon estimated that over 23 million people died. One historian estimated that "a third of the world died."[39]

Moses declared to Israel the consequences of disobedience, and this type of plague applies. Moses warned in Deuteronomy 28:

---

39   I reference the reader to an excellent concise account of this terrible period: John Clifford, Robert DiYanni, *Modern American Prose*. See Barbara Tuchman's essay, "The Black Death," pages 411-420.

21 The Lord shall make the pestilence cleave unto thee …

22 The Lord shall smite thee with a consumption, and with a fever, and with an inflammation, and with an extreme burning …

This church age was warned by Christ of the same terrible judgments awaiting future generations if it failed to repent. Unfortunately, Israel not only failed to repent, but it waxed worse and worse. The context of the Revelation reveals this sad story of judgments unfolding.

And I Will Kill Her Children With Death: In Revelation 16:7 we read: *"True and righteous are thy judgments"* and again in Revelation 18:6, *"Reward her even as she rewarded you."* Historians estimate the total of those who lost their lives fighting against the doctrines and abuses of Papal Rome as no less than 50 million.[40]

24 But unto you I say, and unto the rest in Thyatira, (as many as have not this doctrine, and which have not known. the depths of Satan, as they speak, I will put upon you none other burden:

25 But that which ye have already; hold fast till I come

26 And he that overcometh, and keepeth my works unto the end, to him will I give power over the nations:

27 And he shall rule them with a rod of iron; as the vessels of a potter shall they be broken to shivers; even as I received of My Father.

28 And I will give him the morning star.

29 He that hath an ear, let him hear what the Spirit saith unto the churches.

---

40   H. Grattan Guinness, *The Approaching End of the Age*, 5th Ed. page 212.

REVELATION CHAPTER 3
SEVEN CHURCHES CONTINUED

SARDIS
A.D. 1517-1739
THE REFORMATION

1 And unto the angel of the church at Sardis write; These things saith He that hath the seven Spirits of God, and the seven stars; I know thy works, that thou hast a name that thou livest, and art dead.

The ancient city of Sardis was once the capital of the kingdom of Lydia. By the time of the first century, it had lost its former greatness but was still a considerable city. It is believed that the church was planted there by the companions of Paul. The name Sardis means a *"precious stone."* This is the period of the Reformation because it immediately followed the darkness of Thyatira-the Middle Ages. The Reformation began in A.D. 1517 with the furious bellows of Martin Luther. History records this as the end of the Dark Ages. The Reformation changed the course of western civilization forever.[41] The period of Sardis extends from Luther to the rise of John Wesley. The church witnessed a great upsurge of revival as people began to search for truth in the pages of the Bible. Rome had forbidden its flock to even possess Bibles during her reign of terror. Also during this time, western civilization was blessed with great translations of the Bible from Greek, Latin and Hebrew to the languages of the world.

---

[41]   I recommend these three reader-friendly books on the topic of the Reformation. We are still an evolving product of this reform. Like they say, "The only history you are forced to repeat is the history you haven't read!" (1.) Roland H. Bainton's, *Here I Stand: A Life of Martin Luther;* (2.) R. Tudor Jones', *The Great Reformation;* (3.) Bernard M. G. Reardon's, *Religious Thought in the Reformation.*

Christendom was experiencing the greatest revolt against the corruptions of the Roman Catholic Church—a spiritual and literal war with many campaigns and theaters of battle.

> *2 Be watchful, and strengthen the things which remain, that are ready to die: for I have not found thy works perfect before God.*

The Reformation was indeed glorious and precious—but even it was found to be at fault by our Lord. We must remember that this sixteenth century upheaval was birthed in an age of intolerance and bloodshed. It stands to reason that the process of restoration would take centuries. Therefore, after the Protestant Church solidified many of its doctrines, and territories, it in turn began to persecute the nonconformists who were looking for more truth and liberty. Historians estimate that from approximately A.D. 1600 to 1730, a slothfulness came over the Protestants. Jesus proclaimed this by saying, "You have a name that thou livest, and art dead."

> *3 Remember therefore how thou hast received and heard, and hold fast, and repent. If therefore thou shalt not watch, I will come on thee as a thief, and thou shalt not know what hour I will come upon thee.*

This church age certainly *"received and heard"* the truths of Scripture. Revelation 10 and 11 reveals the drama of this period. It began with the opening of the *"Little Book,"* which is the Bible in print and circulation. Luther's life was a continual maze of religious confusion until the study of the Scriptures revealed to him a new conviction. Luther saw that although there was no way for man to merit God's favor, man could receive through

FAITH God's divine gift of life by the merits of Christ's death and resurrection. *"The just shall live by faith"* (Romans 1:17) was the match that lit the fire. Thank God Luther *received* and *heard* this revelation. With it he brought down an empire of superstition. We, likewise, must both hear and receive the truths of Scripture. If not, our works are dead.

> *4 Thou hast a few names even in Sardis which have not defiled their garments; and they shall walk with Me in white: for they are worthy.*
>
> *5 He that overcometh, the same shall be clothed in white raiment; and I will not blot out his name out of the book of life, but I will confess his name before My Father, and before His angels.*
>
> *6 He that hath an ear, let him hear what the Spirit saith unto the churches.*

For They Are Worthy: The Lord has devastated modern theologies that teach "once saved, always saved" in the loose sense of the understanding. The Bible knows of no such doctrine. Repeatedly, the Scriptures warn that an overcoming life is demanded of the Christian. Paul told the Galatian church that they were *"fallen from grace!"* (Galatians 5:4b). And the writer of the Hebrew epistle warned: *"Looking diligently lest any man fail the grace of God"* (Hebrews 12:15). Now, Christ himself threatens to remove one from the Book of Life if he fails to overcome (Revelation 3:5). The Book of Life means the roll of those who have become heirs of immortality. We must be worthy to walk with Him. This is what the Bible teaches.

PHILADELPHIA

A.D. 1793-PRESENT

THE GREAT AWAKENING

7 And to the angel of the church in Philadelphia write; These things saith He that is holy, He that is true, He that hath the key of David; He that openeth, and no man shutteth; and shutteth, and no man openeth:

8 I know thy works: behold, I have set before thee an open door, and no man can shut it: for thou hast a little strength, and hast kept my word, and hast not denied My name.

The historic city of Philadelphia never attained to the eminence of the other six. It was wanting in worldly stature. It is the perfect type of what would produce the Great Awakening. It was pure. Only it and Smyrna escape censure by the Lord. This is the rise of the evangelical church and its Great Awakening. Both the North American Continent and the British Isles experienced this move of the Spirit. The church was preparing to bring the Word of God to the whole world. This period of Philadelphia will run from this Awakening to the coming of the Lord. We will see in the message to Laodicea (an age which began in the mid-nineteenth century) that these two churches represent the wheat and the tares in the Kingdom.[42] They will exist parallel to one another until the completion of the harvest. The awakenings covered a period of about 180 years. The Great Awakening extended from the late 1730s to the 1740s. The Second Great Awakening extended from the mid-1790s to 1840. And the Third

---

[42]   See Matt. 13:24-43. In this parable of the wheat and the tares, Christ makes it clear that they are both intertwined in the Kingdom. Only at the end of the world (v. 40) will they ultimately be separated. For you rapture buffs, please take notice that the tares are first gathered and destroyed, then the righteous, which remain, will shine forth. The following Scriptures reveal that the righteous remain and inherit the earth: Ps. 125:1; 101:8; 119:119; 37:9-11,29,34-38; Prov. 2:21-22; 10:30; 11:31; Job 21:18; 38:13.

Great Awakening began in 1857-59, and extended through the revival campaigns of Dwight L. Moody.

The Great Awakening in North America was launched by Solomon Stoddard's harvest at Northampton. This man understood the pulpit. He stated: "We are not sent into the pulpit to shew our wit and eloquence, but to set the consciences of men on fire!" This surge was followed by his grandson, Jonathan Edwards, who is most famous for his sermon, "Sinners in the Hands of an Angry God." In the same move of God, George Whitefield rose up and set Philadelphia ablaze. These were two of the most powerful ministers this continent has ever witnessed. In the British Isles, John and Charles Wesley shook the isle—with Whitefield beside them. For America, it was truly a dawning in this new world!

The Second Great Awakening was highlighted by the efforts of Francis Asbury, the great apostle on horseback, and Charles Finney. From 1825 to 1832, under the leadership of Finney, the United States experienced the most intensive evangelistic activity in its history. This was also the rise of the great camp meeting revivals in the southern and western states. The English launched "The Great Century of Christian Advance." The worldwide missionary movement had begun. The Third Great Awakening was known as an awakening of prayer. In New York City, 10,000 people gathered together daily to pray. By 1858, newspapers in the city were competing for coverage of the phenomena. In the Isles, the Awakening touched Ulster, Ireland. This period climaxed with the preaching of D. L. Moody. During his great revival in London, Moody held over 85 meetings during a six month period, and spoke to 2.5 million people. Although not highly educated, he was able through God's guidance to establish three Bible schools. Without proper theological training, Moody redefined Victorian Christianity. Without television or radio, he reached over 100 million people.

If this entire period had only a *"little strength,"* imagine what it will be like when the kingdom of God *"is established into the top of the mountains!"*[43] Philadelphia means "brotherly love."

I Have Set Before Thee An Open Door: This open door was clearly demonstrated during the Awakening. The open door generally means great opportunities for preaching the gospel. Few doors as great as those in the awakenings have been opened. In the gospel of John, Jesus stated: "Verily, verily, I say unto you, I am the door …" (John 10:7).

> *9 Behold, I will make them of the synagogue of Satan, which say they are Jews, and are not, but do lie; behold, I will make them to come and worship before thy feet, and to know that I have loved thee.*

Uriah Smith noted: "Verse 9 probably applies to those who do not keep pace with the advancing light of truth, and who oppose those that do. Such shall yet be made to feel and confess that God loves those, who, not rejecting the past fulfillments of his word, nor stereotyping themselves in a creed, continue to advance in the knowledge of his truth."[44]

> *10 Because thou hast kept the word of my patience, I also will keep thee from the hour of temptation, which shall come upon all the world, to try them that dwell upon the earth.*
> *11 Behold, I come quickly: hold fast which thou hast, that no man take thy crown.*

---

43   This is in reference to the Kingdom's *growth principle*. Isaiah (Chapter 2:1-4) is prophesying about natural Israel. See Heb. 12:22; 1 Pet. 2:9,10. Rise up and shake off that dispensational yoke! You *"are now the people of God."*

44   Uriah Smith, *Daniel and the Revelation*, page 368.

Remember John said that he was in *"the kingdom and patience of Jesus Christ"* (Revelation. 1:9). This is the only place one can receive shelter in the *"hour of temptation."* There are five major warnings in the Hebrew epistle to those who fail to *"hold fast."*[45]

12 Him that overcometh will I make a pillar in the temple of My God, and he shall go no more out: and I will write upon him the name of My God, and the name of the city of My God, which is New Jerusalem, which cometh down out of heaven from My God; and I will write upon him My new name.

13 He that hath an ear, let him hear what the Spirit saith unto the churches.

A Pillar In The Temple: This implies strength, permanence and honor. Again, the symbolic language is clear. The literal temple means nothing. It had already been destroyed. *"Ye are the temple of God"* (1 Corinthians 3:16). Don't let the futurist teaching about a rebuilt temple in Jerusalem fool you. That teaching is the lie of Ribera.[46]

New Jerusalem, Which Cometh Down Out Of Heaven: To swiftly dispel another futurist myth, New Jerusalem is true Israel. One of the seven angels approached John and said, *"Come hither, I will show thee the bride, the Lamb's wife."* John was carried away to a high mountain and showed *"that great city, the holy Jerusalem, descending out of heaven from God"* (Revelation 21:9,10). I advise you to put your dispensationalist books down and believe the Scriptures.

---

45   See Heb. 2:1-4; 3:7-19; 6:4-9; 10:25-31; 12:14-17.

46   For two strong refutations to the futurists' rebuilt temple scheme see my book, *Seventy Weeks: The Historical Alternative,* "The Temple of the Man of Sin," pages 61-65; and H. Speed Wilson's, *Rapture: Prophecy or Heresy,* "Blinding Doctrines of Today," (Daring Publishing Group, Inc.) pages 123-145.

LAODICEA
A.D. 1850-PRESENT
REJECTING THE LUKEWARM

*14 And unto the angel of the church of the Laodiceans write;
These things saith the Amen, the faithful and true Witness, the
beginning of the creation of God:*
*15 I know thy works, that thou art neither cold nor hot: I would
that wert cold or hot.*
*16 So then because thou art lukewarm, and neither cold nor
hot, I will spew thee out of My mouth.*

Laodicea was situated in the valley of the Lycus, near Colosse and
Hierapolis. All three of these churches were named by Paul in his Colossian letter. An epistle, now lost, is believed to have been sent to Laodicea.
This city was extremely proud of its wealth. The condemnation of the
Lord upon it is severe, and its extinction is threatened.

It is clear from this letter that Christ would rather have us acting
hostile towards Him, or zealous for the Lord. This lukewarmness was
most offensive, and hence the Lord declares that they shall be rejected as
one rejects nauseous food.

The name "Laodicea," like the others before, reveals a precious truth
about the letter, for it literally means to be *"under the authority of the
laity."* Government is in the hands of the body, instead of the five-fold
ministry of apostles, prophets, evangelists, pastors and teachers (see
Ephesians 4:11). When this occurs, the prophecy of Paul will come to
pass. He warned:

For the time will come when they will not endure sound doctrine;

but after their own lusts <u>shall they heap to themselves</u> teachers,
having itching ears; And they shall turn away their ears from
the truth, and shall be turned unto fables (2 Timothy 4:34).

About the middle of the nineteenth century, the truth of the gospel was strongly challenged by the rise of a movement popularly called the social gospel. Bible criticism infiltrated the Church. Evolution was proclaimed as truth. Genesis was suddenly seen as untrue. The virgin birth was denied. Claims arose that Daniel did not write his prophecy, but that it was written during the silent 400 years after the prophesied kingdoms had arisen and fulfilled their course. The most daring of all the social gospels was the denial of the deity of Christ.

This criticism had its most furious launch in 1859, when Charles Darwin's *Origin of Species* challenged the biblical account of the creation. Much more disconcerting was the claim written in his *Descent of Man* (1871) that Adam was not fashioned out of the dust of the earth, but was descended from the apes. Prior to Darwin, the German scholar David Friedrich Strauss' work, *Life of Jesus,* denied the divinity of Christ. Another book by the same title, authored by the French writer Ernst Renan, denied that Christ had performed miracles or had risen from the dead. Warfare arose between science and theology. When ministers accepted these lies, Christ left their churches. These are the tares among us. Never forget that both wheat and tares are destined to mature.

17 Because thou sayest, I am rich, and increased with goods, and
have need of nothing; and knowest not that thou art wretched,
and miserable, and poor, and blind, and naked:

All around us we see wealthy churches void of Christ's Spirit. They think that because of their prosperity the Lord has favored them. Not so. Paul warned that the church would see *"Perverse disputings of men of corrupt minds, and destitute of the truth, supposing that gain is godliness."* He went on to command, *"From such withdraw thyself"* (1 Timothy 6:5).

> *18 I counsel thee to buy of Me gold tried in the fire, that thou mayest be rich; and white raiment, that thou mayest be clothed, and that the shame of thy nakedness do not appear; and anoint thine eyes with eye salve, that thou mayest see.*
>
> *19 As many as I love, I rebuke and chasten: be zealous therefore, and repent.*
>
> *20 Behold, I stand at the door, and knock: if any man hear My voice, and open the door, I will come in to him, and will sup with him, and he with Me.*
>
> *21 To him that overcometh will I grant to sit with Me in my throne, even as I also overcame, and am set down with My father in His throne.*
>
> *22 He that hath an ear, let him hear what the Spirit saith unto the churches.*

REVELATION CHAPTER 4
THE HEAVENLY VISION

Chapters 4 and 5 are visions of preparation. It is not until chapter 6 is interpreted that the future begins to be revealed. This is a great interlude. Christ is further revealing Himself to His church. He is sitting upon His heavenly throne in the authority that David prophesied (Psalm 110:1) and Peter confirmed (Acts 2:34,35). He possesses all power and authority. This is the day of His power (Psalm 110:3), and His people are willing to demonstrate this authority. In so demonstrating, all His enemies will ultimately be subdued, and only then will Christ leave His throne and return to the earth. Acts 3:20,21; Hebrews 10:12,13; and 1 Corinthians 15:24-28 prove this assertion. Two great prophets of the Old Testament had similar visions of Christ seated in His glory. These visions, like John's, were given in preparation for further historical revealing. Ezekiel 1 and Isaiah 6 were allowed to record the glorified Christ.

> *1 After this I looked, and, behold, a door was opened in heaven: and the first voice which I heard was as it were of a trumpet talking with me; which said, Come up hither, and I will show thee things which must be hereafter.*

In John 10:9, Jesus proclaimed, *"I am the door."* Only through Christ can the heavenly be seen and understood. *"After this"* is interpreted in some revisions to state *"After these things."* The things which had been stated previously were the letters to the seven churches. Now Christ points John toward the future. Likewise the word *"hereafter"* (literally, *"after these things")* signifies that the vision was describing things yet to be established in the growing Kingdom of God.

Come Up Hither: Oh, what the dispensationalists have attempted to do with these words! To interpret a rapture of the Church from this phrase could only be a result of marvelous blindness. No such doctrine is taught. John ascended, in the Spirit, to observe the visions. That's it. The futurists further attempt to point out that the Church is not mentioned again until Chapter 19:11. We can thank Scofield for this.[47] Furthermore, they say that the Church will not go through the Seals, Trumpets, and Vials of judgment. My friends, they fail to notice that the word "saints" is mentioned several times, as well as "martyrs" and "overcomers." Who are these if they be not the Church? To abide by their argument, one would have to reject the Gospel of John because he doesn't mention the Church either. Chilton argues the point well:

> On the basis of such a curious principle of interpretation we could say with assurance the Revelation doesn't tell us any-thing about Jesus either until chapter 12, because the name "Jesus" does not occur until then (thus "the Lion of the tribe of Judah" and "the Lamb that was slain" [5:5-6] must be terms for someone else). Of course, this method of interpretation involves even more problems for the dispensationalists: *for the word "Church" never again appears in the entire Book of Revelation at all!*[48]

Again, I believe that sanctified common sense has prevailed on this point. The blatant manipulation of the Scriptures by the dispensational-ists is remarkable.

---

47   *The Scofield Reference Bible,* New York, 1909. See note on Rev. 4:1.

48   David Chilton, *The Days of Vengeance,* page 147. The author further elaborates: "In addi-tion, the first fifteen chapters of Paul's letter to the Romans doesn't concern the Church, for the word *Church* doesn't appear there either!"

2 And immediately I was in the Spirit: and, behold, a throne was set in heaven, and one sat on the throne.

3 And He that sat was to look upon like a jasper and a sardius stone: and there was a rainbow round about the throne, in sight like unto an emerald.

John's gaze is directed first of all to the throne of God, and its glory is likened to highly polished stones. Symbolically, Christ is reflecting the glory of God. Some day New Jerusalem will likewise reflect God's glory; hence her similar jeweled description. (See Revelation 21:9-21.) Surely, John did not see a literal pile of jewels. Remember, *symbolic language* is a key to understanding the Revelation. This language must be consistently applied. Not only is glory being reflected, but also mercy. The *"rainbow"* speaks of mercy given after the flood. The *"emerald"* (green) speaks of peace and serenity. Green is the most soothing color to the eye. To behold Christ is to behold his glory, mercy and peace.

4 And round about the throne were four and twenty seats: and upon the seats I saw four and twenty elders sitting, clothed in white raiment; and they had on their heads crowns of gold.

This verse speaks of government in the Kingdom of God. I believe the twenty-four elders represent the Old and New Testament Church twelve apostles plus twelve overcomers from the Old Testament, possibly the leaders of the twelve tribes of Israel. There is a variety of thought-provoking interpretations regarding these elders. Nevertheless, what we have here is a heavenly executive. In Matthew 19:28, Jesus said, *"the Son of man shall sit on the throne of His glory* [which He is presently doing], *ye also* [the twelve apostles] *shall sit upon twelve thrones, judging the twelve tribes of Israel.*" Jesus likened His government (twelve being the number of divine government in Scripture) to a city with twelve foundations, named after twelve apostles. Together with His twelve gates, *"which are the names of the twelve tribes of the children of Israel"* (Revelation 21:12). Again I quote from Chilton's insight relative to the symbolic "Presbytery of Heaven":

But the picture of the twenty-four elders is based on something much more specific than the mere notion of multiplying twelve. In the worship of the Old Covenant there were twenty-four divisions of priests (1 Chron. 24) and twenty-four divisions of singers in the Temple (1 Chron. 25). Thus, the picture of twenty-four leaders of worship was not a new idea to those who first read the Revelation: It had been a feature of the worship of God's people for over a thousand years.[49]

5 And Out of the throne proceeded lightnings, and thunderings, and voices: and there were seven lamps of fire burning before the throne, which are the seven Spirits of God.

The power of God is symbolized. The *"seven Spirits of God"* are described in Isaiah 11:1-5, revealing the seven-fold nature of the Spirit of God. This is beautifully symbolized by the lampstand in the tabernacle of the Old Testament (Exodus 25:31,32,37; 26:35; 27:20); it had seven lamps, but all were joined to one lampstand. Therefore, there is but one God, and His power radiates like seven streams of power through the Holy Ghost. We shall also see the seven-fold nature of Christ depicted in Revelation

---

49   ibid., page 152. Chilton credits his information to Alfred Edersheim, *The Temple: Its Ministry and Services as They Were at the Time of Jesus Christ* (Grand Rapids: 1980), pages 75, 86ff. Ezekiel saw twenty-five men serving in the Temple: the representatives of the twenty-four courses of the priesthood, plus the High Priest. (Ezek. 8:16)

5:6. Jesus is depicted as the Lamb having *"seven eyes,"* depicting the fact that He is the fullness of God's wisdom and truth, and *"seven horns"* proclaiming Him as perfect king.

> *6 And before the throne there was a sea of glass, like unto crystal: and in the midst of the throne, and round about the throne, were four beasts full of eyes before and behind.*
> *7 And the first beast was like a lion, and the second beast like a calf, and the third beast had a face as a man, and the fourth beast was like a flying eagle.*

Verse 6 gives us a picture of peace and tranquillity before the throne. In contrast, the nations of the earth are prophetically pictured as "waters," the connotation being that they are restless and turbulent. This is the state of those whom the *"great whore"* sits upon (Revelation 17:1). Most commentators translate the word *"beasts"* to *"living creatures."* We have similar imagery used in the first chapter of Ezekiel. These living creatures are even more intimately connected with the throne than the twenty-four elders. The Lion, Calf (Ox), Man and Eagle depict God's earthly creation, namely: the beasts of the forest, the beasts of the field, the fowls of the air, and Man who governs them all.[50] The same symbols were also used to depict the four sides of the four-square setting of Israel's camp in the wilderness at Sinai. This positioning formed a cross around the tabernacle, headed by Dan to the north, its banner an Eagle; Rueben to the south, its banner a Man; Ephraim to the west, his banner an Ox; and Judah to the east, his banner a Lion. Still others see the significance portrayed in the gospels, namely: the Gospel of Matthew portraying Christ in His royal office (Lion); Mark accentuating the sacrificial character (Ox);

---

50   4 John S. Fox, *A Flood of Light Upon the Book of Revelation,* page 39.

Luke revealing Christ's human nature (Man); and John revealing Christ's supreme deity (Eagle).

> *8 And the four beasts had each of them six wings about him; and they were full of eyes within: and they rest not day and night, saying, Holy, holy, holy, Lord God Almighty, which was, and is, and is to come.*
>
> *9 And when those beasts give glory, and honor and thanks to Him that sat on the throne, who liveth for ever and ever,*
>
> *10 The four and twenty elders fall down before Him that sat on the throne, and worship Him that liveth for ever and ever, and cast their crowns before the throne saying,*
>
> *11 Thou art worthy, O Lord, to receive glory, and honor, and power: for Thou hast created all things, and for Thy pleasure they are and were created.*

The vision draws our attention to the six wings of the living creatures, which associates them with the seraphim of Isaiah's vision. (See Isaiah 6:1-3.)

They Rest Not: "Oh! happy unrest!" was the joyous acclaim of John Wesley.[51]

---

[51]   Isaiah 62:6-7: "I have set watchmen upon thy walls, O Jerusalem, which shall never hold their peace day or night: ye that make mention of the Lord, keep not silence, and *give Him no rest,* till He establish, and till He make Jerusalem a praise in the earth."

REVELATION CHAPTER 5
THE SCROLL SEALED SEVEN TIMES

1 And I saw in the right hand of Him that sat on the throne a book written within and on the back side, sealed with seven seals.

The book which the apostle sees is not like the books we have today. It was a scroll. John Wesley described the scroll of John's era:

> The usual books of the ancients were not like ours, but were volumes, or long pieces of parchment, rolled upon a long stick, as we frequently roll silks. Such was this represented, which was sealed with seven seals. Not as if the apostle saw all the seals at once; for there were seven volumes wrapped up one within another, each of which was sealed; so that upon opening and unrolling the first, the second appeared to be sealed up till that was opened, and so on to the seventh.[52]

Written Within, And On The Backside: This is a great key in interpreting the Book of Revelation. Not only were the Seals to be opened in successive stages, thus revealing the progressive development of critical historical events, it was also revealing the fact that this prophecy is a *story twice told!* The scroll was written on both sides. As the Revelation is interpreted, the themes of these two stories become quite clear. From Chapters 6 through 11 we see the prophecy revolve around great *secular* events which affect the Church. In Chapter 12 we begin again the Christian era and follow a great *ecclesiastical* struggle with the counterfeit church, until

---

52   Uriah Smith, *Daniel and the Revelation,* page 391.

that spiritual Babylon is destroyed. The prophecy ends by revealing that the Kingdom of God will be established above all the nations-forever.[53]

> *2 And I saw a strong angel proclaiming with a loud voice, Who*
> *is worthy to open the book, and to loose the seals thereof?*
> *3 And no man in heaven, nor in earth, neither under the earth,*
> *was able to open the book, neither to look thereon.*
> *4 And I wept much, because no man was found worthy to open*
> *and to read the book, neither to look thereon.*
> *5 And one of the elders saith unto me, Weep not: behold, the*
> *Lion of the tribe of Judah, the Root of David, hath prevailed to*
> *open the book, and to loose the seven seals thereof:*

I believe the emotional trauma that John experienced here is self evident. He is, no doubt, astonished to discover that not even the twenty-four elders are worthy to open the Seals and unravel the Lord's spectacular secrets. Christ alone—the Lion of the tribe of Judah—was given the authority. John Fox makes an interesting observation about Christ being *"given"* the revelation:

> As we were told clearly at the start of the story (Rev. 1:1),
> even the Lord Jesus Himself did not know the details of these
> things until God "gave" Him this ***"revelation."*** As He Himself
> also admitted, He did not even know when He was to return
> … for He said: *"Of that day and that hour knoweth no man,*

53   2 Elliott stated: "It is to be remembered that the subject of the promised revelation was large and complex … It was to be the same, in effect, as that which in its retrospective delineation constitutes the combined *secular* and *ecclesiastical* history of Christendom: -the former, or secular, comprehending the grand political changes and revolutions of the Roman world, with the agencies instrumental in causing them, whether from without or from within: the latter, or ecclesiastical, the outward fortunes, adverse or prosperous, of the church; its purity or corruptions of doctrine and worship, its general apostasy in the course of time, the coalescing of the apostatizing church with the world, and the separation, sufferings, faith, protection, and ultimate triumph of the saints, that is of the true people, the spiritual church of God." *(Horae Apocalypticae,* Vol.1 page 94.)

no, not the angels which are in heaven, neither the Son, but the Father." (Mark 13:32). It was therefore the Father's privilege to reveal His own secrets to whomsoever He would, and in His own time; and this picture shows that He unveiled them to His beloved Son alone; for this was the *"Revelation of Jesus Christ which God GAVE unto Him..."* (Rev. 1:1).[54]

The Lion Of The Tribe Of Judah: "Judah is a lion's whelp" (Genesis 49:9); see also Isaiah 11:1,10. Jesus was of the tribe of Judah, *the Root of David,* or descended from David.

> *6 And I beheld, and, lo, in the midst of the throne and of the four beasts, and in the midst of the elders, stood a Lamb, as it had been slain, having seven horns and seven eyes, which are the seven Spirits of God sent forth into all the earth.*

John, looking through his tears, expected to see a Lion, but instead he saw an innocent Lamb *as it had been slain,* and on this vital phrase, Adam Clarke commented:

> As if now in the act of being offered, this is very remarkable. So important is the sacrificial offering of Christ in the sight of God; that he is still represented as being in the very act of pouring out his blood for the offenses of man. This gives great advantage to faith; when any soul comes to the throne of grace, he finds a sacrifice there provided for him to offer to God.

Scholars have looked at verse 6 with the understanding that the Greek implies the Lamb appearing with a wounded, bleeding neck. A victim,

---

54   3 John S. Fox, *A Flood of Light Upon The Book of Revelation,* page 40.

it was smitten at the altar.[55] Furthermore, this picture of the Lamb having *"seven horns"* and *"seven eyes"* *is* obviously not a literal portrait of Jesus, but a symbol of Jesus as perfect in kingship and perfect in wisdom.

> *7 And He came and took the book out of the right hand of Him that sat upon the throne.*
>
> *8 And when He had taken the book, the four beasts and four and twenty elders fell down before the Lamb, having every one of them harps, and golden vials full of odors, which are the prayers of the saints.*
>
> *9 And they sang a new song, saying, Thou art worthy to take the book, and to open the seals thereof: for Thou wast slain, and hast redeemed us to God by Thy blood out of every kindred, and tongue, and people, and nation;*
>
> *10 And hast made us unto our God, kings and priests: and we shall reign on the earth.*

There are two critical points to be addressed in this great *"new song."* First, the word "us" in verse 9 is correctly translated *"them."* And in verse 10, "us" again is correctly interpreted *"them,"* and *"we"* should be *"they."* Why the reason for this adjustment? Simple, angelic beings have no need of redemption. Angelic beings will not reign upon this earth- we will. Let's read this with the proper pronouns inserted: *"For thou wast slain, and has redeemed **them** to God ... and hast made **them** unto our God kings, and priests: and **they** shall reign ..."* Second, the proclamation *"they shall reign upon the earth"* means just what it says. It is

---

55   Isaiah 63:4-,5: "Surely he hath borne our griefs, and carried our sorrows: yet we did esteem Him stricken, smitten of God, and afflicted. But He was wounded for our transgressions, He was bruised for our iniquities: the chastisement of our peace was upon Him; and with His stripes we are healed."

our destiny to reign with Christ on this earth. Again, I would like to quote Chilton. I agree with his themes of destiny and dominion; however, we drastically part company beginning with the interpretation of the six seals. I will reveal the truths that great Protestants espoused for centuries, even unto death. Chilton, however, will declare the errors of Alcazar-the preterist scheme. But on the point of reigning we agree, and he stated the issue eloquently:

> Christ has purchased His people out of the nations, not only to redeem them from sin, but to enable them to fulfill God's original Dominion Mandate for man. As the Second Adam, Christ sets His New Creation the task Adam forfeited-this time, however, on the unshakeable foundation of His death, resurrection, and ascension. Salvation has a purpose, a saving to as well as a saving from. Christ has made His people to be kings and priests to our God, and has guaranteed their destiny: They will reign upon the earth. This shows us the direction of history. The redeemed of the Lord, already a nation of kingly priests, are moving toward the complete dominion God had planned as His original program for man. In Adam it had been lost; Jesus Christ, the Second Adam, has redeemed us and restored us to our royal priesthood, so that we will reign upon the earth. Through the work of Christ the definitive victory over Satan has been won. We are promised increasing victories, and increasing rule and dominion, as we bring the Gospel and law of the great King to fruition throughout the world.[56]

---

56   David Chilton, *The Days of Vengeance*, page 179.

Now I suppose that the greatest problem some will have with this verse and the above mentioned interpretation is the phrase, *"new heaven and a new earth."* What is meant by this? How are we going to rule on something which is destined to pass away? This is a great stumbling block for many eschatologists. I think the answer is relatively simple. Remember, the prophets spoke with symbolic language. When Peter prophesied of the *"new heavens and the new earth"* (2 Peter 3:13), he spoke in like language of the prophet Isaiah who stated:*"For, behold, I create new heavens and a new earth: and the former shall not be remembered, nor come into mind"* (Isaiah 65:17). Many scholars view these passages as a revolution of a moral and spiritual nature, and they reference the analogy that Paul uses when he speaks of the change wrought in conversion (2 Corinthians 5:17; Galatians 6:15). Remember, Peter's prophecy yearned for an earth *"wherein dwelleth righteousness,"* not a new planet and an accompanying solar system. And to conclude the point, Daniel prophesied that Christ's Kingdom would last *"for ever, even for ever and ever"* (Daniel 7:18).

> *11 And I beheld, and I heard the voice of many angels round about the throne, and the beasts and the elders; and the number of them was ten thousand times ten thousand, and thousands of thousands;*
>
> *12 Saying with a loud voice, Worthy is the Lamb that was slain to receive power, and riches, and wisdom, and strength, and honor, and glory, and blessing.*
>
> *13 And every creature which is in heaven, and on the earth, and under the earth, and such as are in the sea, and all that are in them, heard I saying, Blessing, and honor, and glory, and power, be unto Him that sitteth upon the throne, and unto the Lamb for ever and ever.*

A final thought on the glory of these doxologies from B. W. Johnson:

> And the picture grows still grander as the heavenly tenants sing their praises of the Lamb. First, the four living creatures and the elders sing a new song; then a countless number of angels, about the throne, the living creatures and the elders join in the chorus. These praises ring through the heavens, and the reverberations reach from heaven to earth, and every creature "in heaven," and on the earth, and under the earth, and such as are in the sea join in the ascription of praise to the Lamb. To these praises the cherubim respond, Amen! and the elders fall down and worship Him that liveth forever and ever.[57]

---

57   B. W. Johnson, *The People's New Testament With Notes.* page 433.

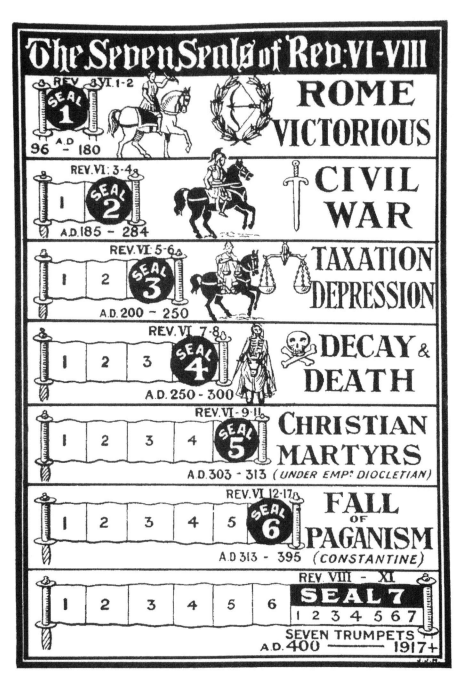

Illustration taken from: *The Pope, Communism and the Coming New World* by Thomas Foster

REVELATION CHAPTER 6
THE FIRST SIX SEALS
PAGAN ROME'S DEMISE

The general subject of the six Seals is the temporary prosperity of the heathen Roman Empire, and its decline and fall before the unfolding progress of the Christian Church. The prophecies revealed in the six Seals are all contained in one small chapter of the Revelation. Logically, these must cover only a small portion of history from John's day onward. It is with this unfolding chapter that the evidence for the historicist interpretation is forcefully initiated. These Seals are not for the distant future as taught by Ribera, neither are they prophecies pertaining to the fall of Jerusalem, Alcazar's counter scheme. They are the clear and consistent metaphors, which have been vindicated by historical fulfillment, pertaining to Pagan Rome's upheaval and demise from the first through the fourth centuries.

From the point of the Seals forward, Elliott briefly summarized the journey which lies before us as we uncover the apocalyptic symbols:

Turning from the prophecy to the history, there seems to me on the whole to be six chief parts, or acts, clearly defined in the sacred prefigurative drama before us ... their historic subject-matter being, respectively as follows:

> I. That of the temporary glory, and then the decline and fall of Rome Pagan, before the power of Christianity: the subject of the six first Seals.
>
> II. The *ravage and destruction of Rome Christian,* after its apostasy, in its divisions both east and west; of the western empire by the *Goths,* of the eastern by the *Saracens* and *Turks:*

the subject of the six first Trumpets.

III. The history of the *Reformation,* as introduced about the middle of the sixth Trumpet.

IV. The supplemental and explanatory history of the *rise* and *character* of the *Papacy* and *Papal Empire,* that sprung out of the Gothic inundations of Western Europe: a part corresponding, as I see it, with the *writing without* on the prophetic roll; and which was exhibited in preparation for the figuration of the Popedom's final overthrow.

IV. The final *overthrow* of the *Papacy* and *Papal Empire,* under the outpouring of the Vials of God's wrath; and the coming of Christ to judgment. Consequent on which follows,

V. The glorious consummation ...[58]

What a wonderful field of historic exploration lies before us. A journey which will take us through nineteen centuries, and bring us to our place in the Book of Revelation.

FIRST SEAL (A.D. 96-180)
ROME VICTORIOUS

1 And I saw when the Lamb opened one of the seals, and I heard, as it were the noise of thunder, one of the four beasts saying, Come and see.

2 And I saw, and behold a white horse: and He that sat on Him had a bow; and a crown was given unto Him: and He went forth conquering, and to conquer.

---

58   E. B. Elliott, *Horoe Apocalypticae,* Vol. IV; pages 107-108.

At the breaking of the first Seal, a horse and its rider cross the landscape. In this series of visions, the color of the horse represents the condition of the people at that particular time, and the rider represents the cause of this condition.

This era begins with the accession of Nerva, on the murder of his predecessor Domitian in A. D. 96, and it includes the reigns of the Emperors Nerva, A. D. 96-98; Trajan, A. D. 98-117; Hadrian, A. D. 117-138; Antoninus Pius, A. D. 138-161; Marcus Antoninus Aurelius, A. D. 161-180; ending with the accession of Commodus in that year.[59]

White Horse: The white horse was symbolic of Roman imperialism at its height. The military conquests of the Roman generals is depicted here. They always rode on white horses in their victory parades. In the Book of Daniel, we have the Persian Empire symbolized by a ram (Daniel 8:3); the Macedonian Empire by a goat (Daniel 8:5), but here the white horse is clearly Rome. The horse was never used by the Jews or Orientals as a beast of burden; historically, the ox and ass were reserved to that office. The horse was reserved for war. The prophets associate the horse with war-like situations; and denoting white, victory is being proclaimed. (Note: this is not the same "white horse" which appears in Chapter 19. The riders have nothing in common.) Rome saw her greatest victory parades during this; time of expansion and conquest. This is *The Golden Age of Rome,* also called *The Age of the Antonines.* Between A. D. 96 to 180, Rome expanded, by military conquest, until it occupied most of the territories of the three preceding empires of Babylon, Medo-Persia and Greece.

The Bow: This bow not only tells of Rome's military character, but it also reveals something very specific about the emperors themselves. We find that the symbol of the bow is strikingly fulfilled with a close look

---

59   Gibbon (Vol. I, page 95) declares that "if a man was called upon to **fix** the period in the history of the world, during which the condition of the human race was most prosperous and happy, he would without hesitation name that which elapsed from the death of Domitian to the accession of Commodus."

at the Emperor Nerva and the dynasty which followed him-specifically Trajan and the Antonines. Before this age, the emperors were of Roman stock. Until the death of Nero, they were of the line of Julius Caesar. Nerva, the founder of a new line of Caesars (Emperors), was of Greek descent, specifically of Cretan stock. The Cretans were known as a race of bowmen, some say the most famous of the ancient world. Ancient Cretan coins, still displayed in the British Museum depict a *Cretan with a bow in his hand!*[60] To quote Elliott, "Yes! the meaning of the bow in the rider's hand is now indeed manifest."

The Crown: The crown mentioned here is the *"stephanos"* or circle of laurels, not the *"diadem"* which is a metal jeweled crown. Again, our Lord has revealed His accuracy, for the *laurel wreaths of victory, not the diadems,* were worn by the emperors of this period. In Revelation 19:11-16 the rider of that white horse wears the diadem, who, of course, is our Lord. The dispensationalists try to tell us that this is Antichrist, yet to come. Someone has not "studied to show himself approved unto God."

SECOND SEAL (A. D. 185-284)
CIVIL WAR

3 And when He had opened the second seal, I heard the second beast say, Come and see.
4 And there went out another horse that was red; and power was given to him that sat thereon to take peace from the earth, and that they should kill one another: and there was given unto him a great sword.

---

60   The reader is urged to examine Elliott's extensive evidence on this point (pictures of the coins included). See *Horae Apocalypticae*, pages 130-138.

Notice that the color of the horse changes from white to red. This represents going from peace to war; from peace to bloodshed.

They Should Kill One Another: This speaks to us of civil war. This is exactly what happened during this second period of Roman history. The law and order of the emperors is displaced by the rule of the sword. This is the beginning of the decline and fall of the great Roman Empire. During this period of time, there were no less than 32 emperors, who in turn were opposed by 27 pretenders, who used the *"great sword."*

The Earth: This is a vital point which will be pointed out several times in this book. The "earth" envisioned by John was the Roman Earth or Empire, not the whole world. The word "earth" at this point in the Book of Revelation is *ghay* pronounced "ge." It means *"a region."* Without this knowledge, it is impossible to interpret the territory in which the Trumpets will blow.

The period of the second Seal is one of the most prolonged and bloody civil commotions in recorded history.[61]

THIRD SEAL (A. D. 200-250)
TAXATION AND ECONOMIC DEPRESSION

5 And when He had opened the third seal, I heard the third beast

---

61   "Peace was taken from the earth" for ninety-two years. During the period of nearly a century, the Roman Empire, that portion of the earth which was the seat of civilization and of the Christian religion, was constantly torn by bloody contests between rival competitors for power. The history of this epoch is epitomized by Sismondi in the following language: "With Commodus commenced the third and most calamitous period. It lasted ninety-two years, from 192 to 284. During that period, thirty-two emperors, and twenty-seven pretenders alternately hurled each other from the throne by *incessant civil warfare. Ninety-two years of almost incessant civil warfare* taught the world on what a frail foundation the virtue of the Antonines had placed the felicity of the *empire" (Sismondi's Fall of the Roman Empire,* Vol. I page 36). A full history of this dark unhappy period is also given in the first volume of Gibbon. During the ninety-two years there were thirty-four emperors, besides nineteen pretenders, known as tyrants. *Of these, all but two died violent deaths.* What could more strikingly represent such a period of civil contention, of incessant civil warfare, of fratricidal bloodshed, than the red horse and its rider, "to whom was given a great sword, and the power to take away peace, that men should kill one another"? I suppose that no such prolonged and terrible period of civil warfare can be pointed out in the history of the world, and there is certainly a wonderful correspondence between the vision and the events of history. (B.W. Johnson, *The People's New Testament,* "The Fulfillment," page 436.)

say, Come and see. And I beheld, and lo a black horse; and he
that sat on him had a pair of balances in his hand.
6 And I heard a voice in the midst of the four beasts say, A
measure of wheat for a penny, and three measures of barley for
a penny,· and see thou hurt not the oil and the wine.

We now go from a red horse to a black horse and its rider. This symbolizes the despair and gloom of the Roman people and their situation. The black horse speaks of a condition of depression. The burden of taxation in the Empire was extremely excessive; endeavoring to pay the high costs of war. Excessive taxation is a terrible curse upon a people.[62]

A Pair Of Balances In His Hand: Balances (scales) mentioned in verse 5 were a common symbol in the empire and represented justice and commerce. This was also the badge of the provincial governors who were assigned to regulate the taxation. The cry of the government at this time was for "taxes to support the armies of Rome." These taxes could be paid with money, or the equivalent value of produce, specifically wheat, oil, and wine. To keep the taxation from being unjust it was necessary to value the produce in terms of money, hence *the voice, "A measure of wheat for a penny … etc."*

Now because of the necessary conversion of produce into money, the Revelation proclaims, *"See thou hurt not the oil and the wine."* The word "hurt" (adikeo) is better translated "be not unjust"-in other words, let the taxation be fair.

---

62   "The results of this oppressive taxation were, as might be expected, a general wasting of the Roman state. Agriculture was insensibly ruined, thus making no preparation for famine; the most fertile provinces became depopulated and desolate; personal suffering and distress prevailed even to despair; and patriotism was gradually extinguished. In short, as Gibbon expressed it, "The industry of the people was discouraged and exhausted by a long series of oppression." (E. P. Cachernaille, *The Visions of Daniel and of the Revelation Explained,* page 181.)

During this period, the Emperor Caracalla granted citizenship to all the free men in the Empire, but only for the purpose of taxing them. Gibbon recorded the oppression as follows:

> The land tax, the capitation, and the heavy contributions of corn, wine, oil, and wheat, exacted from the provinces for the use of the court, the army and the Capital … The great body of Caracalla's subjects were oppressed by the aggravated taxes, and every part of the Empire crushed under the weight of his iron scepter.[63]

Let me mention that the Christians in John's day would quickly decipher the code here referring to the horses. They would see the connection between Revelation 6 and Zechariah 6 in the Old Testament. Both chapters refer to red, black, and white horses, and both metaphors refer to God's judgment on Gentile powers. But the Romans would understand nothing.

FOURTH SEAL (A.D. 250-300)
FAMINE AND DISEASE

7 And when he had opened the fourth seal, I heard the voice of the fourth beast say, Come and see.
8 And I looked, and behold a pale horse: and his name that sat on him was Death, and hell followed with him: and power was given unto them over the fourth part of the earth, to kill with sword, and with hunger, and with death, and with the beasts of the earth.

---

63   John S. Fox, A *Flood of Light Upon the Book of Revelation,* page 45.

The pale horse depicts famine. This is known to be the color of mortification and decay. This signals the coming collapse and disintegration of the Roman Empire.

In verse 8 the word *"hell"* *is* better translated *"hades"* (the grave). After civil war there is always a famine. In the case of the Roman Empire, the famine was devastating. As was prophesied, a fourth of the empire perished. Both Eusebius and Gibbon provide us with graphic historical witness to these judgments. First Eusebius:

> Death waged a desolating war with two weapons, famine and pestilence ... Men, wasted away to mere skeletons, stumbled hither and thither like mere shadows, trembling and tottering. They fell down in the midst of the streets ... then, drawing their last gasp cried out, Hunger! ... Some indeed were already the food of dogs.

How incredibly literal was the fulfillment of this terrible warning that the Romans would fall prey to the "beasts of the earth!" And let the reader turn to the tenth chapter of the first volume of Gibbon's history of Rome, and he will again encounter the confirmation of the prophetic word by an unbiased observer.

> But a long and general famine was a calamity of a more serious kind. It was the inevitable consequence of rapine and oppression, which extirpated the produce of the present and the future harvests. Famine is almost always followed by epidemical diseases, the effect of scanty and unwholesome food. Other causes must, however, have contributed to the furious plague, which, from the years two hundred and fifty to the year two hundred

and sixty-five, raged without interruption in every province, every city, and almost every family of the Roman Empire. *During some time five thousand persons died daily in Rome;* and many towns that had escaped the hands of the Barbarians, were entirely depopulated. Applying this authentic fact to the most correct tables of mortality, it evidently proves, that more than half of the people of Alexandria had perished; and could we venture to extend the analogy to the other provinces, we might suspect that war, pestilence, and famine, had consumed, in a few years, the majority of the human species.

Thus in a series of four consecutive representations, in each of which a symbolic horse and horseman passed forth in vision over the Roman landscape, the coming fortunes of the great military empire of Rome were prefigured.

Though these four symbolisms are briefly proclaimed, they contain within themselves the very spirit of the history of Rome for the next two centuries after John; and are in singular agreement with the best and the most philosophic historians of the Roman Empire. They form an admirable *memoria technica,* in symbol, of those two critical centuries in the decline of heathen Rome.[64]

FIFTH SEAL (A.D. 303-313)
ERA OF THE MARTYRS

9 And when He had opened the fifth seal, I saw under the altar the souls of them that were slain for the word of God, and for the testimony which they held:

10 And they cried with a loud voice, saying, How long, O Lord,

---

64   E. P. Cachemaille, *The Visions of Daniel and of the Revelation Explained,* page 184.

holy and true, dost thou not judge and avenge our blood on them that dwell on the earth?

11 And white robes were given unto every one of them; and it was said unto them, that they should rest for a little season, until their fellow-servants also, and their brethren that should be killed as they were, should be fulfilled.

These verses speak of the Christian martyrs who suffered under the *ten terrible persecutions* unleashed by Pagan Rome, specifically the final (tenth) attempt by Diocletian to root out Christianity from the very face of the earth.[65] This persecution lasted for ten years and is distinguished by the fact that it was the most terrible, most prolonged, and most general persecution known in the history of the ancient church. At the end of the persecutions there were literally hundreds of thousands of martyrs lying symbolically under the altar. They had been sacrificed for the testimony which they held.[66]

These Christians would understand what the altar stood for. It stood for the place of sacrifice in the tabernacle and the temple. The animals of sacrifice were *placed on the altar;* however these martyrs were placed *under the altar,* indicating that they were under the New Covenant and would have eternal life.

The white robes signified that they were righteous before God. Also, the reference to a martyrdom yet to come is mentioned. It must be under-

---

65   The reader is reminded that this persecution's specific divine time measure *(ye shall have tribulation ten days)* was prophesied in the letter to the church at Smyrna (Rev. 2:8-11). The ten days are symbolic of ten years.

66   Early in A. D. 303 secret councils were held in Nicomedia, concerning the destruction of Christianity. "Perhaps," says Gibbon, "it was represented to Diocletian, that the glorious work of the deliverance of the empire was left imperfect so long as an independent people (the Christians) were permitted to subsist and multiply in it." On the twenty-third of February, the first blow was struck. An armed force was sent to destroy the great church of Nicomedia, and to burn the sacred books, so carefully preserved in the day when the printing press was unknown. (B.W. Johnson, *The People's New Testament With Notes,* page 439.)

stood that a *"little season"* to Christ is calculated in God's plan, not our impatient perspectives. This future martyrdom was going to transpire under Antichrist-Papal Rome. In this slaughter over 50 million people would be slain by the apocalyptic beast.

The persecution of the fifth Seal was terminated with the rise of Constantine, A.D. 313. His ascension fulfilled the events of the sixth Seal.[67]

SIXTH SEAL (A.D. 313-390)
THE FALL OF PAGANISM AND ROME DIVIDED

12 And I beheld, when He had opened the sixth seal And lo, there was a great earthquake; and the sun became black as sackcloth of hair, and the moon became as blood;

13 And the stars of heaven fell unto the earth, even as a fig tree casteth her untimely figs, when she is shaken of a mighty wind:

14 And the heaven departed as a scroll when it is rolled together; and every mountain and island were moved out of their places:

Those who fail to understand the symbolism of the Book of Revelation here would envision the end of the world (solar system) and so it would be if this was literal. But these are symbols.[68]

---

67   A final note on this Seal. At the commencement of the persecution, Diocletian, Maximian and Galerius united in erecting pillars commemorating the success in having destroyed the Christian superstition." A medal of this period represents Maximian as Hercules destroying the seven-headed Hydra of Christianity.

68   Those who insist that the opening of the sixth seal portrays the end of the world should bear in mind, not only that the chain of events continues on through the 7th, 8th, 9th, 10th and 11th chapters, and that it is only when the Seventh Angel sounds his trumpet (11:16) that the proclamation is made that "the kingdom of the world is become the kingdom of our Lord and his Christ," but they should keep in mind also that the scenes beheld by John are not literal pictures of the events, but symbolic visions. (B. W. Johnson, *The People's New Testament With Notes,* page 441)

Earthquakes in the prophetic scriptures represent great political upheavals. In the Old Testament, we have seven judgments which are depicted in prophetic metaphors (see Ex. 19:18; Ps. 18:7, 15; 60:2; Isa. 13:13-14; 24:19-20; Nah. 1:5).

The *sun, moon* and *stars* are symbolic of earthly dignitaries, great political authorities and great lights in the political or religious heavens (see Gen. 37:8-10; Dan. 8:5-10; Isa. 13:9,10, 17-20; 34:4-10; Hos. 10:8). Their falling to the earth symbolizes that the government, which is defined by the text of the prophecy (Pagan Rome), is being defeated and removed from the political heavens.

And The Heaven Departed As A Scroll: This speaks of the pagan government disappearing from sight (see Isa. 34:4; 51:6; Ps. 102:25- 26).

And Every Mountain And Island Were Moved Out Of Their Places: This speaks of the "other nations" which were affected by the demise of Pagan Rome (see Job 9:5-6; 14:18-19; 28:9-11; Isa. 41:5, Ezek. 38:20; Nah. 1:4-8; Zeph. 2:11).

> *15 And the kings of the earth, and the great men, and the rich men, and the chief captains, and the mighty men, and every bondman, and every free man, hid themselves in the dens, and in the rocks of the mountains;*
> *16 And said to the mountains and rocks, Fall on us, and hide us from the face of Him that sitteth on the throne, and from the wrath of the Lamb;*
> *17 For the great day of His wrath is come; and who shall be able to stand?*

With the defeat of the firm pagan Maxentius in A.D. 313, the persecutions ceased and the Christian Emperor Constantine, the new political "sun," ascended the throne. This was a mighty political earthquake that totally displaced all pagan authority. To them, it was as if the world had fallen. Such a unique event was portrayed to John as the darkening of the imperial pagan Roman world.

It is now evident that this *"great day of God's wrath"* is not the end of the age. In this context, we have depicted Christ's righteous judgment on the tyranny of the previous three centuries. The historicist Fox comments on this great event and the future implications relevant to the empire in the West:

> Under Constantine's tolerant Christian rule, the Roman earth thereafter had a God-given opportunity to repent: but this it eventually failed to do, hence we shall continue later in the story to see the complete disruption of the Roman Empire in the year A.D. 476. Meanwhile, as an initial step in the process, God began to disintegrate it in the year A.D. 395 by splitting it up into two opposing halves; the Western half becoming ruled by one Emperor (Honorious), and the Eastern half by another (Arcadius). Thus the Sixth Seal brings Rome's history up to the point of the Constantine "earthquake," but has not yet reached the final obliteration of the Roman Empire. We shall see this portrayed as we pass on to unfold the period governed by the Seventh and last Seal, during which period seven angels appear (as shown in chapter eight and onwards) sounding "Seven Trumpets."

These prophecies released by the Seals were all in their correct time, chronology, and correct order as proven by the fulfillment of Pagan Roman history.

We shall see that in less than one century after the conclusion of the sixth Seal, the whole of the Western Roman Empire completely collapses forever, and is subdivided into ten kingdoms as prophesied by Daniel 2 and 7.

REVELATION CHAPTER 7
144,000—THE SYMBOLIC
NUMBER OF GOVERNMENT

A VERY IMPORTANT OBSERVATION NEEDED!

No matter how you interpret this chapter, one irrefutable fact is staring you in the face! This sealing occurs between the 6th Seal, the fall of Rome's Pagan religious dynasty and the first 4 Trumpets, the Gothic invasions of Chapter 8. As you will see, Jesus is protecting his people (the migrated House of Israel) in Western Europe from being demolished by the Gothic hordes who complete the fall of Rome Pagan in the west.

This is not a future occurrence! These are not 144,000 futuristic converted Jews!

Read on…

> *1 And after these things I saw four angels standing on the four corners of the earth, holding the four winds of the earth, that the wind should not blow on the earth, nor on the sea, nor on any tree.*
> *2 And I saw another angel ascending from the east, having the seal of the living God: and he cried with a loud voice to the four angels, to whom it was given to hurt the earth and the sea,*
> *3 Saying, Hurt not the earth, neither the sea, nor the trees, till we have sealed the servants of our God in their foreheads.*
> *4 And I heard the number of them which were sealed: and there*

were sealed a hundred and forty and four thousand *of all the tribes of the children of Israel.*

5 Of the tribe of Judah were sealed twelve thousand. Of the tribe of Reuben were sealed twelve thousand. Of the tribe of Gad were sealed twelve thousand.

6 Of the tribe of Asher were sealed twelve thousand. Of the tribe of Naphtali were sealed twelve thousand. Of the tribe of Manasseh were sealed twelve thousand.

7 Of the tribe of Simeon were sealed twelve thousand. Of the tribe of Levi were sealed twelve thousand. Of the tribe of Issachar were sealed twelve thousand.

8 Of the tribe of Zebulon were sealed twelve thousand. Of the tribe of Joseph were sealed twelve thousand. Of the tribe of Benjamin were sealed twelve thousand.

9 And after this I beheld, and, lo, a great multitude, which no man could number, of all nations, and kindreds, and people, and tongues, stood before the throne, and before the Lamb, clothed with white robes, and palms in their hands; And cried with a loud voice, saying, Salvation to our God which sitteth upon the throne, and unto the Lamb.

PART I: 144,000
"THE EXCLUSIVE COMPANY"

In this great interlude, between the Seals and Trumpets of judgment, we find the 144,000, and we also find a great multitude. As we look closer, we discover that the 144,000 is an **exclusive number;** and the other, "the great multitude" an **all-inclusive number, a** great company which no man could number. We are now going to pursue one of the most daring teachings in this great book. I believe the 144,000 are truly a revelation to the Church. In order to unveil the symbolic language, it will be necessary that I cut some traditional doctrinal nerves. I pray you have the capacity to follow the operation. Let me open this discourse with two broad statements:

First, I do not believe that these 144,000 are only literal Israelites, or futuristic Jews, as the dispensationalists teach. When we examine the tribes that are named, we immediately notice that the tribe of Dan is left out, and the tribe of Manasseh is added on. Why did God do this? Didn't the text state, *"of all the tribes of Israel"*? The omitting of Dan was a signal that much more is being implied. After all, you should understand by now that this is a book of signs and symbols.

Second, I believe that the 144,000 represent an exclusive part of Christ's New Testament church. Those who are redeemed by His blood, baptized in His name, and sealed with the Holy Spirit of promise are an exclusive company. Now the burden of proof is demanded. Now we can plow into divine revelation.

In Revelation 2:9, 3:9, John stated candidly that, when a Jew is mentioned in the Book of Revelation it doesn't mean a literal Jew, but a symbolic Jew. The apostle Paul has already taught us God's definition of true Jews. He stated, *"For he is not a Jew, which is one outwardly; neither is that circumcision, which is outward in the flesh: But he is a Jew, which is one inwardly; and circumcision is that of the heart, in the spirit, and not in the letter; whose praise is not of men, but of God"* (Romans 2:28,29). This is God's recognition of His New Testament people under the New Covenant. The only Jew God recognizes now is that one who is the inward Jew, circumcised of the heart. Paul again wrote, *"For we are the circumcision, which worships God in the spirit, and rejoice in Christ*

Jesus, and have no confidence in the flesh" (Philippians 3:3). Also see 1 Peter 2:9,10.

The Kingdom in this age is the true circumcision. (Matthew 21:43). The Jerusalem in the Book of Revelation is Zion. We find this in Revelation 3:12, and very specially in Revelation 21:2 which states, "*And I John saw the holy city, new Jerusalem, coming down from God out of heaven, prepared as a bride adorned for her husband.*" REMEMBER THE CHURCH IS CHRIST'S BODY, TRUE ISRAEL IS HIS BRIDE. Furthermore, John stated, "*And I looked, and lo, a Lamb stood on the mount Zion, and with Him a hundred forty and four thousand, having His Father's name written in their foreheads*" (Revelation 14:1).

A VERY IMPORTANT RECOMMENDATION!

If you are under the impression that the Jews currently living in the Jewish state, in the ancient land of Israel, are the only remnant of the House of Israel and the House of Judah, God's chosen people of whom the Bible tells the history and destiny of, then you are misinformed by the Dispensationalists. Here is where you need to go if you want to understand your Bible:

TRUTH IN HISTORY
P.O. BOX 808
OWASSO, OKLAHOMA 74055
WWW.TRUTHINHISTORY.ORG

THE BRIDE OF CHRIST IS A VERY DEEP SUBJECT. THE DIFFERENCE BETWEEN THE BODY AND THE BRIDE MUST BE UNDERSTOOD.

Now that we understand that the number 144,000 is symbolic, we can seek the deeper meaning. How does this symbolism apply to the Body of Christ? What is Christ trying to tell His Church?

The number 12 (Bible scholars are very much aware of this in the Scriptures) is the number of divine government. When we look at Jerusalem in the Book of Revelation, we see that the New Jerusalem, which is the bride of Christ, has a series of twelves in its matrix: 12 gates; 12 angels; the names of the 12 tribes on the gates; 12 foundation stones, and the names of the 12 apostles of the Lamb on the stones. The 12 gates are 12 pearls, and the tree of life yields 12 fruits in the restored paradise of God (see Revelation 21:12-21; 23:2). So all of this isin harmony with our Lord's own words to the apostles when he said, *"Ye also shall sit upon twelve thrones, judging the twelve tribes of Israel"* (Matthew 19:28).

In addition, the New Jerusalem lies four square with 12,000 furlongs on each side. The walls are 144 (12 X 12) cubits high. And God tells us, *"out of **Zion** shall go forth the law, and the word of the Lord from **Jerusalem**"* (Isaiah 2:3).

Those who overcome in this life, those who have repented and been Spirit-filled, those who have been baptized in the name of Jesus (Acts 2:38), will rule and reign with our Lord Jesus Christ in the New Jerusalem. This is an exclusive part of the Bride of Christ.

In verse 1 we read of *winds,* or destructive forces (These were the 4 Gothic invasions being held back until the symbolic sealing); the *earth,* which speaks of earthly power, carnal power, the power of men as opposed to the power of God; the *sea,* defined as elements of storm, nations in a state of restless agitation; and *trees,* the great and powerful ones of the world. Ezekiel 12:22-24 proves this. What do these metaphors tell us? They reveal that nothing will be able to stop Christ from building His Church, and even the gates of hell will not prevail against it. Nothing will prevent the sealing of these exclusive members of Christ's Bride.

Paul stated, *"For by one Spirit are we all baptized into one body..."* (1 Corinthians 12:13). Likewise, to the Ephesian church he writes, *"in whom also after that ye believed, ye were sealed with that holy Spirit of promise"* (Ephesians 1:13). Paul was speaking of Christians who are sealed, not Jews in the millennium. These are believers who have received the baptism in the Holy Ghost, which is the sealing of the Spirit. This is one of the requirements for being counted among the 144,000; they were sealed (Revelation 7:3).

In chapter fourteen, John further identified the exclusive company. He stated, *"These are they which were not defiled with women; for they are **virgins**... These were redeemed from among men, being the **first fruits** unto God..."* (v. 4). Specifically, John symbolizes this company with the terms *"virgins"* and *"first fruits."* Let us now endeavor to find like symbolism applied to the Church the Bride. First, James uses this terminology in stating, *"Of His own will begat He us with the word of truth, that we* [True Israel] *should be a kind of **first fruits** of His creation"* (James 1:18): And second, Paul employed the other metaphor by stating, *"For I am jealous over you with godly jealousy: for I have espoused you* [True Israel] *to one husband, that I may present you as a chaste **virgin** to Christ"* (2 Corinthians 11:2).

This is what the Bride of Christ is going to be like on that great day when she has matured and *"made herself ready"* (Revelation 19:7). You cannot live your life the way you want to and expect to be in the New Jerusalem on that great day. God is not speaking about any denomination, He is speaking of His Bride that will rule and reign with him, the symbolic 144,000.

Notice also that these 144,000 are baptized in the name of the Lord Jesus Christ. How do we know this? We know because they have their Father's name written in their foreheads (Revelation 14:1).

When I was properly baptized into the name of Jesus, I took upon me the name of the Father—according to the Word of God. Isaiah revealed that the child was going to be the *"Everlasting Father"* (Isaiah 9:6). Further, John has already revealed that the overcomers had the name of God written upon them. Also, the name of the city is written upon them, so they are the inhabitants of the New Jerusalem. *"Him that overcometh will I make a pillar in the temple of my God… I will write upon him the name of my God, and the name of the city of my God, which is new Jerusalem, which cometh down out of heaven from my God"* (Revelation 3:12).

I think this is it in a nutshell. It is so beautiful. When we come to understand the Book of Revelation, we again see the beauty of our God. Likewise, we see the demands that He makes on His Church. However, if the demands are great, how much greater the rewards must be.

So before we precede, let me summarize the 144,000. They are the exclusive elect of the Bride of Christ, true overcomers, baptized in His name, sealed with the Holy Ghost-the true Bride of Christ. Apostle Paul says in l Corinthians 12:27, ***"Members in particular."*** This is the mighty Church that was founded on the day of Pentecost. We are placed in this Church by the baptism in the Holy Ghost.

PART II: THE GREAT MULTITUDE "THE INCLUSIVE COMPANY"

In this chapter of the Revelation, we read about an all inclusive congregation: *"A great multitude, which no man could number"* (v. 9). Who are these that sing the song of salvation, having washed their robes and made them white in the blood of the Lamb? I believe, and have believed for many years, that these can properly be termed, **"the friends of the Bridegroom."**

Now before you panic, please give very close attention to the argument which I am about to embark upon. Each verse will be critical in our examination. I am convinced that this is a balanced presentation of how people stand before their God.

My friends, there is an exclusive company mentioned here, as we have seen, the 144,000, the number of government in the kingdom of God. And *we* have already examined the requirements to be a part of this company. But there is another multitude which cannot be numbered. These are friends who have been saved by faith. Please examine the following verse closely. John the Baptist made a startling assertion. John was never baptized with the Holy Ghost. He was never in the Body of Christ. Therefore, he is not part of the Bride. John the Baptist revealed that he is content to be a *"friend of the bridegroom"*:

> *He that hath the bride is the bridegroom: but the friend of the bridegroom, which standeth and heareth him, rejoiceth greatly because of the bridegroom's voice:* ***this my joy therefore is fulfilled*** (John 3:29).

In Luke's gospel we read the parable of the great supper. Jesus stated, *"A certain man made a great supper, and bade many: And sent his servant at supper time to say to them that were bidden, Come, for all things are now ready"* (Luke 14:16-17). A great supper has been made. All things are ready.

Now in John's gospel we read: *"Greater love hath no man than this, that he lay down his life for his friends"* (John 15:13). Jesus laid down his life for the friends of the Bridegroom, as well as to redeem his Bride (True Israel). I believe that the Lord laid down His life for all the redeemed, from Abel right through to the second coming. Scripture vindicates this. The Old Testament saints looked forward to the cross: Isaiah could say that Christ would be bruised for his iniquities (Isaiah 53:4,5). Job could say that he knew that his redeemer lived (Job 19:25-27). And David could proclaim that as far as the east is from the west, the Lord had removed his transgressions (Ps. 103:12). The one who would do this would be David's greater son, Jesus Christ.

Matthew records for us the parable of the marriage feast. I believe this is critical in our search for the friends. Jesus said, *"The kingdom of heaven is like unto a certain king, which made a marriage for his son. And sent forth his servants to call them that were bidden to the wedding..."* (Matthew 22:2,3). Notice that the Bride is not the issue. The parable goes on to reveal that not all were interested in the opportunity, but finally the wedding was furnished with guests. Now notice very carefully that in the following verses the king came to judge the "friends" not the bride! At this wedding were both a bride and *a great company called friends.*

> *And when the king came in to see the guests, he saw there a man which had not on a wedding garment And he saith unto him, Friend, how earnest thou in hither not having a wedding garment?* (Matt. 22:11-12)

Everyone who is invited to the wedding feast must wear a wedding garment, one that has been washed in the blood of the Lamb. It doesn't matter whether it's the bride or the friends-all must be in proper attire. What did our Lord call the bidden guests? Friends, the same term that John the Baptist applied to himself. I believe that there are the *Bride,* the *friends,* and the *wicked lost* in the Word of God. It is the Bride that occupies the governmental aspect of the Kingdom of God. To them, the 144,000 is applied to the rulership over the nations, not to the friends. They have eternal life and sing the song of salvation, but they don't carry the weight and authority of government. Let's examine closer the requirements pertaining to Kingdom government.

> *Jesus answered, Verily, verily, I say unto thee, Except a man be born of water and of the Spirit, he cannot enter into the kingdom of God* (John 3:5).

I believe the birth of water is the act of baptism by immersion, calling on the saving name of the Lord Jesus. I believe the birth of the spirit is as it was on the day of Pentecost, with the mighty baptism in the Holy Ghost. It is interesting and vital to note that when Jesus addressed the disciples at Caesarea Philippi, He informed them that He had given them the "keys" (plural) to the kingdom of heaven (Matthew 16:19). This means that more than one door needs to be unlocked. Peter understood this authority and proclaimed the gospel of the kingdom at Pentecost. He commanded, "*Repent, and be baptized everyone of you in the name of Jesus Christ* [water birth] *for the remission of sins, and ye shall receive the gift of the Holy Ghost* [spirit birth] (Acts 2:38). These are the true 144,000. It is this apostolic doctrine that separates those who are saved by faith (the friends) and those who possess kingdom authority (the Bride).

Luke recorded a startling assertion made by our Lord in response to the messengers of John who had been inquiring as to whether Jesus was the Messiah. Jesus said:

> *For I say unto you, Among those that are born of women there*

is not a greater prophet than John the Baptist: **but he that is least in the kingdom of God is greater than he** (Luke 7:28).

He that is least in what kingdom? He that is least in what part of the kingdom? This is the part that will be inhabited by the Spirit baptized Bride of Christ. None of us will ever live a greater life of sacrifice for the Lord than did John the Baptist. But we have a greater experience than John because of our baptism in the Holy Ghost and the subsequent speaking in other tongues. John never experienced this gift from God. Henceforth, his joy is fulfilled in being a friend of the Bridegroom.

It seems that there are two great aspects of the Kingdom: the Old Testament saints, and the New Testament Church with its friends. But our Bible tells us that except we all repent, we will all likewise perish. That which is demanded at all times in the Word of God is true heart repentance.

I believe there are those all down through the age of the New Covenant who have not been baptized in water, and have not been baptized with the Holy Ghost. I believe if they repented and turned to God with all their hearts, and had their sins washed in the precious blood of Jesus by faith, they would sing the song of salvation with the great multitude. They are the friends of the Bridegroom. I believe they are in the same category as the Old Testament saints. The saints of the Old Covenant looked forward to the cross. The New Testament saints looked back to the cross, but they all looked to the same cross; the same Jesus; the same Lamb of God who takes away the sins of the world. Now the words of the Hebrew epistle become clearer:

And these all, having obtained a good report through faith, received not the promise: God having provided some better thing for us, that they without us should not be made perfect (Hebrews 11:39,40).

This is talking about the Old Testament saints and the friends of the Bridegroom. We are all justified by faith (that is understood), but this Scripture reveals that there is still something better for us. And those who attain to it are what Paul terms as *"members in particular"* (1 Corinthians 12:27). They will take their place in the resurrection, and we will take ours. Jesus said, *"In my Father's house are many mansions: if it were not so, I would have told you. I go to prepare a place for you"* (John 14:2). And the Hebrew epistle reveals that our place (those who are sealed with the Spirit and possess the Father's name) is *"some better thing!"* Now maybe we can unveil Paul's great teaching on the various aspects of the resurrection of the dead, which he so powerfully revealed in his first epistle to the Corinthians:

> *There are also celestial [heavenly] bodies, and bodies* **terrestrial** *[earthly]: but the glory of the celestial is one, and the glory of the terrestrial is another. There is one glory of the sun and another glory of the moon, and another glory of the stars: for one star differeth from another star in glory. So* **also is the resurrection of the dead...** (1 Corinthians 15:40-42)

My friends, somehow it sounds balanced. It is very special knowledge that Christ is revealing. Yes, there is a New Jerusalem. It is the celestial glory of God, inhabited by the 144,000; the true Zion from which will proceed the laws of God. And there is a new earth; the terrestrial glory yet to be manifested; inhabited by the great multitude. Can you handle this? The 144,000 are an exclusive part of the the Bride of Christ, the "something better" of the New Testament Church, born of the Spirit, the water and the blood (I John 5:8).

The Bible teaches that a threefold cord is not easily broken. I believe that this is what I have presented; I have tried to rightly divide this glorious chapter. Let me summarize this cord: First, Revelation seven presents 144,000 and a great multitude. Second, the Gospels reveal a bride and her friends. Third, Paul reveals heavenly bodies and earthly bodies which will appear in the resurrection. Is it possible that we have put our foot in an even place (Psalms 26:12)?

> *11 And all the angels stood around about the throne, and about the elders and the four beasts, and fell before the throne on their faces, and worshipped God,*
>
> *12 Saying, Amen: Blessing, and glory, and wisdom, and thanksgiving, and honor, and power, and might, be unto our God for ever and ever. Amen.*
>
> *13 And one of the elders answered, saying unto me, What are these which are arrayed in white robes? and whence came they?*
>
> *14 And I said unto him, Sir, thou knowest. And he said to me, These are they which came out of great tribulation, and have washed their robes, and made them white in the blood of the Lamb.*

Look again at the fifth Seal. This was the terrible climax of pagan Rome's attempt to destroy the Christian Church-Diocletian's persecution. *"These are they which came out of great tribulation,"* is in reference to these martyrs. Isaiah proclaimed that *"Of the increase of His government and peace there shall be no end"* (Isaiah 9:7). The Revelation has revealed that the persecutions of Pagan Rome did not hinder the increase of God's government. Actually, they fueled its growth. Chapter seven is a glorious proclamation of this principle.

A further understanding of this teaching will appear again in Chapter 14. The 144,000 are proclaimed after another period of intense persecution, which was unleashed by the second beast of Chapter 13, Rome Papal, which is later revealed as Babylon the Great, who was seen by John at the end of her domination to be *"Drunken with the blood of the saints, and with the blood of the martyrs of Jesus."*

> 15 *Therefore are they before the throne of God, and serve Him day and night in His temple: and He that sitteth on the throne shall dwell among them.*
> 16 *They shall hunger no more, neither thirst any more; neither shall the sun light on them, nor any heat.*
> 17 *For the Lamb which is in the midst of the throne shall feed them, and shall lead them unto living fountains of waters: and God shall wipe away all tears from their eyes.*

Keep in mind the symbolic nature of this prophecy. When John referred to the *"sun light on them, nor any heat"* he referred to wicked, oppressive government. The day will come when all governments, hostile to the kingdom of God, will fall. As Daniel envisioned, they *"became like the chaff of the summer threshing floors; and the wind carried them away, that no place was found for them"* (Daniel 2:35). (See also Revelation 22:3-5.)

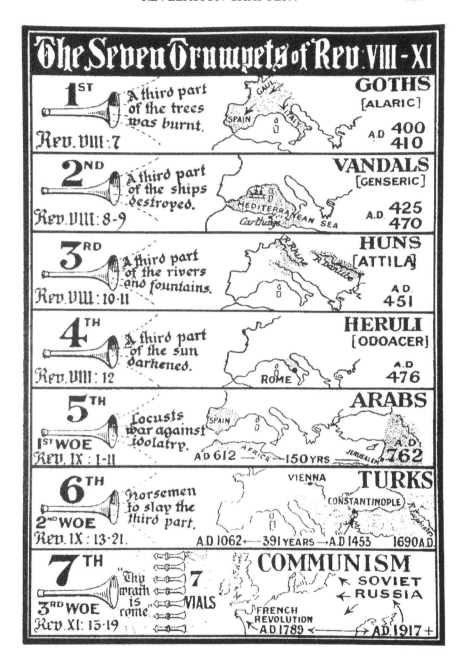

Illustration taken from: *The Pope, Communism and the Coming New World* by Thomas Foster

REVELATION CHAPTER 8
THE SEVENTH SEAL:
REVEALING THE FIRST SIX TRUMPETS
(THE DESTRUCTION OF THE WESTERN EMPIRE
BY THE GOTHS & THE DESTRUCTION OF THE
EASTERN EMPIRE BY THE SARACENS & TURKS)

THE 144,000 HAVE BEEN SEALED!

1 And when He had opened the seventh seal, there was silence in heaven about the space of half an hour.
2 And I saw the seven angels which stood before God; and to them were given seven trumpets.

The seventh Seal is divided into seven subsections of judgments known as Trumpets. In these next two chapters, we will witness the Revelation having prophesied the fall of the Western Roman Empire at the hands of the invading Gothic hordes; the conquest of the Saracens in the south and east, and the remaining eastern, and final third, of the empire conquered by the Turks.

Silence In Heaven…Half An Hour: This solemn apocalyptic phrase is used here to denote calm before the storm, or possibly the oppressive silence before the eruption of a terrible battle. It is prophetic terminology designed to emphasize the events which are about to follow in the first four Trumpets-four invasions, encompassing seventy-six years of war and devastation at the hands of the *Goths, Vandals, Huns* and *Heruli.* [69]

Seven 'Trumpets: In the Old Testament the blowing of trumpets was often used to proclaim that God was about to judge the enemies of His people. After the blowing *of "seven trumpets of Ram's horns"* the great city of Jericho fell (Joshua 6:16). So likewise the metaphor is applied, with the blowing of seven Trumpets in the Book of Revelation another seemingly invincible power will fall, the Roman Empire (both Pagan Rome, and ultimately Papal Rome too).

> *3 And another angel came and stood at the altar, having a golden censer; and there was given unto him much incense, that he should offer it with the prayers of all saints upon the golden altar which was before the throne.*
>
> *4 And the smoke of the incense, which came with the prayers of the saints, ascended up before God out of the angel's hand.*
>
> *5 And the angel took the censer, and filled it with fire of the altar, and cast it into the earth: and there were voices, and thunderings, and lightnings, and an earthquake.*

This *"angel"* must be the Lord Jesus Christ himself. We know this because he possesses the *"golden censer"* which was found only inside the Ark of the Covenant (a type of Christ) residing in the Holy of Holies

---

69   But what of the *half-hour's* predicated *duration* of the silence, or rather the *"as it were half-an-hour I?"* I incline to consider St. John's *"as it were,"* as meaning that it appeared to and affected him, as the half-hour's stillness before a storm might do in common life. At the same time the alternative seems open to him who prefers it-while explaining the *silence* to mean stillness from the threatened tempest, as before-yet to interpret the *half-hour* on the *prophetic year-day scale,* as but a *very short interval,* even as of a *few days.* So that in any case the interval between the opening of the 7th Seal, and the first outbreak of the tempest of barbarian invasions, was indicated as but very small. For on the half-hour's ending, the previous check upon the threatened tempest, and the spirits riding them, was evidently to be withdrawn [Rev. 7:1-31]. Just accordant with which (if I may anticipate for a moment) is the record of history. Theodosius died in Jan. 395; the epoch, I think, of the 7th Seal's opening; and "before the winter ended," says Gibbon, "the Gothic nation was in arms"-that "tempest of barbarians," as he elsewhere calls it, "was to subvert the foundations of the Roman empire." And so, too, Mr. Hallan: *"The fourth century set in storms."* (E. B. Elliott, *Horae Apocalypticae,* Vol. IV, Part II, page 303.)

(Hebrews 9:4). In the tabernacle in the wilderness, only the High Priest could enter into the holiest place. This *"angel"* also gathers or mediates the prayers of the saints; only Jesus has this authority (1 Timothy 2:5). The prayers he is gathering are those belonging to the martyrs who fell under Pagan Rome. *"How long, O Lord, holy and true, dost thou not judge and avenge our blood on them that dwell on the earth?"* (Revelation 6:10). The Trumpets reveal that those prayers, which *"ascend up before God,"* are now going to begin to be answered.

> *6 And the seven angels which had the seven trumpets prepared themselves to sound.*

On the death of the Emperor Theodosius in AD. 395, the Goths, who had already moved into the lands of the empire during the fourth century, revolted from their allegiance to Rome as a civil power. The Goths revolted and the call to arms was sounded throughout the empire. "Before winter had ended," said Gibbon, "the Gothic nation was in arms."

Such a revolution was not only like an earthquake, but also like the thunderings and lightnings in that it gave warning of the approaching storms of judgment about to break on the empire with these swift and devastating invasions.

It is important to note that in the judgments released by the seven Trumpets, the phrase, *"the third part,"* is repeatedly used. And we see that judgments were to fall on particular third parts of the prophetic earth (ghay/region). It is remarkable that during the fourth century, which saw the fulfillment of the sixth Seal in the fall of Roman heathenism, that the empire was on three occasions divided into three parts, under the rule of three emperors. First, at Constantine's conversion, A.D. 312, there was a five-part empire under the rule of three emperors. Second, at his death in AD. 337 the empire was tripartite. Third, the years AD. 383-387 saw trisections in the empire. Such trisections seemed to be forewarnings of the prophesied judgments in this chapter.

It is impossible to obtain any detailed judgment on the actual boundaries of the third parts mentioned in Revelation 8 and 9 until we see the fulfillment of their prophecies in history. Wonderfully, we have a confirmation of these prophecies in that on three different occasions the Goths, Saracens (Arabs), and the Turks each invaded and scourged a third part of the whole Roman territory:

First: By the **GOTHS** in the West (Rev. 8:7-12).[70]

Second: By the **SARACENS** in the East and South (Rev. 9:1-12).

Third: By the **TURKS** in the East (Rev. 9:13-21).

Before we open the first four Trumpets let us take note that they only occupy the last seven verses of Chapter 8. Hence, we should expect their prophecies to be fulfilled quickly in proportion to the small space allotted to them. Also, these first four Trumpets release judgments on the same western third of the Roman Empire. We will see these first four Trumpets' judgments fall on the empire's land, sea, rivers, and her leaders. The time span will go from A.D. 400-476.

---

70   Let the reader note that there were five great destroyers of the Western Empire, two of the earliest associated nearly as one cycle of invasion, this being *Alaric* and *Radagaisus*. The other three were: *Genseric, Attila* and *Odoacer*.

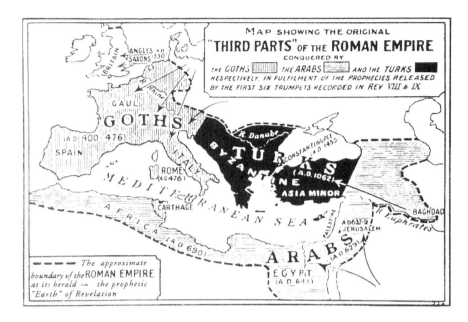

Illustration taken from: *The Pope, Communism and the Coming New World* by Thomas Foster

FIRST TRUMPET
A.D. 400-410
THE GOTHS

7 The first angel sounded, and there followed hail and fire min-gled with blood, and they were cast upon the earth: and the third part of the trees was burnt up, and all green grass was burnt up.

The origin of this desolation was from the north as signified by the "hail." In Europe hail storms sweep down on the continent from the north. The historian Claudian compared the invasions by the Goths to a "*hailstorm.*" All history books on the Roman Empire state that between the years A.D. 400-410, the Goths, led by Alaric, came down from the north.[71] They attacked Gaul, Spain and Italy. John prophesied that these warriors would conduct a "scorched earth" policy, and so the Goths fulfilled their prophecies. Everything in their path was burned or destroyed. So great was this threat that the Romans evacuated Britain to help strengthen the northern borders and defend against this terrible horde. Remember, the Roman Empire's territory had not seen the face of a foreign enemy for eight hundred years.[72]

SECOND TRUMPET A.D. 425-470
THE VANDALS

8 And the second angel sounded, and as it were a great mountain burning with fire was cast into the sea: arid the third part of the sea became blood;
9 And the third part of the creatures which were in the sea, and had life died; and the third part of the ships were destroyed.

This prophecy foretold the coming of the Vandals, under the leader Genseric, historically referred to as the "Tyrant of the Sea." They waged great naval warfare in the Mediterranean and around its coasts, destroy-

---

71   396 Alaric's invasion of Greece. 400-403, His first invasion of Italy. 406, Radagaisus with 300,000 Vandals from the Baltic, marching by way of the upper Danube, invade Italy. Defeated and killed under the walls of Florence, the remains of his army retire from Italy, and cross the Rhine into France. 408, Alaric's first siege of Rome. 409, Second siege. 410, Third siege and capture. In the same year Alaric died.

72   It is strange, also, how the infidel Gibbon has chosen the very language of inspiration to describe some of the events of this period. I will quote a few phrases found in his thirty-first chapter that are descriptive of the great invasions of Alaric and the Goths. "The tremendous sound of the Gothic *"trumpet"* stirred the hosts to invasion. "At the first sound of the *trumpet* the Goths left their farms" to rush on in invasion. "The Gothic *conflagration"* consumed the empire. "Blood and conflagration and the burning of trees and herbage marked their path." (B. W. Johnson, *The People's New Testament With Notes,* page 447.)

ing Rome's navy and ships.[73] The great port at Carthage was captured in A.D. 439. These Vandals, a branch of the Goths, ravaged Gaul and Spain, as well as their sea exploits. Many portions of the sea were turned to blood as the Roman ships were sunk and their sailors butchered. After the Vandals had captured the great base of Carthage, they sailed out for the next 30 years, destroying not only Roman ships but also pirating the seas. Finally, Rome itself was taken and ravaged for fifteen days. Neither age nor sex was spared. The spoil of eight centuries of Roman plunder was now loaded upon the Vandal fleets, and the capital was abandoned.

THIRD TRUMPET
A.D. 451
THE HUNS

10 And the third angel sounded, and there fell a great star from heaven, burning as it were a lamp, and it fell upon the third part of the rivers, and upon the fountains of waters;
11 And the name of the star is called Wormwood: and the third part of the waters became wormwood; and many men died of the waters, because they were made bitter.

The great "star" in the military heavens was the king of the Huns, Attila *"the scourge of God."* This warrior was deemed by some to be greater than human. "The barbaric princes," said Gibbon, "could not presume to gaze with steady eye on [what they deemed] his divine majesty." Attila made desolate the valleys of the Rhine, upper Danube and Po Rivers. "The Huns," Gibbon wrote, "were the masters of the great river." They devastated the Italian Alps, the source of the rivers, causing pollution

---

73   For six centuries no ship hostile to Rome had disputed the mastery of the sea, but now it is turned into a theater of war and devastation.

and bloodshed in these fountains. One historian wrote, "Many had died and still continue to die, that drank of the water, through famine, disease, and pestilence." Before A.D. 440, the Romans knew little or nothing about this Hungarian nation. Its emergence was like a *blazing meteor.* About this time there appeared, with a meteor-like flash in the heavens, Attila, assembling upon the banks of the Danube, with 800,000 men.

And finally, Wormwood is bitter in its context, and is associated often in the Bible with gall (Deuteronomy 29:18); it is also equated with judgment. In this prophecy, it is in reference to the poisoning of the great European rivers previously mentioned.[74]

FOURTH TRUMPET
A.D. 476
THE HERULI

12 And the fourth angel sounded, and the third part of the sun was smitten, and the third part of the moon, and the third part of the stars; so as the third part of them was darkened, and the day shone not for a third part of it, and the night likewise.

This verse is symbolic of the ruling powers of the western third of the Roman Empire. As we have mentioned on several occasions, the *sun, moon* and *stars* are symbolic for the political heavens of Rome. In A.D. 476, the Heruli, led by Odoacer, conquered Rome itself, ending its imperial rule. Odoacer's command was "that the name of the office of Roman emperor of the west should be abolished." The last pitiful emperor,

---

74   Historians estimate that up to 300,000 men lay slaughtered in the rivers. The fury of the conflict made these waterways turn to blood. Henceforth, the "Wormwood" or deadly bitterness in the waters.

Romulus-Augustus, was banished. This is the cessation of Imperial Rome in the West. This occurred 76 years after the sounding of the first Trumpet in A.D. 400.

Fox makes an interesting observation pertaining to the metaphorical use of the *earth, sea, rivers,* and *sun* in the Trumpet judgments:

> Verses 7, 8, 10 and 12 speak of the four symbols "Earth," "Sea," "Rivers," and "Sun," the latter typifying the brightest center of the prophetical earth, i.e., the ruling center Rome itself. It is interesting to note that in God's judgment of Pagan Rome, and later in his judgments on Papal Rome, the exact same symbols are used. Further on, in Chapter 16, we shall reach the first of the seven "Vials" of God's wrath being poured out in judgment upon the Papal Roman earth; and there also the same picture is repeated again, with the same symbols used, and in the same order, viz: the "Earth," "Sea," "Rivers" and "Sun."[75]

> 13 *And I beheld, and heard an angel flying through the midst of heaven, saying with a loud voice,* Woe, woe, woe, *to the inhabiters of the earth by reason of the other voices of the trumpet of the three angels, which are yet to sound!*

Three more Trumpets are yet to sound, and they are further revealed as "Woes" or catastrophes. We will see what these represent:

1. The Saracen's conquest of the Southern and Eastern third.
2. The Turkish conquest of the remaining Eastern third.
3. The third "Woe" being the pouring out of the seven Vials Papal judgments.

---

75   John S. Fox, *A Flood of Light Upon the Book of Revelation*, pages 62-63.

A BRIEF "VITAL" INTERLUDE
CONCERNING ANTICHRIST

You need to understand, at this point in prophecy and history, that the Early Church anticipated this event, the fall of Rome's ancient empire, as fraught with consequences relative to the rise of Antichrist. His manifestation was understood to be connected with the dissolution of the empire, and its subsequent subdividing into ten Gothic kingdoms. (This will be taught later.) Furthermore, these second through fourth century fathers interpreted Paul's teaching on the "let" and hindrance (letteth) to Antichrist's manifestation, as the then existing Roman Empire. Let's spend a minute on this vital point. Its timely relevance should be self-evident. Paul wrote in his second epistle to the Thessalonians, Chapter 2:

> *5 Remember ye not, that, when I was yet with you, I told you these things?*
> *6 And now ye know what withholdeth that he* [the man of sin] *might be revealed in his time.*
> *7… only he who now letteth* [hinders] *will let, until he be taken out of the way.*

The word "letteth" (let) can properly be interpreted "restrain." What was hindering the emergence of this man of sin? In the primary case, the apostle speaks of it in the neuter gender—"you know **WHAT** withholds." Then he used the masculine gender—"HE who now hinders." The only logical conclusion is that the hindrance or restrainer will be both neuter and masculine. As long as the Roman Empire was under pagan rule, the man of sin could not take his place of authority in the seven-hilled city of

Rome. Thus, the "hindrance" in the primary neuter gender is fulfilled in the Roman Empire, and the same "hindrance" in the masculine gender was fulfilled in the despotic emperors. They had to be taken out of the way first. We have just seen how this happened with the Gothic invasions. In A.D. 476, Pagan Rome vanished in the West, only to be replaced by apostate Papal Rome.[76] The following quotes will help us understand this issue.

> *Chrysostom, Bishop of Constantinople, A. D. 390, writes, "By the 'Hindrance' Paul means the Roman Empire."* This was also believed by Augustine, Bishop of Hippo, A.D. 400.

> Jerome, A.D. 400, declared, *"If St. Paul had written openly and boldly that the man of sin would not come until the Roman Empire was destroyed, a just cause of persecution would then appear to have been afforded against the Church in her infancy."* And he went on to state, *"The Roman world rushes to destruction, and we bend not our neck in humiliation …*
> *The hindrance in antichrist's way is removing, and we heed it not … In that one city the whole world hath fallen."*

> Tertullian: *"We pray for the Roman Emperors and empire, for we know that convulsions and calamities are threatening the whole world, and the end of the world itself is kept back by the intervention of the Roman empire."*

> Evangrius: *"The Roman emperors are driven from their kingdoms: wars rage: all is commotion: Antichrist must be at hand."*

---

76   Hindrance information taken from Thomas Foster's *The Antichrist-Who Is He?*

And Theodoret, A. D. 431, from his more distant bishopric in Syria, after long and studious consideration of the prophecies, *confidently reasserted* that it needed but the dividing of the Roman Empire into ten kingdoms-and then Antichrist would be revealed, and the fearful consequences would follow.[77]

This has been the consistent voice of the historicist school for century after century. On the other hand, the futurist view was cleverly formulated by Ribera to mock the Protestants. It was Ribera who taught that the hindrance was the Holy Spirit. If it was the Holy Spirit, Paul would have boldly said so, since he had no hesitations in other chapters when writing about this subject.

In conclusion, we see that Paul had good reason for refusing to openly name the hindrance; to do so would have brought swift and terrible destruction to the infant church in Thessalonica. He had already caused a disturbance when he was there speaking against Caesar. *"**Remember ye not, that, when I was yet with you, I told you these things**?"* (2 Thessalonians 2:5)

---

77   For further study on this remarkable insight see Elliott's *Horae Apocalypticae,* Vol. 1, Part II, pages 362-369.

REVELATION CHAPTER 9
SEVEN TRUMPETS CONTINUED

FIFTH TRUMPET
(A.D. 612-762, 150 YEARS)
THE FIRST "WOE"—RISE OF
MOHAMMEDANISM FULFILLED
IN THE SARACENS

1 And the fifth angel sounded, and I saw a star fall from heaven unto the earth: and to him was given the key of the bottomless pit. 2 And he opened the bottomless pit; and there arose a smoke out of the pit, as the smoke of a great furnace; and the sun and the air were darkened by reason of the smoke of the pit.

The eastern section of the Roman Empire, along with the African provinces, survived the Gothic scourge in the West. The capital was Constantinople, known as the New Rome. At the same time there developed a new Greek church in the East; it practiced relic worship and developed a superstitious trend, and would ultimately be judged by God. John's writings in Chapter 9 record the judgments he saw coming upon this remaining idolatrous territory. These were fulfilled in the 5th and 6th Trumpets, or the first two "Woes."

Chapter 9 reveals the rise of the Arabian or Saracen Empire, which was deceived and motivated by the false teachings of Mohammed. This *"false prophet"* opened the *"bottomless pit"* in the year A. D. 606 when he retired to his cave and formulated his religious doctrines. In A. D. 612, his empire emerged, and in A. D. 762, after previously being defeated by the "Hammer of Western Christendom," Charles Martel, their aggression ceased.[78] The *"smoke"* of their surge darkened the *"sun"* which represents the bright rulership from Constantinople, not destined to be destroyed in this woe, only darkened.

I Saw A Star Fall: A "star" indicates a prince or ecclesiastical ruler. John sees a fallen star; a prince degraded from supremacy and power. This fits Mohammed perfectly. He was from the princely house of Koreish, the governors of Mecca. They possessed the "keys of Caaba," symbolic of their rulership. At Mohammed's birth, his grandfather possessed this authority (star), but just after Mohammed's birth his father died, and then his grandfather. Therefore, the "keys of Caaba," the governorship of Mecca, passed into other hands. Mohammed was now a fallen political star.

> *3 And there came out of the smoke locusts upon the earth: and unto them was given power, as the scorpions of the earth have power.*

These destroying "locusts" symbolize destroying armies. Time and time again, the Lord speaks in the Old Testament about the locusts coming out of Arabia. The destroyers of ancient Nineveh were likened to locusts. "Make thyself many as the locusts" was the command of the Lord (Nahum 3:15). And in Exodus we read that it was "the east wind [that] brought the locusts" (Exodus 10:13). In other words, they came from Arabia.[79]

---

78   A. D. 606, The cave experience. 612, Mohammed announced his mission. 622, Hejira (opening year of the Mohammedan calendar): Flight from Mecca. 629, Saracens issue from Arabia. 732, Checked in Tours by Charles Martel. 755, Caliphate divided. 762, Settlement at Bagdad.

79   Elliott commented: "I say the very word for locust might almost to a Hebrew ear suggest Arab: the names of the one and of the other being in pronunciation and in radicals not dissimilar; of the locusts (arbeh), of an Arab (arbi)."

4 And it was commanded them that they should not hurt the grass of the earth, neither any green thing, neither any tree; but only those men which have not the seal of God written in their foreheads.

We read in this verse that it was forbidden of them (locusts) to destroy nature in their judgment. Remember, the Goths destroyed the vegetation in the West, "all green grass burnt up" (Revelation 8:7). Here in the East though, the Arabians were forbidden by the Koran to hurt the green grass or the trees. However, they were allowed to hurt the apostate churches and corrupt Christians. Here we have the Lord using these locusts to fulfill his will in judgment.[80]

Hurt... Only Those Men As Have Not The Seal Of God: Mohammed declared his commission to be against idolaters and unbelievers-especially the mariolatrists (those who worship Mary as the queen of heaven) and saint worshipers of the Roman Empire.

5 And to them it was given that they should not kill them, but that they should be tormented five months: and their torment was as the torment of a scorpion, when he striketh a man.
6 And in those days shall men seek death, and shall not find it; and shall desire to die, and death shall flee from them.

The Mohammedan Arab's plan was not to kill their enemies, but to forcibly convert them to the Moslem religion or make them pay tribute. With a fury they attacked the corrupt churches in the East. These churches

---

80   *"It was said unto them... ,"* by their false prophet, in his book the Koran, repeated by Caliph Aboubekr, and oft quoted after: "Destroy no palm trees, nor any fields of corn, cut down no fruit-trees." This policy enabled them to form flourishing kingdoms out of conquered countries (compare Deut. 20: 19,20); and was in marked contrast with that of other conquerors, such as the Goths, who left desolation behind them. (E. P. Cachemaille, *The Visions of Daniel and the Revelation Explained,* page 260.)

were filled with images of the Virgin Mary and the saints, which Moslems could not tolerate.

"Ye Christian dogs, ye know your option, the Koran, the tribute, or the sword." Threats such as those revealed a fulfillment of the prophecy which states, "And in those days shall men seek death."[81]

Tormented Five Months: This divine time measure must be interpreted with the consistent year-for-a-day code applied to Daniel and the Book of Revelation. The *"five months"* prophetic period depicts 5 X 30 or 150 prophetical "Years." The most fitting beginning date appears to be A. D. 612, for it is the date of Mohammed's public proclamation, which advocated the propagation of his religion by violence and the sword. His cry was, "There is one God, Allah is his name, and Mohammed is his prophet." Exactly "five months" or 150 prophetical years later, the Moslems ceased their aggression and moved their capital back to Bagdad, on the Tigris. This occurred in A. D. 762. Henceforth, the locusts took their flight far to the east away from Christendom. "War," said Gibbon, "was no longer the passion of the Saracens."

It is *the* unanimity of several historians that the deliverances of Christendom from the Saracens were events which, at the time, could not have been anticipated. By all judgment, Europe should have fallen into their hands. Europe to this very day owes its existence, its religion, and its liberty to the victory of Charles Martel in A. D. 762.

7 And the shapes of the locusts were like unto horses prepared unto battle; and on their heads were as it were crowns like gold,

---

81   This statement is made clearer by examining a parallel one in Jer. 8:3, where it is said of the Jews taken by the Babylonian captivity: "And death shall be chosen, rather than life, by all the residue of them that remain of this evil family, which remain in all the places whither I have driven them." And likewise we read in Job 3:20, "Wherefore is light given to him that is in misery, and life unto the bitter soul? Which long for death, but it comes not, and dig for it more that for hid treasures: which rejoice exceedingly when they can find the grave." This is clearly a strong proverbial expression of great punishing wretchedness.

and their faces were as the faces of men.

8 And they had hair as the hair of women, and their teeth were as the teeth of lions.

9 And they had breastplates, as it were breastplates of iron; and the sound of their wings was as the sound of chariots of many horses running to battle.

10 And they had tails like unto scorpions, and there were stings in their tails: and their power was to hurt men five months.

This metaphorical language is exact to the most minute detail. B. W. Johnson summarized as follows:

The Arabians, unlike the Goths, Vandals and Huns, were an army of horsemen, and moved over a country almost with the swiftness of the locust. Let the reader note the following facts concerning the Arabs: 1. They came forth from the home of the locust (and the horse). 2. They all fought on horseback. 3. They wore upon their heads something like crowns of gold. The historians often speak of them as the "turbaned Arabs." Ezekiel 23:42, speaking of the Sabeans, which were an Arabian tribe, says, *"The Sabeans of the wilderness who put upon their heads beautiful crowns."* The yellow turbans of the Arab horsemen, at a little distance, would strikingly resemble *"crowns of gold."* 4. The locusts had *"the faces of men."* The Jews and Arabs wore long patriarchal beards. The Romans and northern races shaved the face. John noted that these locusts have the distinguishing mark of manhood in the east, the unshorn beard. 5. To the faces of men is added *"the hair of women."* The female distinction is long hair, and evidently John beholds, as

the riders rush by, long hair flowing from their shoulders and streaming in the air. Did the Arabs in the seventh century wear long hair? Pliny, who was the contemporary of John, speaks (Nat. His. 7:28) of "the turbaned Arabs with their uncut hair." Ammianus Marcellinus in the fourth, and Jerome in the fifth century, each speak of the long-haired Arabs. An Arabian poem, *Antar,* written in Mohammed's time, often speaks of the hair of its heroes flowing down upon their shoulders. I quote: "He adjusted himself, twisted his beard, and folded his hair under his turban, drawing it up from his shoulders."
6. But the locusts had *"breastplates, as it were breastplates of iron."* The historians of the Arabian wars constantly speak of the iron coats of mail. Mohammed, in the Koran, said: "God has given you coats of mail to defend you in your wars."

And There Were Stings In Their Tails: Johnson unfortunately omitted this point. This "scorpion" metaphor was fulfilled in the fact that the Saracens were well skilled in fighting rearward over their horses' tails. This is the dread of the scorpion, with its tail-pain and torment are inflicted.

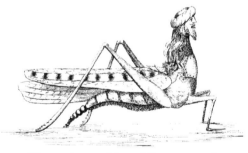

11 And they had a king over them, which is the angel of the bottomless pit, whose name in the Hebrew tongue is Abaddon, but in the Greek tongue hath his name Apollyon.

Figure A.   **Literal Interpretation**

Abaddon and Apollyon are words that essentially mean "destroyer, or the one who exterminates." It is evident that the character of this Mohammedan inspiration is emphasized. Mohammed received his revelation from hell, not from Jesus Christ, the God of the Christian. And one day Islam will bow its knee and confess that Jesus is "the" Lord.[82]

12 One woe is past; and, behold, there come two woes more hereafter.

This verse announces that although the Saracenic Woe, with its 150-year-time measure, has passed, the end of the age would not come until two more terrible "Woes" had run their prophetic courses. The rest of this chapter is devoted to the prophetic substance of the second "Woe" or the Turkish Empire. The historian Keith truthfully says: "There is scarcely so uniform an agreement among interpreters concerning any other part of the Apocalypse as respecting the application of the fifth and sixth trumpets, or the first and second woes, to the Saracens and Turks. *It is so obvious that it can scarcely be misunderstood.*" Today this man would tear his garments if he viewed the prophecy section of a Christian bookstore.

RISE OF THE TURKISH EMPIRE
SIXTH TRUMPET (A. D. 1062-1453)
THE SECOND "WOE"

13 And the sixth angel sounded, and I heard a voice from the four horns of the golden altar which is before God,
14 Saying to the sixth angel which had the trumpet, Loose the four angels which are bound in the great river Euphrates.

John sees the sixth trumpet release multitudes of military horsemen from the valley of the Euphrates, whose object was to subjugate the remaining *"third part"* of the area of the Pagan Roman Empire (the eastern

---

82   I know this to be true because the Bible states (emphatically) that Christ will, "...put down all rule and all authority and power" (1 Cor. 15:24).

third that was untouched by the Goths and the Arabs). History describes for us the rise of a great military power that arose from the eastern delta of this Euphrates in the early parts of the 11th century.

A few years before the end of the first Christian millennium, a race of people known as the Tartars, formidable by their numbers and fierceness, left the area of the Caspian Sea and moved southwestward until they arrived and settled on the eastern banks of the Euphrates. A large area east of the river fell to their influence. Persia became a province, and India was subjugated as far as the ocean. But for two generations they were *"bound by the river Euphrates"* from moving towards the vulnerable countries in the West. Their restraining is a historic mystery to some, but to others the Book of Revelation had revealed the scenario. Finally, after being bound up for over 60 years, in the year A.D. 1062, they crossed the Euphrates and surged against the eastern Roman Empire. These people were called the Turkomans or Turkmans; most refer to them as the *Turks.*

Loose The Four Angels: We have the implication of four powers being involved. It is remarkable that history records these people being divided into four bodies, which formed four kingdoms, under the four grandsons of the leader who established the empire of the Turks in western Asia. This prince was named Togrul. However, it was his son, Alp Arslan, the "valiant lion" who led the Turks across the river. He died in battle and was succeeded by Malek Shah. History further records that the mighty empire under Shah was divided into four principalities under his four sons. So this great prophecy accurately revealed four angels or messengers of destruction. Prophetically, the great river Euphrates had overflowed its banks.

> *15 And the four angels were loosed, which were prepared for an hour, and a day, and a month, and a year, for to slay the third part of men.*

We come now to one of the most spectacular divine time measures in the Bible. John sees a period which includes a prophetic *"hour"* (approximately 2 months); a prophetic "day" (1 year); a prophetic *"month"* or 30 days (30 years); and a prophetic *"Year"* of 360 calendar days (360 years). *Combined,* this time measure would total just over 391 years-the time given to the Turks to *"slay the third part of men,"* or conquer the remaining third part of the territory which once belonged to Pagan Rome, but at this point in history is known as the Byzantine Empire, with its capital in Constantinople. This prophecy was wonderfully fulfilled in the year A.D. 1453. Remember, in A.D. 1062 the Turks crossed the river Euphrates and began their slaughter. The prize was Constantinople, a city which had endured for a thousand years after the fall of Pagan Rome in the West. On May 29, 1453, *(just over 391 years after the Turks crossed the Euphrates)*[83] the city, which had previously been the center of Eastern Greek Christendom, fell, and the great church of Hagia Sophia (Justinian's great church) was turned into a Mohammedan mosque. Catastrophically, the Byzantine Empire was no more. And from this point forward the Turks would make no more significant territorial gains.[84]

16 And the number of the army of the horsemen were two

---

83   This author has studied the various historicist arguments concerning this, and several other divine time measures. For example, Elliott contends that *the solar year* (366 days and 6 hours) should be attached to the time measure. Others insist that the *calendar* or *prophetic year* (360 days) is applicable. Nevertheless, the exact "era" is clearly understood by all historicists. It would take "marvelous blindness" to miss it. The exactness in the dating, is a matter of scholarship, and conclusions reached by sanctified common sense. Even at that, the great Elliott concluded that relative to this Turkish time measure, "the question is an open one" (referring to the application of the solar or calendar year). Please reference the chapter entitled "Prophetic Periods."

84   VERY IMPORTANT NOTE: Reader, please notice that John does not record the end of the second woe until Rev. 11:14. This is done for a brilliant reason. The Turks continued to fight against western Christendom for another 200 years. But they did not expand the territory they had gained in the 391 years of conquest. These wars were called the *Crusades.* ALSO, the events that encompass the 10th and 11th chapters (which entail the Reformation) must occur during the time frame between the beginning of this second woe Rev. 9:13, and its conclusion Rev. 11:14.

hundred thousand thousand: and I hear the number of them.

Many manuscripts read the above phrase, relative to the numbers, in the following way. "The number of the armies of the horsemen," it is said, "was myriads of myriads." This numeral phrase is indefinite, but according to its implied use in the Scripture, is expressive of large numbers, which is applicable to the Turkish "millions." Gibbon speaks of "the myriads of the Turkish horse overspreading the Greek frontier." Further he expounds that "both men and horses, proudly compute by millions."[85]

And I Heard The Number Of Them: John heard a report of might and numbers, much more emphatically than common impressiveness would bring upon the ear.

> *17 And thus I saw the horses in the vision, and them that sat on them, having breastplates of fire, and of jacinth, and brimstone: and the heads of the horses were as the heads of lions; and out of their mouths issued fire, and smoke, and brimstone.*
> *18 By these three was the third part of men killed, by the fire, and by the smoke, and by the brimstone, which issued out of their mouths.*
> *19 For their power is in their mouths, and in their tails: for their tails were like unto serpents, and had heads, and with them they do hurt.*

Constantinople at the time of its invasion was almost an impregnable fortress, and had repeatedly held out against many invasions. But the Turks made remarkable use of the cannon, and they battered breaches into the walls. This was the first time a cannon was ever used

---

85   Gibbon, vii. 287, page 351.

in a major siege. How amazingly this prophecy revealed the fact that it would be by these means that Constantinople would fall. Artillery had arrived for battle![86] The conquest was enhanced by the use of *"fire, and smoke, and brimstone."* Brimstone or sulphur is the basis for the invention of gunpowder. Remember, the Arabs only had *"stings,"* but the Turks now have "fire." This fire was issued out of the mouths of their cannons which would trail behind the Sultan's armies. However, when the battle would begin, the cannons were swung around and positioned to destroy. Hence the symbol of the power being also *"in their tails."*

It is relevant that the *horsetail* was adopted by the Turks as a standard. They were the only nation that had chosen so strange an ensign. The authority of a Turkish pasha was marked by the number of horsetails-one, two, or three-that he was entitled to display. It was his badge of authority. [87]

To further expound on the Turkish metaphors, I reference Elliott's insights and analysis:

> "I saw the horses in the vision, and them that sat on them, having breastplates of *fire,* (i.e. of fire-color,) and *jacinth,* and *sulphur;"* or of red, blue, and yellow. On which it is the just remark of Mr. Daubuz, "that from their first appearance the Ottomans have affected to wear warlike apparel of scarlet, blue, and yellow..."

Elliott further clarified the symbolic language:

---

86   The Sultan Mahomet possessed 67 cannons. The smallest fired a 200-pound stone shot. The largest, 3 feet in bore, hurled a 1,200-pound ball. Sixty oxen were needed to draw it. These cannons could only be fired seven times a day because it took so long to clean them between blasts.

87   "Dark Muchtar his son to the Danube sped, Let the yellow-haired Giaours view his horsetail with dread." (Byron: *Childe Harald,* Can. II, 72.)

It is marked prominently in the prophecy before us. It is marked prominently *also in the history.* It was to "the fire and the smoke and the sulphur," to the artillery and firearms of Mahomet, that the killing of the third part of men, i. e. the capture of Constantinople, and by consequence the destruction of the Greek empire, was owing. Eleven hundred years and more had now elapsed since her foundation by Constantine. In the course of them, Goths, Huns, Avars, Persians, Bulgarians, Saracens, Russians, and indeed the Ottoman Turks themselves, had made their hostile assaults, or laid siege against it. But the fortifications were impregnable by them. Constantinople survived, and with it the Greek empire. Hence the anxiety of the Sultan Mahomet to find that which would remove the obstacle. "Canst thou cast a cannon?" was his question to the founder of cannon that deserted to him, "of size sufficient to batter down the wall of Constantinople." Then the foundry was established at Adrianople, the cannon cast, the artillery prepared, and the siege began… the fortifications which had stood for ages against hostile violence, were dismantled on all sides by the Ottoman cannon, many breaches opened, and, near the gate of St. Romanus, four towers leveled with the ground.[88]

20 And the rest of the men which were not killed by these plagues, yet repented not of the works of their hands, that they should not worship devils, and idols of gold,. and silver, and brass, and stone, and of wood; which neither can see, nor hear, nor walk: 21 Neither repented they of their murders, nor of their sorceries,

88   E. B. Elliott, *Horae Apocalypticae,* Vol I, Part II, pages 480,481.

nor of their fornications, nor of their thefts.

Before we enter into Chapter 10, we must understand how verses 20 and 21 form a link between these two chapters.

The rest of the Roman world that was not affected by these two trumpets was, of course, western Roman Catholic Europe. She refused to recognize that these judgments, in the form of "Woes," were being sent by God; instead, she organized the Crusades to fight the Turks.

There were some important benefits that arose out of the Turkish woe, as revealed by this sixth trumpet. When the scholars in Constantinople saw the approaching Turks, they fled from the city, taking with them their valuable manuscripts, including copies of the Bible which had been translated into Greek from Latin. They brought these copies of the Scriptures to Europe, especially England, which sowed the seed for the soon-coming glorious Reformation. Furthermore, the arrival of the scholars from Constantinople, who settled in the universities of western Europe, brought with them their knowledge of Greek and their precious Greek manuscripts of the Bible. This greatly helped the Reformation. In A.D. 1458, only five years after the fall of the eastern capital, Greek was being taught for the first time in Europe. The Reformation would soon follow to rock the world.

So we must conclude that verses 20 and 21 could only refer to the idolatrous church of Rome. By this time in history she had already killed hundreds of thousands of Albigenses and Waldenses. She had declared open war (Inquisitions) on all who opposed her sorceries, her thefts (indulgences), and her idolatries. She refused to learn from the fate of her eastern sister who was falling under the terrible hand of God. Therefore, we shall see later that the third "Woe" must fall on this European Roman Church in the form of "Vials."

We have now followed the opening of the seals and the blowing of the trumpets to the sixth trumpet under the seventh seal. By searching out historical facts, God's Word is proven to be wonderfully accurate. But much more lies ahead, waiting to be unveiled.

Read on.

VERY IMPORTANT NOTE:

It is clear that the main purpose of the first 2 WOE's were to bring judgement upon the Roman Earth. However, it is also clear that these demonic Islamic forces had one major goal – to invade Western Europe and destroy the House of Israel. As we have seen, they were thwarted by God's divine time measures.

If you possess a "love of the truth" and have the courage to pursue it, and want to understand your Bible, I highly recommend:

JUDAH'S SCEPTRE AND JOSEPH'S BIRTHRIGHT

An analysis of the Prophecies of the Scriptures in regard to the Royal Family of Judah and the Many Nations of Israel, the Lost Ten Tribes.

—By J.H. ALLEN

REVELATION CHAPTER 10
THE EVE OF THE REFORMATION
("CHRIST" REVEALED IN THE "LITTLE BOOK")

1 And I saw another mighty angel come down from heaven,
clothed with a cloud; and a rainbow was upon his head, and his
face was as it were the sun, and his feet as pillars of fire;
2 And he had in his hand a little book open: and he set his right
foot upon the sea, and his left foot upon the earth,

The 10th and 11th chapters should not have been separated, because they relate to one series of events, the Reformation. You need to keep this in mind when attempting to unveil the symbolism. The sixth trumpet has already blown, and the Euphratean horsemen have already completed their territorial mission in *"an hour, and a day, and a month, and a year."* The remaining remnants of the old Roman Empire, as John knew it, have fallen, and the state of European Catholicism is described in the last verses of Chapter 9. The events which we are going to interpret still belong to this sixth trumpet and will include all of Chapter 10 and verses 1-15 of Chapter 11. Having discovered that the Byzantine (Greek) Empire fell in A.D. 1453, the logical conclusion is that this chapter entails events subsequent to that date.

We, of the historicist school of prophetic interpretation, believe that this is *unquestionably* symbolic of the discoveries made by the Reformers, led by Martin Luther. Indeed, the seeds were sown in earlier centuries by Wycliffe and Huss, but it was fully commissioned by God in the 16th century.

This "mighty angel" could only be Jesus Christ because only He has the right to open the Book (Revelation 5:3). His sudden descent symbolizes the sudden discovery by the Reformers that Jesus was the *"one mediator between God and men,"* not the priesthood or the pope of Rome.

Just as John had seen the rainbow of divine mercy (Revelation 4:3), so did the Reformers awaken to the mighty truth of the mercy of God as expressed in our Lord Jesus Christ. The face of the angel as the *"sun,"* symbolizes how they saw Jesus as the *"son of righteousness,"* and not the pope, or any other false mediator.

Whatever the Romish clergy may claim now, there is no student of history who can deny that before the Reformation, Rome had taken the Bible away from the people. The full authority of the Catholic Church opposed its circulation, and in many instances people were burned to death for no other crime than having a Bible in their house. For almost a thousand years, the whole of Christendom had been in this hellish darkness. Christ had been displaced from his church by false mediators. But almost miraculously from A.D. 1517 onwards, a new and glorious gospel truth began to spread like a fire throughout Europe. As we will see in the next chapter, whole nations began to shed Rome's smothering yoke.

John sees the angel, with a *"little book"* in his hand, symbolically verifying the claims written therein. I believe this little book was the "Bible." Because the movable type printing press was invented,[89] the large hand written Bible was now a "little book." Rome had closed it, but thanks to the courage of the Reformers, it was open again. If you had lived in this time or previously, you would not have been able to get a Bible for love or money. Today, it is still the best selling book in the world-a result of the Reformation.

The Reformation was preceded by a period called the Renaissance (New Learning), also foretold by the Word of God. With the movement

---

89   Johann Gutenberg was a German printer and is generally considered the first European to print from movable type. He made his great invention in 1436 or 1437. He founded a print shop in Mainz where he issued the Mazarin Bible. Mainz became the center of this new printing trade. His invention is marked by historians as one of the most significant turning points in history.

of eastern scholars into Western Europe the study of classical languages helped spread the fires of the Reform. The impact of the Reformation and the printing of the Bible spread wider and wider. The fall of Constantinople, together with the Renaissance, which it brought, added to the earlier influence of Wycliffe and other Reformers, resulting in the glorious Reformation.

Many consider Wycliffe, Huss, and Luther to be the "threefold cord" of the Reformation. Wycliffe's writings influenced John Huss of Bohemia. Huss' writings then stirred Martin Luther of Germany. Luther then challenged the papacy, bringing on an event which changed western civilization forever. Thank God. Show me a man today with the courage of Luther.

I believe the following brief summary of Biblical achievements will help you grasp the importance of this era:

A.D. 1453 Flight of Greek scholars to western Europe.

A.D. 1453 The acceleration of printing in Holland and Gennany.

A.D. 1458 Greek language first taught in European universities.

A.D. 1476 Caxton introduces printing into England.

A.D. 1516 Erasmus printed his Greek New Testament.

A.D. 1518 Zwingli printed the first Swiss New Testament.

A.D. 1522 Luther's New Testament in German-57 editions.

A.D. 1526 Tyndale's English New Testament. Also Swedish Bible.

A.D. 1537 The Bible in Danish. Also Matthew's English Bible.

A.D. 1539 "The Great Bible" in every English church by command.

A.D. 1611 King James authorized version.

For centuries the Bible had been sealed in a tomb of dead languages, and it was impossible for the common people to read it. This angel, however, had in his hand a book open, significant of the fact that these determined Reformers would now present the Bible, open, to the world.

> *3 And cried with a load voice, as when a lion roareth: and when he had cried, seven thunders uttered their voices.*
>
> *4 And when the seven thunders had uttered their voices, I was about to write: and I heard a voice from heaven saying unto me, "Seal up those things which the seven thunders uttered, and write them not."*

Here we have the tremendous challenge of Christ (the Lion of the tribe of Judah), through the mouths of the Reformers, challenging the doctrines of Catholicism.[90] Within 14 days after Luther nailed his 95 theses to the church door at Wittenburg, all of Germany was aroused. And within 30 days all of Europe was so aroused that Rome was forced to reply. With this in mind, it is not difficult to interpret the *"seven thunders"* John hears answering the Lion's roar.

Again, I will extract from B. W. Johnson's *The People's New Testament With Notes:*

"The seven thunders uttered their voices when the angel cried in a loud voice. John was forbidden to record what they uttered. Certain facts will help us to understand what is meant. 1. The apostate power which had taken away and *closed* the book of the New Testament was called the seven-hilled city, and is alluded to in Revelation as the woman that sat on

---

90   2 The period of time between the Leipzig debate with Eck in July 1519, and the Diet of Worms in April 1521, was an exciting time for Luther. In May, 1520, he published a pamphlet entitled, *On Good Works*. Its effect was far reaching. It emphasized his new conviction that man is saved by faith alone. On June 15, 1520, Pope Leo X excommunicated Luther in a papal bull. Luther burned this document and replied, "As thou hast wasted the Holy One of God, so may the eternal flames waste thee," and further retaliated with a tract entitled: *Against the Execrable Bull of Antichrist*. Swiftly following, Luther published what became known as "The Three Great Reformation Treatises": 7b *the Christian Nobility of Germany-a* call to reject the abuses fostered by Rome; *The Babylonian Captivity of the Church* in which Luther destroyed Rome's claim that men could only be saved through the priesthood and its sacramental system; and *The Liberty of the Christian Man* containing the sum of the Christian life.

seven mountains (17:9). 2. The word *thunder* has been constantly used to describe the threatening, blasphemous, and authoritative fulminations issued by the seven hilled power against its enemies. To illustrate this, Le Bas says in his life of Wycliff [sic], page 198: 'The *thunders* which shook the world when they issued *from the seven hills,* sent forth an uncertain sound, comparatively faint and powerless, when launched from a region of less devoted sanctity.' These ecclesiastical thunders derived their power from the fact that they were hurled from the seven-hilled city. Very appropriately the bulls and anathemas of Rome may then be called the *seven thunders.*

3. It is a historic fact that the *opening of the book* by the Reformation called forth the loudest voices of *the seven thunders.* The anathemas that had been wont to shake the nations were hurled at Luther and his supporters.

"John says that he was about to write what they uttered. His act was symbolic. He becomes himself a part of the symbolism. His act shows that the voices of the *seven thunders* claimed a record as of divine authority. There was something uttered, and what was uttered was so presented that John was about to record it in the Word of God. Then he heard a voice from heaven which bade him seal up what was uttered and write it not. When we remember that the *thunders* that issued from the Vatican were regarded by the nations as the voice of God, and that the pope claimed to be the vicar of Christ, we can understand the meaning of John's symbolic purpose to record them as a part of the Word of God, and also that of the heavenly voice which forbade them to be written. It simply represents what *did* take place among the reformers. There was an open book offered to the world. This resulted in the voices of the thunders of the seven-hilled city. At first there was a disposition on the part even of Martin Luther, to listen to these thunders as divine, but finally he committed the papal bull issued against his teachings to the flames to be rejected and it was rejected by the Reformers."

> 5 *And the angel which I saw stand upon the sea and upon the earth, lifted up his hand to heaven,*
> 6 *And sware by him that liveth for ever and ever, who created heaven, and the things that therein are, and the earth, and the things that therein are, and the sea, and the things which are therein, that there should be time no longer:*

Many reformers who read these verses realized that this was a message for them. *"There should be time no longer"* is more correctly translated, *"That there should be no more delay"* (Living Bible). This phrase has mystified some people, but it should not. If we study its context, it most surely means that the time granted for repentance to apostate Christianity had finally run out. God's final offer to the "mystery of iniquity" was the Reformation. Rome treated the offer just as the Jews treated God's last offer to their nation; she did her utmost to destroy the messengers of the gospel.

> 7 *But in the days of the voice of the seventh angel, when he shall begin to sound, the mystery of God should be finished, as He hath declared to His servants the prophets.*

This verse simply reminds us that we are still in the period of the sixth trumpet (second woe). The seventh and last trumpet is the one for further revealing of the time, and the prophecies, relative to the complete unfolding of this book, and the consummation of this age.

8 And the voice which I heard from heaven spake unto me again, and said, Go and take the little book which is open in the hand of the angel which standeth upon the sea and upon the earth.
9 And I went unto the angel, and said unto him, Give me the little book. And he said unto me, Take it, and eat it up; and it shall make thy belly bitter, but it shall be in thy mouth sweet as honey.
10 And I took the little book out of the angel's hand, and ate it up; and it was in my mouth sweet as honey: and as soon as I had eaten it, my belly was bitter.

During the 16th century the people received the Word of God with great eagerness. They wanted more truths taught to them. But they soon found out that as they preached the Word of God and as nation after nation converted to the biblical principles of Christ and as they proclaimed truth and confronted error, that the papal sword had become unsheathed. The Scriptures were so sweet to them, but millions were destined to fall under this papal sword of bitterness.

11 And he said unto me, Thou must prophesy again before many peoples, and nations, and tongues, and kings.

Here now is portrayed another consequence of eating the book. *"Thou must prophesy again before many peoples, and nations, and tongues, and kings."* Prophecy is not just foretelling future events. It is also the ability to declare the true message of God. The apostles clearly declared the truths of Christ. Apostolic preaching had almost ceased for many ages before its revival with the Reformation. This command proclaims the revival of apostolic preaching which is destined to affect all nations. In other words, it will fill the earth.

I believe in the unrestricted providence of our God. If we go back to the first advent of Christ, we can see how the Lord had wonderfully prepared the Roman world to receive the Word of God. The Greek Empire had been conquered by the Romans. But the Greek culture had conquered the Roman Empire. There was a common tongue throughout the whole Roman earth, which enabled the swift spreading of the gospel.

So now we see how the Lord was preparing Europe for the receiving of the little book. We have the flight of Greek scholars to western Europe, the advent of the printing press, and the ability to make cheap paper out of rags and wood pulp. Our Lord is wonderful. He has never been caught off guard. His purpose has been and will be fulfilled. We are so fortunate to be living in a time where we can look back and see the glory of the Lord through His prophetic word. Why do we listen to the futurists and preterists who pervert this great truth? Let's read and understand what a living God we serve.

"We have also a more sure word of prophecy; whereunto ye do well that ye take heed, as unto a light that shineth in a dark place, until the day dawn, and the daystar arise in your hearts" (2 Peter 1:19).

REVELATION CHAPTER 11
THE TWO WITNESSES

"JAM NEMO RECLAMAT, NULLUS OBSISTIT!"

"There is an end of resistance to the papal rule and religion: opposers there exist no more."

The Latin Proclamation of Triumph, May 5, 1514

"My pen is ready to give birth to things much greater. I know not myself whence these thoughts come to me. I will send you what I write, that you may see if I have well conjectured in believing that the Antichrist, of whom St. Paul speaks, now reigns in the court of Rome."

Luther writing to his friend Link,
before the approaching disputation with Eck.

1 And there was given me a reed like unto
a rod: and the angel stood, saying, Rise, and measure the temple
of God, and the altar, and them that worship therein.
2 But the court which is without the temple leave out, and mea-
sure it not; for it is given unto the Gentiles; and the holy city
shall they tread under foot forty and two months.

The significance of these verses is masterfully expounded by the historicist scholar B. W. Johnson. He, like many others, identifies and reveals this symbolic language without violating the consistent historical unfolding of this great prophecy. After Johnson's observations are considered, I will explain the meanings of some other terms:

"This prediction will be fulfilled if, under the sixth trumpet, before the seventh is blown, a corrupted church, corrupted during long ages of apostasy shall be compared with some divine standard. Or, in other words, *after 1453 there ought to be an effort to reform the Church, and to conform it to the New Testament.* Let us ask, who shall measure the church? It had been measured for hundreds of years, not by the Bible, but by the decrees of councils, and by the decisions of popes. There was during all this time a voice, almost suppressed, asking that it be measured by the divine standard, but it was stifled. This prophecy, however, implies a movement of commanding power which shall seek to apply the divine reed to the measurement of the church. Who now, according to John, shall make the measurement; what shall be the standard? Not popes, not councils, not apostolic fathers, but the reed is given to an apostle, the living representative of the apostolic body. The Twelve to whom were given 12 thrones, to judge the 12 tribes of Israel, shall also measure the church of Jesus Christ in the day signified by the symbolism employed. How? The reed was not their own creation but was given to them. There is but one divine measure that has ever been given. The New Testament, written by apostles, given to them by inspiration, is the divine standard with which the church, the worship and the worshipers, must be tested. Not the traditions of men, not the decisions of councils, not the decrees of synods, or conferences, not the creeds of any uninspired body that ever met on the face of the earth, but the standard measure is the New Testament.

"This is not the only place where the *reed* is named as the appointed instrument for the measurement of the Church. If the reader will turn to the 21st chapter, he will find that the New Jerusalem, the Holy City, is measured by an angel with a golden reed. In Ezekiel, chapter 40, the prophet sees an angel measure with a reed the temple such as has never been seen by mortal vision. The temple itself is just equal to the measure, and it is composed of many chambers, all equal in size to the reed, to each other, and to the temple itself, of which they are parts. This strange symbolism, this representation of what is apparently impossible, most beautifully represents the character of the true church, when it has reached the fullness of the divine measure, and appears as the New Jerusalem. The whole temple is just the size, neither larger nor smaller than the reed. The true church corresponds exactly with the divine measure of the Word. It neither adds to itself things unknown to the apostles, nor omits the things therein enjoined. As the temple of Ezekiel was composed of chambers, each of which was the same size of the temple, so the church is composed of many congregations, each of which should correspond exactly to the measure of the whole body. These individual congregations, which make up the spiritual temple, should not differ from each other in name, in creeds, in rites, in observances, as do the sects of modern times. In the true church, when fully restored, there will be one Lord, one faith, one baptism, one spirit, one hope, one name, one practice.

"The symbolism recorded by the apostle evidently describes the measurement of the church, its worship, and of its worshipers by the divine standard of the New Testament. Our next inquiry is whether history records the fulfillment. Do we find taught in history, subsequent to 1453, which can be regarded a fulfillment of the prophecy? Earlier reformers, such as Waldo, Wycliff, and Huss, made an attempt to reform the church, but the whole world dates the beginning of the Protestant Reformation with Luther. It was in 1517 that he nailed his theses to the doors of the church in Wittenberg, by which he broke with Rome. It was held by the papacy, which then lorded over Christendom that the writings of the Fathers, tradition, and the decrees of councils were not only an additional measure, but might even set aside the Word of God. The great Reformation planted itself upon the principles maintained by Martin Luther. The Bible as the cornerstone and only rule of faith and practice in the Christian church. Protestantism has not always been true to its principles, *but it has always conceded that the final standard of measurement is the Word of God*,"[91]

Measure The Temple: For centuries the Christian church understood that the temple of this verse was the Greek word *naos* which is th,e spiritual temple.[92] This has absolutely nothing to do with the temple that had once stood in Jerusalem. It had already been destroyed by Titus more than 20 years before John received this revelation. Also, everywhere in the New Testament, after the Jews had finally rejected the gospel in the stoning of Stephen (Acts 7:51- 60), the word naos is used only to designate the church of Jesus Christ. Peter, in his epistle, called believers "lively stones in the temple [naos] of God" (1 Peter 2:5).

As Johnson so properly revealed, the Church [many believe True Israel] is the Holy City in the Book of Revelation. Hebrews 12:22-24, and Matthew 5:14, prove to us that *Mount Zion, The Holy City,* and *Heavenly Jerusalem* is the New Testament Church of the firstborn. The symbolism is used throughout the Book of Revelation. History has proven the Word of God, and shown us many aspects of this Holy City. Furthermore, history has revealed that the true Church was [again the House of Israel] *"tread under foot"* (persecuted) for 1,260 years at the hands of the papal powers. Therefore, the unmeasured court could only be the Roman Catholic system. The Bible does not measure it, it condemns it, and exposes it. (That's why they burned so many Bibles.) The Reformers made no attempt

---

91   B.W. Johnson, *The People's New Testament With Notes,* pages 456-457.

92   Paul writes in 1 Cor. 3:16, "Know ye not that ye are the temple (naos) of God, and that the Spirit of God dwelleth in you?" It is a remarkable thing that the despensationalists try to teach you that this temple is literal. Having eyes, they see not.

to reform this Roman church in their endeavor to progress in the ways of the Lord. They simply did like John the Revelator and rejected it.

But The Court Which Is Without The Temple Leave Out: The phrase *"leave out"* is more perfectly translated *"cast out."* An example of this is seen at the first Diet of Augsburg, held A.D. 1525, just while the Reformation was accelerating. This apology was delivered by the Elector, written by Melancthon. The following points were insisted on:

First, that every minister of God's Word is bound by Christ's express precept to preach the leading doctrine of the gospel, *justification by faith in Christ crucified,* and not by the merit of human performances; whereas men had by the Romish doctrines been drawn from the cross of Christ, to trust in their own works, and in superstitious vanities.

Second, that it became the princes (those over whom the Pope and the bishops had exercised hitherto and usurped authority, but to whom the authority in these matters rightfully belonged) simply to consider whether the new doctrines, as they were called, were or were not true; and if true, to protect and promote them.

Third, that the Roman pope, cardinals, and clergy did not constitute the church of Christ, though there existed among them some that were real members of that church, and opposed the reigning errors: the true Church consisted of the faithful, and none else, who had the Word of God and by it were sanctified and cleansed; while, on the other hand, what St. Paul had predicted of *Antichrist's* coming, and *sitting in the temple of God,* had its fulfillment in the papacy…[therefore] the Reformers were not guilty of schism, either because they had convicted Antichrist of his errors, or made alterations in their church worship and regulations, whereby the Romish superstitions were ***cast out!*** Such was the manifesto of the Reformers.

3 And I will give power unto my two witnesses, and they shall prophesy a thousand two hundred and threescore days, clothed in sackcloth.
4 These are the two olive trees, and the two candlesticks standing before the God of the earth.

Before I reveal the simple interpretation of the *"two witnesses,"* let's deal with the divine time measure of *"a thousand two hundred and threescore days."*

Ezekiel 4:6: *"I have appointed thee each day for a year."*

The synonymous applications of the 1,260 "day-years" is simply phrased three different ways in the Bible so as to identify the **doctrinal, temporal** and **persecuting** periods given to Papal Rome. We will later see that when great Babylon is ultimately destroyed, God divides her judgment into three parts (Revelation 16:19). She terrorized in three historic phases; likewise, she will fall in three complete and terrible judgments. *"Great Babylon came in remembrance before God."*

"forty and two months" (Rev. 11:2)
"a thousand two hundred and threescore days" (Rev. 11:3)
"a time, and times, and half a time" (Rev. 12:14)

A. D. 254-A.D. 1514

Rome is supreme in her doctrinal authority. This period runs from the *"Edict of Stephen,"* which asserted that the bishop of Rome was the

Supreme Pontiff, to the *"5th Laterine Council"* where the papacy pro-claimed doctrinal victory. *"Jam nemo reclamat, nullus obsistit!"*

A. D. 533-A. D. 1793

Rome is supreme in her temporal (political) authority. This period runs from *"Justinian's Decree,"* which stated that all must be subject to the Bishop of Rome, until the destruction of Rome's temporal power which began with the *"French Revolution."* NOTE: The decree was enforced by arms, and the title *Rector Ecclesiae,* or "Lord of the Church" was bestowed (D'Aubigne's *Reformation,* Vol. I, p. 42).

A. D. 606-A.D. 1866

Rome enters the time given her to persecute and overcome the saints of the Most High (see also Daniel 7:25): From the *"Phocas Decree"* which made Boniface III the first official pope, to the last massacre (burning) of Protestants in Barletta, Italy.

THE TWO WITNESSES
THE OLIVE TREE—THE CANDLESTICK

Let's begin this revealing with a very simple question: What is *a witness?* Simply answered, *a witness is evidence for a case.* I emphasize this point because we are continually taught that a witness must be a person. That is not true. You are now prepared to investigate this portion of the prophecy armed with sanctified common sense.

Please also notice that the two witnesses do not just appear for the first time; rather, they are already there and are being given power for a special time of emergency.

The Lord gives power to these witnesses to "preach" for 1,260 years, in symbolic sackcloth, a type of Israel in mourning. The word "witness" used here is the same word that John uses in Chapter 17, verse 6 *(martus or martyrs)*. In Chapter 17, John said that the woman (harlot church) had made herself drunk on the blood of the martyrs. We are presented with the same group of people, but we're given the time in which the woman has to drink their blood (persecuted them unto death): it was for 1,260 years. Let's see who these witnesses are *according to the Bible*.

The reason why we have two witnesses is because it is written in the Mosaic law that *"at the mouth of two witnesses… shall the matter be established"* (Deuteronomy 19:15; 2 Corinthians 13:1). Let me give it to you simply, then I'll expound. The Old Testament reveals that the House of Isreal and the House of Judah are God's two witnesses. However, during the time of the Reformation, the tools used to proclaim this witness were the Word of God and the True Church.

The following is an excerpt from:

THE BOOK OF REVELATION
FROM AN ISRAELITE
& HISTORICIST INTERPRETATION
BY CHARLES A. JENNINGS

—Available at Truth In History

First, let us ascertain from the Old Testament who God refers to as His two witnesses. In Isa. 43:10 it is stated, unto Jacob, which is inclusive of both houses of Israel. "Ye are my witnesses saith God, and my servant whom I have chosen..." The prophet is referring to Jacob yet he says, Ye are my witnesses, which denotes more than one or a plurality of witnesses. In Isa. 44:8 it is stated, "Fear ye not, neither be afraid: have not I told thee from that time, and have declared it? Ye are even my witnesses. Here again, God speaking through the prophet unto Jacob, His servant, states that the house or the family of Jacob are His witnesses. End quote.

THE MANIFISTATION OF THE TWO WITNESSES DURING THE REFORMATION:

The Word of God

John 5:39 *"Search the Scriptures; for in them ye think ye have eternal life: and they are they which testify (witness) of me."*[93]

The True Church

Acts 1:8 "Ye shall be my witnesses"[94]

---

93   As we know, the Bible is divided into two great divisions, which are called the *Old* and *New* Testaments. Note further that the term *testament* is a word that signifies to bear witness. It is derived from a Latin word, *testor,* which means, I testify.

94   During the time of the Reformation, great works on the martyrs began to appear. It is relevant to this issue to note the titles of these works. In A.D. 1556, Flacius Illyricus, who is justly called "the parent of ecclesiastical history; reflecting, as it did, a light really wonderful on the facts of the history of the Christian Church, hitherto covered with darkness, and corrupted by innumerable fables," wrote a work that was published under the title *Catalogus ':lestium,* or *Catalogue of Witnesses.* Almost in the very same year appeared Fox's Martyrology: in other words, rendering the Greek of the title into English, *The History of Christ's Martyrs and Witnesses.* In 1571, it was ordered that a copy of this book be placed in all the churches of England. Matthew 5:14 *"Ye are the light of the world"*

In the Book of Zechariah chapter 4, verses 1-4, 11-14, we have two olive trees shown supplying oil to *one candlestick.* This oil lights the candlestick. In Revelation chapter 1, verse 20, the Lord revealed to John that a candlestick represents a church. Applying this revelation to Zechariah's prophecy, we have the Old Testament church in Israel as a candlestick. Acts 7:38 states, *"This is he, that was in the church in the wilderness..."* A church cannot exist without being fed by the Word of God.

Now, why does the one candlestick in Zechariah become two candlesticks in the Book of Revelation and form one of the witnesses? Answer: The New Testament Church is the second candlestick. Yet both of these form one witness. Remember in Acts, Jesus said, *"Ye are my witnesses."* The Church of the Old Covenant and the New Covenant are seen by God as one witness throughout the ages.

In Zechariah's vision the two olive trees were present and were supplying oil to the Old Testament church. I believe that in this vision the olive trees represented the two major segments of the Old Testament, the law and the prophets. When Paul was in Rome, it was said of him that *"there came many to him into his lodging; to whom he expounded and testified the kingdom of God, persuading them concerning Jesus, both out of the law of Moses and out of the prophets..."* (Acts 28:23). David testified, *"The entrance of Thy words giveth light,"* and *"Thy word is a lamp unto my feet, and a light unto my path."* I believe that these olive trees are now symbolic of the prophets of the Old Testament and the apostles of the New Testament. Therefore, the second witness must be the Bible.

Though by no means exhaustive, these considerations and declarations are sufficient to reveal the prophecy, and seriously refute the incredibly fanciful speculations of the dispensationalists.

5 And if any man will hurt them, fire proceedeth out of their mouth, and devoureth their enemies; and if any man will hurt them, he must in this manner be killed.

6 These have power to shut heaven, that it rain not in the days of their prophecy: and have power over waters to turn them to blood, and to smite the earth with all plagues, as often as they will.

Fire Proceedeth Out Of Their Mouth: By the use of this phrase, the reader is informed of the authority that these witnesses possess. In Jeremiah we read, *"Wherefore thus saith the Lord God of hosts, Because ye speak this word, behold, I **will make my words in thy mouth fire,** and this people wood, and it shall devour them"* (Jeremiah 5:14). And the rest of this verse is understood through the teachings of our Lord. He stated this divine principle, *"For with what judgment ye judge, ye shall be judged: and with what measure ye mete, it shall be measured to you again"* (Matthew 7:2). Furthermore, it could not be that there would be no natural rain on the earth for 1,260 years: a spiritual drought is surely intended. *"The days come, saith the Lord God, that I will send a famine on the land: not a famine of bread, nor a thirst for water, but of hearing of the words of the Lord"* (Amos 8:11).

History contains many illustrations of the fulfillments of these two verses. The nations of Europe such as France and Spain, who persecuted the Christians and their Scriptures (by burning the Word of God), felt the awful judgments of revolutions and wars much more intensely than those nations who turned to the truth of the Bible during the Reformation. As long as these nations of Europe persecuted the Church during the time of the Dark Ages, there is recorded a continuous account of the shedding of blood along the waterways of Europe. This is why verse 6 states that *"they have power over waters to turn them to blood, and to smite the earth with all plagues, as often as they will."* This is symbolic language.

> *7 And when they shall have finished their testimony, the beast that ascendeth out of the bottomless pit shall make war against them, and shall overcome them, and kill them.*

When they have *completed* their testimony is the literal meaning.

This beast is the fourth beast of Bible prophecy as revealed by the prophet Daniel, Chapter 7. It is the Roman Empire, both pagan and papal. History reveals that the papal church persecuted the witnesses with much more intensity than did the pagan empire. This verse reveals that there would come a time when the papal "beast" would make war with the witnesses, kill them, and overcome them.

By the 12th century, the church had completed its testimony (verified the evidence) against the papal wild beast. An example of this is seen in the life of Peter Waldo and the poor men of Lyons, A.D. 1170. This marked the rise of the Waldenses, who were persecuted from 1179 onwards, excommunicated by the Council of Verona, A.D. 1184, and in turn, valiantly opposed the errors and corruptions of the church. Waldo preached: (1.) That the pope is the Antichrist. (2.) That the Mass is an abomination. (3.) That the host is an idol. (4.) That purgatory is a fable. The result of this was that the mature beast now declares open war upon the heretics. It began with the *3rd Lateran General Council of 1179,* and accelerated with the *Inquisitions.* These were designed to exterminate the Bible church, and to prevent the Scriptures from being used. The results: The Bohemian Brethren, in A.D. 1499, sent men throughout Europe to see if there were any witnesses left, who had a similar testimony to their own, and they found none. So successful had been the papal war of extermination.

The systematic slaughter of the saints, which began in the 12th century, commenced under Innocent III, whose accession is the 666th year from the rise of the papacy at Justinian's edict. Gibbon recognized the era of Innocent III as that of the meridian of papal greatness.

Have we forgotten the **Inquisition?**

> *8 And their dead bodies shall lie in the street of the great city which spiritually is called Sodom and Egypt, where also our Lord was crucified.*
>
> *9 And they of the people, and kindreds, and tongues, and nations, shall see their dead bodies three days and a half, and shall not suffer their dead bodies to be put in graves.*
>
> *10 And they that dwell upon the earth shall rejoice over them, and make merry, and shall send gifts one to another; because these two prophets tormented them that dwelt on the earth.*

On December 16, 1513, a papal bull was issued calling the remaining Bohemian brethren to present their case before the *Ninth Session of the Fifth Lateran Council* to be held on May 5, 1514. No Protestant showed.[95] The Romanists hailed this as a great victory. As a result of this, the orator of the session ascended a platform, and amidst great applause from the Latin assembly he boasted that memorable exclamation of triumph: *"Jam nemo reclamat, nullus obsisgit!"* *"There is an end of resistance to the Papal*

---

[95]   Concerning the opening of the 16th century, the famous historian of the Council of Trent, *Cardinal Pallavicini,* had this to say: "In the West the true faith flourished [Catholicism], with scarce any contamination attached to it: there remaining only, *almost invisible,* certain minute stains of ignoble and despised heresies, followed by a little flock of rustic and rude men: the remnant either of the Waldenses, or of the followers of John Huss, who had been condemned and burnt a century before, in the Council of Constance." E.B. Elliott, *Horae Apocalypticae* 4th ed., Pt. III, page 414.

rule and religion: opposers there exist no more" and again, *"The whole body of Christendom is now seen to be subjected to its Head [the Pope]."* This brought great rejoicing in the Roman hierarchy, causing great feasts to celebrate the end of the Protestants. Gifts were exchanged to herald the momentous occasion.[96] It was as if the witnesses were dead. There was nothing heard from them.

The Street Of the Great City: The *"street"* or *"meeting place"* of that great city is St. Peter's in Rome (Revelation 17:18). With an overwhelming voice, the Reformers referred to the Roman Catholic Church of that time as "spiritual" Sodom and Egypt. Sodom for her impurity, and Egypt for her idolatry. Many times the martyrs condemned this institution for crucifying the Lord with her persecutions of the true Church and her daily Masses. Even the dead (heretics) were denied the privilege of Christian burial.[97]

> 11 *And after three days and a half the spirit of life from God entered into them and they stood upon their feet; and great fear fell upon them which saw them.*

---

96   "All which considered," says Leo [Pope Leo X], "Our soul exults in the Lord: and we judge that thanks should be given to God for it, and that, among all the faithful in Christ, there should be those signs of joy which on similar occasions are wont to be observed." So, "for the greater joy," a plenary Papal Indulgence was granted, and then the Te Deum was sung. And if the making merry in banquetings was another of the customary modes of expressing joy on public occasions of festivity, it too was acted out both by Leo himself and by his Cardinals, very notably, on this auspicious occasion. The splendor of the dinners and fetes given by Leo and the Cardinals on the triumphant close of the Council-a splendor unequalled since the days of Pagan Rome's greatness is made the subject of special record by the Historian of Leo X. E.B. Elliott, *Horae Apocalypticae,* 4th ed., Pt. III, page 438.

97   "At length in the 12th century Christendom, as a public body, moved in the matter. Thus in the 3rd Council of Lateran, A. D. 1179, Christian burial was denied to heretics: the same in the 4th Lateran Council A.D. 1215, and the Papal Decree of Gregory IX, A.D. 1227: the same again in that of Pope Martin, immediately after the Council of Constance, A.D. 1422: which Council ordered that *Wycliff's* body should be exhumed ... and the ashes of *Huss,* instead of burial, should be collected and cast into the Lake of Constance. I may add that *Savonarola's* ashes were similarly cast into the Arno, A. D. 1498, and that in the first Bull entrusted to the Cardinal Cajetan, against *Luther,* as well as that afterwards, this was one of the declared penalties, that both Luther and his partians should be deprived *'ecclesiasticae sepulturae.'"* [Christian burial] E. B. Elliott, *Horae Apocalypticae,* 4th ed., Pt. III, page 435.

Exactly three and a half years after the Lateran Council opened on May 5, 1514, when no Protestant showed up to state their case, the spirit of strength entered into Martin Luther, and on October 31, 1517, he nailed his *95 Theses* (points for debate) on the door of the Wittenberg church. The mighty Reformation had started on its way and nothing was going to stop it. It exploded upon Europe. This time Rome was not able to silence it. It was proclaimed at the Diet at Nuremberg, 1523, that "The *heretics Huss and Jerome* seem now to be *alive again* in the person of *Luther."*

The great Elliott boasted, "So that whole interval is *precisely, to a day,* three and a half years; *precisely, to a day,* the period predicted in the apocalyptic prophecy! - Oh wonderful prophecy, is the exclamation that again forces itself on my mind!" He went on to quote other vindications of this remarkable insight:

"The fire ill-smothered," says he [Pope Leo] at the close of 1513 and of 1514, "was blown up again by Luther's bellows, and spread its flames far and wide, more than ever before."

Popish Annalist Raynaldus

"Every thing was quiet; every heretic exterminated: and the whole Christian world supinely acquiescing in the enormous absurdities inculpated on them [by the Romish Church], when, in 1517, the empire of superstition received its first attack [its death blow almost] from Martin Luther."

Elliott quoting the *Encyclopedia Britannica*

"At the commencement of the 16th century, Europe reposed in the deep sleep of spiritual death, under the iron yoke of the papacy. There was none that moved the wing, or opened the mouth, or peeped: when, suddenly, in one of the universities of Germany the voice of an obscure monk was heard, the sound of which rapidly filled Saxony, Germany, and Europe itself; shaking the very foundations of the Papal power, and arousing men from the lethargy of ages."

Mr. Cuninghame

12 And they heard a great voice from heaven saying unto them, Come up hither, and they ascended up to heaven in a cloud; and their enemies beheld them.

From this point onwards, none were able to stop the acceleration of the Reformation. It was a determined and sovereign move of the Holy Spirit, destined to affect the whole world. The Bible churches of today are still a product of this courageous reform. In understanding the symbolic nature of this prophecy, it is clearly understood that these witnesses didn't literally ascend into heaven, rather they "ascended back into *heavenly places in Christ* Jesus" (Ephesians 2:6), and it was evident that their power was from above.

"We are not the first ones who applied the anti-Christian kingdom of the papacy: this, many great men have dared to do many years before us and that, frankly and openly, under the greatest persecution. The old divinely-ordained witnesses confirm our doctrine, and the bodies of these saints arise as it were among us with the newly vivified Gospel, and awaken much confidence."[98]

Martin Luther, 1528

---

98   Thomas Foster, *The Pope, Communism, and the Coming New World*, page 58.

13 the same hour was there a great earthquake, and the tenth part of the city fell, and in the earthquake were slain of men seven thousand: and the remnant were affrighted, and gave glory to the God of heaven.

After Luther's surge of the Reformation, the Roman Catholic Church was torn apart in western Europe. Fortunately, this changed the direction of the Church for all time. The massive floodgates of reform had been opened. Not only would the European land mass be shaken, but across the channel the effects would accelerate.

The English Reformation occurred under King Henry VIII and his son, Edward VI. The same causes that Luther and the other reformers were espousing were present in England. (Wycliffe had stirred the nation two centuries earlier, and his light was still shining. Even though his Lollard followers had been crushed, the memory of this "morning star of the Reformation" had never been entirely forgotten.) The ratio between these religious grievances and the national, political and economic motives is argued to this present day in academia. It was not till after the death of Henry VIII that England became, in the Christian sense, Protestant.

The story of Henry's needing a male heir to preserve the Tudor line is well known and can easily be researched. He would not wait on Rome, so in 1529 he called a parliament which declared the English church independent of Rome. By 1533, the English church was so far removed from the Roman Church that the Archbishop of Canterbury was able to grant the king his long-sought divorce.

The next year Parliament took the last step needed to establish the total independence of the English national church. All contacts with Rome were severed, and Henry was declared by the "Act of Supremacy" to be absolute head of the Church of England. Therefore, this kingdom was severed, from the once universal church. *England was the first nation to break away from Rome's European spiritual city.* This is the fulfillment of the verse which states, *"and the tenth part of the city fell."*

In the visions of the Revelation, earthquakes are consistently interpreted to be great political upheavals. Certainly the Reformation was one of the major earthquakes of all time. The effects of this earthquake, as we have seen, caused *one tenth* of a great city to fall away. In Revelation 17:18, Rome (as a spiritual empire) is identified as that great city. Through the leadership of Henry VIII, Edward VI, Queen Elizabeth, and James I, the British Monarchy became the head of the Church of England, not the pope. However, the remainder of verse 13 states, *"and in an earthquake were slain of men seven thousand,"* and understanding this will help us pinpoint this epic turmoil in Reformation Europe. To do this, we must look at the events which led up to the revolt of the Netherlands.

The Holy Roman Emperor Charles V had a son named Philip II (1556-98). Philip is noted in history as Spain's "most Catholic king." This king's reign is referred to as the "golden age of Spain." During the time of Philip, Spain was the nerve center of the Catholic Reformation. Also, by the time of Philip, the Spanish Inquisition had reached its apex. This Inquisition was a furious killing field of which Rome has yet to repent. Its attempted introduction into the Netherlands led to rebellion.

The Netherlands then consisted of 17 provinces. The humanism of Erasmus, as well as the teachings of Luther, took early root in the nation, soon followed by Anabaptist ideas. But in the 1550s a militant, disciplined Calvinism spread rapidly and soon became the dominant form of Protestantism. The revolt was tripart in nature. First, there was a reaction against centralization. Second, a patriotic fervor surfaced. Third, there was a religious protest against inquisitorial Catholicism.

The year 1566 marked a drastic acceleration of the revolt. Calvinist mobs began to break images of the saints and smashed the stained glass windows in Catholic churches throughout the 17 provinces. Philip reacted by sending in the Duke of Alva with ten thousand troops. Alva instituted what came to be known as the "Council of Blood." He boasted that he had executed over seventeen thousand people. This council lasted for 6 years, and the people of the Netherlands never forgot this hellish scourge. In 1576, Antwerp was sacked by Spanish troops in what is known as the "Spanish Fury." All 17 provinces were frightened into submission and agreed to stay together with the pacification of Ghent.

Within three years, all moderation lost influence. The majority of Catholics looked to Spain for protection. The 17 provinces divided. The Calvinists fled to the Dutch provinces of the north, beyond the great rivers where they were able to set up adequate defenses. The Catholics went south to the Walloon provinces. In 1579, the seven Dutch provinces in the north formed the Union of Utrecht. It was the foundation of the United Provinces or Dutch Netherlands. They formally declared their independence from Spain in 1581. The prophetic Word of God was fulfilled, *"and in an earthquake were. slain of men seven thousand."*

All in the futurist school, preterist school and many even in the historicist school have wrestled with the interpretation of this verse. However, I reference *Horae Apocalypticae* (Pt. III, pages 457-467).[99] Here, Elliott interprets this verse with unmatched scholastic genius. He proves that the word "thousands" is properly interpreted *chiliads,* meaning provinces or counties. It is important to see how simply and beautifully history falls into proper perspective with this enlightenment.

Thus, we look for seven chiliads of the papal city to break away about the time England (one tenth of the city) rebels. You have already read the history of this fulfillment. The Union of Utrecht formed these seven

---

99   Also, E.P. Cachemaille, *The Visions of Daniel and the Revelation Explained,* pages 356-371.

chiliads that fell away. These are the seven provinces ("thousands" KJV) that fell away as a result of the Reformation: HOLLAND, ZEALAND, UTRECHT, FREISELAND, GRONINGEN, OVERYSSEL and GUIDER-LAND. The Revelation is not a mystery; it is a revelation.

> *14 The second woe is past; and, behold, the third woe cometh quickly.*

Now, I hope you have followed this glorious scenario and have seen that the events from Revelation 9:13 to Revelation 11:14 occurred during the time of the sixth trumpet or second woe. During this period, the Reformation occurred and the Turks conquered a "*a third part of men*" and continued to war with papal Europe until the Treaty of Carlowitz in A. D. 1699.

So now we are introduced to the era of the "*seventh trumpet,*" when God pours the final "vials" of judgment on the Roman earth.

> *15 And the seventh angel sounded; and there were great voices in heaven, saying, The kingdoms of this world are become the kingdoms of our Lord, and of His Christ; and He shall reign for ever and ever.*

The phrase "*are become*" is more correctly translated "*are becoming*" (as the Concordant translation and others render it).

Since the time of this mighty Reformation, nation after nation has rejected the religion of Rome and adopted biblical Christianity. This process will continue until all kingdoms have been converted, then the end will come (1 Corinthians 15:24-28). This verse simply vindicates the growth principle of Christ's Kingdom (see Daniel 2:35,44; Matthew 13:31-

33). Truly, the Reformation accelerated the process of *"the kingdoms of this world becoming the kingdoms of our Lord."*

Furthermore, this verse tells us that there is yet another "Woe" to come, so it cannot be speaking about the end of the age.

> *16 And the four and twenty elders, which sat before God on their*
> *seats, fell upon their faces, and worshipped God.*
> *17 Saying, We give Thee thanks, 0 Lord God Almighty, which*
> *are, and wast, and art to come; because Thou has taken to Thee*
> *Thy great power, and hast reigned.*

The psalmist David revealed to us, and Peter confirmed the prophecy, that upon ascending to the throne (Acts 2:30-35), Christ began to rule in His *"great power"* through the Church-the true Zion. Notice carefully the words of the 110th Psalm, verses 1-3a: *"The Lord said unto my Lord, Sit thou at my right hand, until I make Thine enemies Thy footstool. The Lord shall send the rod of Thy strength out of Zion: rule Thou in the midst of Thine enemies. Thy people shall be willing in the day of Thy power..."* And the prophet Daniel clarified the picture even more. He states, *"And there was given Him dominion, and glory, and a kingdom, that all people, nations, and languages, should serve Him: His dominion is an everlasting dominion, which shall not pass away, and His kingdom which shall not be destroyed"* (Daniel 7:14).

So Christ has taken His great power and reigned, and will continue to do so (through the willing people of Zion) until all His enemies are conquered. All nations *"should serve Him,"* but unfortunately some will just have to be conquered. That's what the Bible teaches.

> *18 And the nations were angry, and Thy wrath is come, and*

the time of the dead, that they should be judged, and that Thou
shouldest give reward unto Thy servants the prophets, and to
the saints, and them that fear Thy name, small and great; and
shouldest destroy them which destroy the earth.

Again, it is the psalmist David who has revealed to us why these nations are angry. They are in rage because the Kingdom of God is attacking their hellish gates. David records their fury as they try to resist Zion: *"Why do the heathen rage, and the people imagine a vain thing? The kings of the earth set themselves, and the rulers take counsel together, against the Lord, and against His Anointed, saying, Let us break their bands asunder, and cast away their cords from us; He that sitteth in the heavens shall laugh: the Lord shall have them in derision"* (Psalm 2:1-4). Do you see this clear picture? It's much different from that painted by the escapist futurists.

John also included reference to the resurrection of the dead. Oh, what a glorious hope! The Scriptures reveal to us that our present afflictions are not even worthy to be compared with the glory that will be revealed in us (2 Corinthians 4:17). However, it is our Lord who confidently proclaimed the resurrection of those in the grave. He stated, *"Marvel not at this: for the hour is coming, in the which all that are in the graves shall hear His voice, And shall come forth; they that have done good unto the resurrection of life; and they that have done evil, unto the resurrection of damnation"* (John 5:28,29).

19 And the temple of God was opened in heaven, and there was seen in His temple the ark of His testament: and there were lightnings, and voices, and thunderings, and an earthquake, and great hail.

At this point in the Book of Revelation we have reached the end of the first half, having completed 11 of the 22 chapters. Remember, John saw the Scroll written in two halves. This verse summarizes the end of the age. The true temple (naos) of God, the Body of Christ, is revealed standing firm in the approaching upheaval of nations. Jesus is typified by the "Ark" standing in the midst of His Church. This scene seems to typify the proclamation in Hebrews Chapter 12, verses 25-29, which state with great authority: *"See that ye refuse, not Him that speaketh. For if they escaped not who refused Him that spake on earth, much more shall not we escape, if we turn away from Him that speaketh from heaven: Whose voice then shook the earth: but now He hath promised, saying, Yet once more I shake not the earth only, but also heaven. And this word, Yet once more, signifieth the removing of those things that are shaken, as of things that are made, that those things which cannot be shaken may remain. Wherefore we receiving a kingdom which cannot be moved, let us have grace, whereby we may serve God acceptably with reverence and godly fear: For our God is a consuming fire."*

AN ANALYSIS OF PART I

Revelation 11:18 closes the first great division of the Book. It brings one series of visions which reaches from the time of John to the end of the world systems as they presently exist in their illegitimate form. It will aid those who have carefully studied the preceding chapters to examine the results in a condensed analysis.

The first four chapters provide the application for the metaphorical pattern (symbolic language) used in this prophecy and reveal Christ's analysis of the seven successive church periods.

THE FIRST SEAL · The White Horse. Rome victorious. The glorious period of Pagan Roman history; 6:2. A.D. 96-180.

THE SECOND SEAL - The Red Horse. Civil War; 6:3,4. A.D. 185-284.

THE THIRD SEAL . The Black Horse. Taxation and Economic Depression; 6:5,6. A.D. 200-250.

THE FOURTH SEAL · The Pale Horse. Era of Famine and Disease. 6:7,8. A.D. 250-300.

THE FIFTH SEAL · Era of the Martyrs. The last effort of paganism to destroy the Christian name; 6:9-11. A.D. 303-313.

THE SIXTH SEAL· The Fall of Paganism and Rome Divided; 6:12-17. A.D. 313-395.

THE FOUR WINDS · A vision of destructive forces that destroyed the Roman Empire, but was held back until the 144,000 of the House of Israel were sealed. The four winds represent four northern invasions, also indicated by four Trumpets; 8:1-13. Fulfilled A.D. 400-476.

THE FALL OF THE OLD ROMAN EMPIRE

THE FIRST TRUMPET (under the Seventh Seal) - The Gothic Invasion fulfilled by the Invasion of Alaric; 8:7. A.D. 400-410.

THE SECOND TRUMPET - The Vandal Invasion. The Conquest of the Seas by Genseric; 8:8,9. A.D. 425-470.

THE THIRD TRUMPET - The Invasion of Attila, the Hun. The Scourge of the Rivers; 8:10,11. A.D. 451.

THE FOURTH TRUMPET - The Final Overthrow of Rome by Odoacer and the Heruli; 8:12. A.D. 476. These four Trumpet invasions are the four winds which were withheld.

THE FALL OF THE EASTERN OR NEW ROMAN EMPIRE

THE FIFTH TRUMPET - 1st WOE - Rise of Mohammedanism. The Saracen Empire; 9:1-12. A.O. 612-762.

THE SIXTH TRUMPET - 2nd WOE - Rise of the Turkish Empire. The Euphratean Angels Loosed; 9:13-21. A.D. 1062-1453.

REVIVAL OF BIBLICAL CHRISTIANITY

THE LITTLE BOOK and the Seven Thunders - Symbols of the Reformation of Luther; 10:1-11. A.D. 1517.

THE OLD PATHS SOUGHT - The Church Measured; 11:1,2. From A.D. 1517 to the present time.

THE TWO WITNESSES - The Two Houses manifested in True Church with the Word of God. In sackcloth for twelve hundred and sixty years pronounced slain in 1514. Resurrected. October 31, 1517.

THE PROGRESSIVE VICTORY OF THE "STONE KINGDOM"

- The Kingdoms of this World *are becoming* the Kingdoms of our Lord; 11:15-18. The process is now accelerating.

NATIONS ARE ANGRY

WRATH IS COME

TIME OF THE DEAD

DESTROY THEM FROM THE EARTH

PART II
THE OTHER SIDE OF THE SCROLL
BEGINNING AGAIN THE CHRISTIAN ERA

REVELATION CHAPTER 12
THE WOMAN AND THE DRAGON

I believe that the first series of visions ends with Chapter 11, verse 18. Those visions have shown us how judgments were inflicted on great powers which opposed and persecuted the Church, or in any way affected its destiny. The context of the prophecies deals with great secular powers known to the apostles, and then is followed by the revelation of wicked spiritual powers. The "wicked city" is dealt a severe blow by the exaltation of the witnesses, and this inaugurates the seventh trumpet and the final triumph of Christ's Kingdom.

Note on Chapter 11:19. I believe it is clear that this verse belongs to Chapter 12. B.W. Johnson commented: "The reader will observe that the language with which the first series opens in Revelation 4:1, is quite similar to the opening words of the verse that begins the second series. *'I saw a door opened in heaven'* is the opening sentence of the prophecy (4:1), language which implies that the secrets of heaven are to be revealed. In chapter 11:19, it is said that *'The temple of God was opened in heaven.'* Even the ark of the Testament in its most secret place is brought to view. There is to be a revelation of facts connected with the temple of God. We have already shown that the reference is not to the Jewish temple, which no longer existed, but to the spiritual temple, the church of Jesus Christ… The *thunders, earthquake, etc.,* foreshadow the commotions, revolutions, and judgments which will take place in the fulfillment of the symbols."

1 And there appeared a great wonder in heaven; a woman clothed with the sun, and the moon under her feet, and upon her head a crown of twelve stars:

When we look at the woman of Chapter 12, her apparel describes her as representing the twelve tribes of *Israel-natural Israel*. (Remember, we are beginning again the Christian Era.) In searching for the meaning of this symbolism our thoughts go back to the days of the origin of Israel, and Joseph's dream. *"And he dreamed yet another dream, and told it to his brethren, and said, Behold, I have dreamed a dream more; and, behold, the sun and the moon and the eleven stars made obeisance to me. And he told it to his father, and to his brethren. and his father rebuked him, and said unto him, What is this dream that thou kast dreamed? Shall I [the sun] and thy mother [the moon} and thy brethren [the 11 stars] indeed come to bow down ourselves to thee to the earth?"* (Genesis 37:9,10) Thus Jacob, who fathered the twelve tribes of Israel, gives us the interpretation. Therefore, the woman of this verse must symbolize natural Israel from whom the Messiah was born-the Branch of the lineage of David of the royal tribe of Judah. Therefore, Chapter 12 takes us back to the days of the advent of Jesus Christ.

> *2 And she being with child cried, travailing in birth, and pained to be delivered.*
> *3 And there appeared another wonder in heaven: and behold a great red dragon, having seven heads and ten horns, and seven crowns upon his head.*

The Roman imperial sign was the sign of the dragon. When the Book of Revelation talks about the dragon, it is talking about Imperial Pagan Rome; implying that it is under the power of Satan.

The *"seven heads"* speak of Rome's seven mountains. The *"seven crowns"* speak of Rome's seven historic forms of government. And the *"ten horns"* perfectly identify this dragon as the fourth beast of Daniel Chapter 7—the Roman beast.[100] The Romans worshiped the dragon; this is important to remember. It is interesting to note that the rise of Constantine is depicted on ancient Roman coins with the cross erected over the fallen dragon.

> *4 And his tail drew the third part of the stars of heaven, and did*
> *cast them to the earth: and the dragon*
> *stood before the woman which was ready to be delivered, for to*
> *devour her child as soon as it was born.*
> *5 And she brought forth a man child, who was to rule all nations*
> *with a rod of iron: and her child was caught up unto God, and*
> *to his throne.*

A Third Part Of The Stars Of Heaven: Verse 4 further identifies the dragon as Pagan Rome prior to the time of Christ. *"And his tail drew the third part of the stars of heaven, and did cast them to the earth…"* The stars in the firmament of John's vision symbolize the ruling powers of a third of the prophetic earth. It is a picture of Rome pagan conquering a third of the prophetic earth and displacing its rulers.

History records for us that just prior to the advent of our Lord, the Romans conquered Palestine and the area of the Near East (B.C. 63). This third of the remaining unconquered rulers was now displaced by Roman authority. This is the third of the prophetic earth dictated by the context of this vision.

The Roman dragon is now standing before the woman (Israel) waiting to devour the man child, the Messiah. We must remember that Satan

---

100   The identifying relevance of Rome's "seven mountains" and "seven historic forms of government" is clearly revealed in Chapter 17. Please be patient, we'll get there. Also, we will see the "crowns" shift from the seven heads of Rome *pagan* to the ten horns of Rome *papal* in Chapter 13:1

could also calculate the time of Messiah as prophesied in Daniel Chapter 9. He knew exactly when to control the land of the Messiah's birth. And we know the story of the birth of the Lord and his flight to Egypt, evading the sword of the Roman governor, Herod. It is so clear. This is no mystery; it is a revelation.

So it is evident how Satan attempted to use the Roman Empire to destroy the Christ. The Roman Empire was satanic. It was ruled by Satan himself. We also see here how his calculations were thwarted, and Jesus was called up unto God and His throne (Acts 1:9-11).[101] And He will remain enthroned, ruling in the midst of His enemies (Psalm 110:2b), until they are all conquered (1 Corinthians 15:24-28). Then, and only then, will He return to the earth (Acts 3:21). Try to stick that into dispensationalist/futurist theology.

> *6 And the woman fled into the wilderness [Europe], where she hath a place prepared of God, that they should feed her there a thousand two hundred and threescore days.*

And The Woman Fled Into The Wilderness: Notice something. Many historical writers interpret the woman of this chapter as the Church all the way through the context of the prophecy. I cannot believe this. At the beginning of this chapter it was established that the **woman** who brought forth the man child was the nation Israel. But, between the birth of our Lord and His ascension, Jesus told the Jews (Judah nation) that the Kingdom would be taken from them and given to a nation. That nation was the Church (Matthew 21:43), clearly manifested in the woman's seed, Israel in Europe. This New Testament Church had its beginnings in Jerusalem on the Day of Pentecost in the land of Israel. By the time we reach John's day in A.D. 96, the *kingdom is taken from the Jews* of the Judah nation and given

---

101   See also Psalm 2:7-9 and Isaiah 9:6,7.

to the House of Irael's Church, bringing forth the fruits. The woman, as we will go on to establish, from verse 6 onwards in this chapter, is Israel which was eventually scattered to the nations and become known as (Gentiles).

A Thousand 'Two Hundred And Threescore Days: This is a period of 1,260 years. In fulfillment of this prophecy, the true Church and truth were subdued by the rising Roman Catholic Church from A.D. 254 to A.D. 1514. The true Church went through a time of spiritual wilderness, clothed in symbolic sackcloth, subdued and subjugated by a false and counterfeit violent church.

> *7 And there was war in heaven: Michael and his angels fought against the dragon; and the dragon fought and his angels,*
> *8 And prevailed not; neither was there place found any more in heaven.*
> *9 And the great dragon was cast out, that old serpent, called the Devil, and Satan, which deceiveth the whole world: he was cast out into the earth, and his angels were cast out with him.*

What does the Bible mean by this? Let's look at it from three points of view. Not the futurist, preterist or even the historicist view, but from three points of view in the Word of God. Please read the following Scriptures very carefully:

> *Now is the judgment of this world: now shall the prince of this world be cast out* (John 12:31).

> *I beheld Satan, as lightning, fall from heaven* (Luke 10:18).

> *… that through death He* [Jesus] *might destroy him*

that had the power of death, that is, the devil (Hebrews 2:14).

Remember that we have seen in the fulfillment of the seven Seals, the fall of heathenism in the Roman Empire, specifically under Constantine in the fourth century. The dragon of imperial Rome and devil worship is cast down. It is not very well known that during the rule of the pagan emperors, from the days of Nero through the time of Diocletian, that millions of Christians suffered martyrdom. And so with the rise of Constantine, the dragon was cast down. But the greater revelation has been presented. As a result of the victory of Christ, the devil was cast out of heaven. He no longer has the authority to accuse the brethren (Romans 8:1). This understanding is vindicated in the next verse:

10 And I heard a loud voice saying in heaven, Now is come salvation, and strength, and the kingdom of our God, and the power of his Christ: for the accuser of our brethren is cast down, which accused them before our God day and night.

NOW IS COME: **Salvation**

Strength

and the "KINGDOM OF OUR GOD!"

The ramifications of this revelation are enormous. The Book of Revelation has just revealed that with Christ's victory came the Kingdom-even a strong kingdom! How can this be? Haven't the dispensationalists been telling us that the strong kingdom is yet to come? However, in John 10:35 Jesus states, *"The scriptures cannot be broken."* Either John the Revelator broke the scriptures or the dispensationalists did. You choose. As for me, I choose to believe the power of these Scriptures. I believe that we have obtained a strong Kingdom. I believe Jesus would have this to say to the dispensationalists, *"Ye do err, not knowing the scriptures, nor the power of God!"* (Matthew 22:29) Amen.[102]

> *11 And they overcame him by the blood of the Lamb, and by the word of their testimony; and they loved not their lives unto the death.*
>
> *12 Therefore rejoice, ye heavens, and ye that dwell in them. Woe to the inhabiters of the earth and of the sea! for the devil is come down unto you, having great wrath, because he knoweth that he hath but a short time.*

Regardless of the destruction caused by the devil, we who are in "heavenly places in Christ" rejoice at the continual growth of the Kingdom of God.

Stone..................Becomes...............MOUNTAIN

REFERENCE Daniel 2:34,35.

In Chapter 13 we will see that this *"great wrath"* was executed against the Church through the papacy for a little less than thirteen centuries.

> *13 And when the dragon saw that he was cast unto the earth, he persecuted the woman [Israel manifesting in the Christian Church] which brought forth the man child.*

---

102   The following verses should help you grasp the present reality of Christ's growing Kingdom. It does not instantaneously appear in total power. Remember Isaiah 9:7, "Of the INCREASE of His government and peace there shall be no end." Furthermore, Daniel revealed that "there was given Him dominion, and glory, and a kingdom, that all people, nations, and languages, SHOULD SERVE HIM [some initially won't]: His dominion is an everlasting dominion, which shall not pass away, and His Kingdom that shall not be destroyed (Dan. 7:14). Now, fundamental question: Has Christ been given this kingdom yet? YES HE HAS ! ! ! ! Wash that dispensationalism out of your minds with the "water of the word." Luke 22:29 states, "I appoint unto you a kingdom, as My Father has appointed unto Me."

14 And to the woman were given two wings of a great eagle, that she might fly into the wilderness, into her place, where she is nourished for a time, and times, and half a time from the face of the serpent.

When Satan saw that through the Pagan Roman Empire he had failed to destroy the Church, he began adding to his tactics. History shows us that he developed that counterfeit church through which he could not only kill the saints of God, but through which he could also create the greatest apostasy of lies and deception the world has ever seen. It still sits in Rome.

Two Wings Of A Great Eagle: These wings were the power and protection of God Himself. Christ promised Israel that He would build a church. The devil has never been able to stop divine construction. These wings also signify the haste with which this remnant Church was to seek her own safety from the man of sin. This metaphor is used to describe God's deliverance of ancient Israel. Through Moses He said to them: *"Ye have seen what I did unto the Egyptians, and how I bare you on eagles' wings, and brought you unto myself"* (Exodus 19:4).

In nature the eagle is the natural enemy of the snake (serpent). It has the ability to swoop down on the snake and destroy it at will. Remember, the witnesses had fire coming out of their mouths (Revelation 11:5). As verse 14 goes on to say, this Christian Church would be nourished in the wilderness for almost 13 centuries. This was the terrible time of the *"little horn"* about which Daniel forewarned (Daniel 7:25).

15 And the serpent cast out of his mouth water as a flood after the woman, that he might cause her to be carried away of the flood.

16 And the earth helped the woman, and the earth opened her mouth, and swallowed up the flood which the dragon cast out of his mouth.

The interpretation of these verses is as simple as this: The *"waters"* in the Book of Revelation speak of multitudes of peoples (Revelation 17:15). We remember when we studied the seven Trumpets, that in the fifth century A.D. the Goths, the Huns, and the Vandals—these barbarian hordes—came into the Western Roman Empire like a flood. And they destroyed Rome. We now read that these floods were swallowed up by the earth. When we further examine history, we find out that these barbarians soon settled into the lands which they had invaded and conquered. They were then swiftly converted to Christianity. And so the earth swallowed up the flood of extermination. Although the false church continued to rise, the true Church was preserved and sealed, borne on the wings of an eagle.

17 And the dragon was wroth with the woman, and went to make war with the remnant of her seed, [Israels Seed] *which keep the commandments of God, and have the testimony of Jesus Christ.*

Went To Make War: On St. Bartholomew's Day, 1572, 10,000 Huguenots (Protestants) were killed in a terrifying massacre in Paris. Catholic extremists falsely alarmed Catherine de Medici with reports that the Huguenots were plotting to remove her from the throne. This led to a plot which called for a treacherous and wholesale massacre. After this war, the French king went to Mass to thank God that so many heretics were destroyed. When Rome received the news, it had a grand procession, led by Pope Gregory XIII, to the church of St. Louis. Gregory then ordered the papal mint to make coins commemorating the event. The coins depicted an angel with a sword in one hand and a cross in the other, before whom a group of Huguenots, with horror on their faces, were fleeing. The words *Ugonottorum Stranges 1572* which signify "The Slaughter of the Huguenots, 1572" appear on the coins.

Enough said, more to come.

REVELATION CHAPTER 13
THE ANTICHRIST AND THE PAPACY
(THE UNIFYING DOCTRINE
OF THE REFORMATION}

1 And I stood upon the sand of the sea, and saw a beast rise up
out of the sea, having seven heads and ten horns, and upon his
horns ten crowns, and upon his heads the name of blasphemy.

It has been pointed out by many eminent historicist commentators that this *"beast"* was first called the Pagan Roman Empire. This is
an assertion of the fourth beast of Daniel 7. All empires are pagan and
idolatrous which are inspired by the devil himself. This was the case with
the Roman Empire.

In Daniel 7, there is an account of a remarkable prophetic dream
which Daniel had in the first year of the reign of Belshazzar. This dream
must be understood before we can proceed any further in the Book
of Revelation. The futurists have distorted this prophecy in the same
manner as the 70 weeks of Daniel 9. This was done by ripping contextual
historical sequence apart and throwing pieces of the prophecy into the
future-Ribera's future. I will prove that their interpretation is a Jesuit lie.

Let's examine this startling vision. It is relevant to the opening verses
of Chapter 3. I shall quote in a partly abridged version from Daniel 7:1-8.
I am extracting this portion from my book, *Seventy Weeks: The Historical
Alternative.*

1 In the first year of Belshazzar, king of Babylon, Daniel had a
dream … he wrote the dream, and told the sum of the matters.
2 Daniel spake and said, I saw … four winds of heaven strove

upon the great sea.

3 And FOUR GREAT BEASTS [not five!] came up from the sea, different one from another.

4 The first was like a LION, AND HAD EAGLE'S WINGS

5 And behold another beast, a second, LIKE TO A BEAR, and it raised itself on one side, and it had THREE RIBS in the mouth of it, between the teeth of it.

6 After this I beheld, and lo another, LIKE A LEOPAR.D, which had upon the back of it FOUR WINGS OF A FOWL; the beast had also FOUR HEADS; and dominion was given to it.

7 After this I saw in the night visions, and beheld a FOURTH BEAST, dreadful and terrible, and strong exceedingly … and it had TEN HORNS.

8 I considered the horns [of the fourth beast],

and, behold, there came up among them another LITTLE HORN, before whom there were THREE of the first horns plucked up…

An outline of the true historical interpretation will help to orient you as you read part of the vision's fulfillment.

DANIEL 7:3-8

v.4 BABYLON

v.5 MEDO-PERSIA

The three ribs: Babylon

Egypt

Lydia

v.6 GREECE

The four heads: Cassander-ruled Greece

                           Lysimachus-ruled Asia Minor

                           Seleucus-ruled Syria and Babylon

                           Ptolemy-ruled Egypt

v.7 ROME (Pagan)

v.8 ROME SUB-DIVIDED (west)

The ten horns: Vandals   Heruli

                           Suevi   Franks

                           Ostrogoths   Huns

                           Visigoths   Allemani

                           Lombards   Burgundians

v.8 LITTLE HORN (Papacy)

The three

plucked up: Lombards

                    Vandals

                    Ostrogoths

A Brief Summary of the Four Beasts

Babylon

The first of these four great beasts was *"like a lion, and had eagle's wings."* In this vision in Daniel 7 the empire which had been represented by the most costly and precious of metals in Daniel 2 was now represented by the king of beasts with the wings of the king of birds. The vision was fulfilled in the ancient Babylonian Empire and its magnificent capital city, Babylon, whose splendor has become legendary.

This empire of golden grandeur and lion's strength is referred to in Isaiah 13:19 as *"the glory of kingdoms, the beauty of the Chaldees' excellency."* Isaiah 14:4 called it *"the golden city."* (*"Thou art this head of gold,"*

Daniel 2:38.) And Jeremiah described it as *"the praise of the whole earth"* (Jeremiah 51:41).

Medo-Persia

The Persian Empire was represented in Daniel 2 by the great image's breast and arms of silver. In Chapter 7 the imagery of a bear, rising up on one side (until this point it had been at rest) and with three ribs in its mouth is used to represent the same empire.

In 550 B.C. the Persian, Cyrus, captured Ecbatane, capital of the kingdom of Media, and deposed Astyages their king. He amalgamated Media with the Persian kingdom, hence the rise of the Medo-Persian empire.

Croesus, king of Lydia, whose name is still proverbially linked with great riches, attacked the Persians. But he was smashed by Cyrus, who in turn took Sardis, his capital.

Cyrus then attacked Nabonidus and the main Babylonian army. Having successfully routed them, he marched on the city of Babylon itself and captured it. His son Cambysees conquered Egypt. Three ribs in the mouth of the bear represent Lydia, Babylon, and Egypt. The conquest of Egypt by the Persians was further established by Darius I (521-486 B.C.), then completed by Xerxes (486-467 B.C.).

Greece

In Daniel 7 the ancient Greek Empire is likened to a leopard with four heads and four wings. This is perfect symbolism for the rise and later four-fold subdivision of the great Grecian Empire with its military genius, Alexander the Great.

The leopard is a very swift animal, and this was an important fact of Alexander the Great's tactics in the military prowess and conquests which built his empire.

The wings on the leopard also represent his swiftness and agility of military maneuver; and the four heads represent the four subdivisions of his empire after his death (Cassander, Lysimachus, Selucus and Ptolemy). Darius III was conquered by Alexander at the three battles of Grancius, Issus, and Guagamela. He had a dream of forging Europe and Asia together into a single political, cultural, and possibly, linguistic unit. He died before this dream could be fulfilled.

Rome

Daniel 7 prophesied that the fourth successive empire (Roman) would be *"dreadful and terrible, and strong exceedingly; and it had great iron teeth; it devoured and brake in pieces, and stamped on the residue with the feet of it: and it was diverse from all the beasts that were before it; and it had ten horns."*

This is the predicted rise of the ancient Roman Empire which succeeded the Greek and existed from B.C. into A.D. During its reign of conquest, our Lord and Savior Jesus Christ lived and died for the sins of the world. And during the era of the Roman Empire, the New Testament canon was completed.

When one reads Edward Gibbon's *Decline and Fall of the Roman Empire,* it becomes clear that as the Romans deteriorated morally, their empire started to come apart at the seams until the fifth century A.D. It was only a matter of time until the whole structure, especially the western half of the empire, simply fell to pieces in the face of the militaristic incursions of what the Romans called "barbarian hordes." In 410 A.D., the reigning emperor, Honorius, recalled all his legions from Britannia back to Europe to help defend their European frontiers.

This only helped stave off final disaster until 476 AD. In that tumultuous year, Romulus Augustus, the last western Roman emperor, was deposed by Odoacer, the leader of the Heruli (the fourth Trumpet, Revelation 8:12). In fulfillment of Daniel 2 and 7, the western empire began its subdivision into 10 different kingdoms (Vandals, Suevi, Visigoths,

Ostrogoths, Heruli, Franks, Allemani, Huns, Lombards, and Burgundians). Daniel had predicted that these ten *"toes"* or *"horns"* would *"not cleave one to another."* Historically, this was precisely fulfilled. Instead, they cleaved to papal ideology.[103]

We have now seen prophecy and history bring us to the point of the "little horn" of Daniel 7:8,24.

Dear reader, take a breath and get your bearings. This is the same historical juncture that Revelation 13:1-3 is addressing. A great transition has taken place. In Daniel 7 we have a "little horn" arising victorious from a great struggle with three other horns. However, it is portrayed in the Book of Revelation as the second beast (papal) arising from the mortal head wound of the first beast (pagan). Nevertheless, what is being implied is that these transitions should not have occurred. Both Daniel and John captured the amazing survivability of this determined beast. History vindicated the predictions. Let's go on and see the fulfillment of Daniel's prophecy and then we'll return to the Revelation. This has been a necessary and vital interlude.

Daniel 7:8,24 states:

8 I considered the horns, and, behold, there came up among them another little horn, before whom there were three of the first horns plucked up ...

24 And the ten horns out of this kingdom are ten kings that shall arise: and another shall rise after them; and he shall be diverse from the first, and he shall subdue three kings.

---

103   Britannia is also included by most scholars, but from a historical perspective we do well to remember that under the decree of Honorius, Britain was totally evacuated. This took place 66 years, at least a generation, before Romulus Augustulus was deposed. Britain was also invaded by the Anglo-Saxons before 476 A.D.

All that is needed is a look back in history to see if this prophecy was fulfilled. If it was not fulfilled, then it is, as the futurists say, "yet to come." However, if we can identify three of the horns (nations or kings) which struggled against, and were plucked up by, the infamous little horn, then dispensationalism takes another deserved rebuke. Titus 2:15!

Guess what, a college western civilization freshman could figure this one out. It's a shame that the futurists can't. This is not a future occurrence. Neither is it a complicated matter of research. This event perfectly unfolded in unbroken historical chronology.

In the year 533 A.D. the horn of the Vandals in Africa, Corsica, and Sardinia, and shortly after, that of the Ostrogoths in Italy were rooted up by Justinian's forces under Belisarius. The Lombard horn, the third horn, was eradicated by Pepin and Charlemagne.

By the year 752 A.D. the three horns which posed a threat to the rise of the "little horn" (the usurping bishop of Rome) were completely plucked up by the roots. Exactly as predicted, this great prophecy was fulfilled. Why do we let the futurists throw this into the future and tell us the little horn is yet to come? This is what Ribera taught. It's exactly what Rome wants the Protestants to believe. The Reformation fathers knew better.

Let me finish my thoughts on the subject. Don't worry, I haven't forgotten the Book of Revelation. Though I do need to write a commentary on Daniel.

The diversity of this little horn was seen by Daniel. It would claim not only temporal, but spiritual domination as well. We also know that it was unmistakenly to be a Roman power. The fourth beast of Daniel seven was Rome. It was to emerge preeminent among ten new kingdoms in its revived papal form. The exact identity was enhanced with the prediction that it would defeat three kingdoms that resisted its rise. It would also "speak great words against the Most High." Libraries are filled with texts documenting these "great words" of contempt for true Bible Christianity. I believe Guinness correctly identified this apostasy:

> Is not the papacy sufficiently diverse from all the rest of the kingdoms of western Europe to identify it as the little horn? What other ruling monarch of Christendom ever pretended to apostolic authority, or ruled men in the name of God? Does the pope dress in royal robes? Nay, but in priestly garments. Does he wear a crown? Nay, but a triple Tiara, to show that he reigns in heaven, earth, and hell! Does he wield a scepter? Nay, but a crosier or crook, to show that he is the good shepherd of the church. Do his subjects kiss his hand? Nay, but his toe! Verily this power is "diverse" from the rest, both in great things and in little. It is small in size, gigantic in its pretensions.[104]

In concluding this interlude, Daniel said that this terrible little horn would make *"war with the saints,"* and prevail for a defined period of time against them. Is Daniel saying that the saints of God will have to face Antichrist? Yes he is, and yes they did. For 13 centuries God's saints were *"worn out"* by the one *"whose look was more stout than his fellows."*

This is going to be a blunt and bloody chapter in the Book of Revelation. I hope you are willing to be reminded of some history that the ecumenical movement would like you to forget. Be assured, God has not forgotten.

Now before we move on to verse 2, let me point out another important revelation concerning verse 1. The previous chapter (Revelation 12:3) opened with a reference to the dragon's pagan empire described as having

---

104 H. Grattan Guinness, *Romanism and the Reformation*, page 28.

"seven heads, and seven crowns upon its HEADS" depicting rulership from the seven-hilled city of Rome itself, or depicting a seven-fold phase of government (KINGS, CONSULS, DICTATORS, DECEMVIRS, MILITARY TRIBUNES, CAESARS AND DESPOTIC EMPERORS) which historically unraveled in Pagan Rome prior to the advent of the papacy (the eighth form of government). Here, however, in Revelation 13:1, the crowns have moved from the seven HEADS on to the ten horns, viz. *"...and upon his HORNS ten crowns"* depicting individual kingdoms in Europe each with its own sovereign rule. Upon the *"seven heads,"* however, John saw written *"the name of blasphemy"* of spiritual wickedness (as we will see in verses 5 and 6), depicting the rise of the papacy speaking great words against the Most High, as foretold in Daniel 7:25. It is all so simple when applied to its true historical context.

> *2 And the beast which I saw was like unto a leopard, and his feet were as the feet of a bear, and his mouth as the mouth of a lion: and the dragon gave him his power, and his seat, and great authority.*

Notice that this beast was like a leopard, with the feet of a bear and a mouth of a lion. So this fourth beast (Rome) was to take *"in parts,"* the territory of the Grecian Empire, the Medo-Persian Empire and the Babylonian Empire. This is exactly what Rome did. Check your historical atlas. Also in this verse, we see the rise of the papacy. Its power came from the dragon himself. This *"great authority"* is the masterpiece of Satan. It still causes cowardly Protestant ministers to tremble!

> *3 And I saw one of his heads as it were wounded to death; and his deadly wound was healed, and all the world wondered after the beast.*

It is important to point out that the word *"world"* here does not mean the whole globe. It is the Pagan Roman world. The Greek word used is *Ghey;* it means a *region*. We often get confused in the Book of Revelation by not knowing the meaning of these words.

So what this is speaking of is a *dramatic change of government* in the Roman earth. Royal authority was going to be shared by the 10 horns in the Western Empire. Again, let me remind you not to confuse the Western Roman Empire with the Eastern Roman Empire. It was the West falling under judgment and transition at this time. In the first and second Woes (Revelation 9) we saw the judgment fall on the other two-thirds of the empire. Now the Book of Revelation is focusing on the struggle in the west between the remnant true Church and the persecuting papal beast.

And I Saw One Of Its Heads As It Were Wounded: This wounded head was the seventh form of government-the Emperors. Specifically, it was the last Emperor, Romulus Augustus, who received the mortal head wound of the Book of Revelation (the fourth Trumpet, Revelation 8:12). Roman government should have perished from the earth. However, it didn't. The wound was healed with the transition and rise of papal authority. And the Roman world wondered at the survivability of this beast. It had now taken on its second form in the Book of Revelation-the papal form.

> *4 And they worshipped the dragon which gave power unto the beast: and they worshipped the beast, saying, Who is like unto the beast? who is able to make war with him?*

The prophetic earth bowed to the authority of this new papal power. The popes rose to such heights of authority, who could "make war with him"?

5 And there was given unto him a mouth speaking great things and blasphemies; and power was given unto him to continue forty and two months.

This is as good a time as any to proceed on with another lengthy but necessary interlude. (This is my gift to the scholars who desire exhaustive references. The reader may proceed to the next verse commentary without losing the interpretation of the chapter.) During this interlude we investigate the "Identification of Antichrist." That's what this entire chapter is about. It was so clear to the Reformation fathers. However, I intend to extract my witnesses from the Romish authorities themselves. It's amazing that so many of them understood the identity of this mysterious blasphemous power, and yet the present-day Protestants are still trying to figure this out. God help us. Let's call for a changing of the guard. Likewise, let's attempt to avoid the pollution of our fathers.

I will extract this testimony from Baron Porcelli's book, *The Antichrist,* revised 1927. I will present a threefold cord of "Catholic" witnesses, in 24 testimonies, which will not easily be broken, combined in:

A - Identifying the city of Rome as the Babylon of the Apocalypse;

B - The Bishop of Rome as the successor of Caesar seated at Rome;

C - The Papacy and Church of Rome as the Antichrist of Scripture.

A - Testimony of Romish Writers on the Apocalypse

(1.) The Jesuit, Sylvester J. Hunter, in his "Outline of Dogmatic Theology" (Vol. I., p. 410) said: "There is no room for doubt that by the Babylon of the Apocalypse is meant the city of Rome. And down to the time of the Reformation it was the unanimous judgment of all writers

... that the Babylon of St. Peter's Epistle is the same Rome."

(2.) Cardinal Newman, before he joined the Church of Rome, in 1840 described the city of Rome as "a doomed city," clearly pointed to "amid the obscurities of the fearful Apocalypse."

(3.) Bishop Bossuet, of Meaux (1690), in his work on the Apocalypse, taught that Babylon is a symbol of Rome Pagan (Pref. sur l'Apocalypse).

(4.) Bishop Walmsley (1771) did the same.

(5.) Cardinal Baronius ("Annals," sec. xvi., p. 344) said: "By Babylon is to be understood Rome." "Rome is signified by Babylon; it is confessed of all."

(6.) Cardinal Bellarmine ("De Rom. Pont.," c. iii. 2, Preterea, Tome I., p. 232, Colon 1615): "John, in the Apocalypse, calls Rome Babylon."

(7.) Bishop Bossuet also admitted that "all the Fathers" taught that the Babylon of the Apocalypse is Rome ("Pref. sur l'Apocalypse").

(8) Similar avowals might be cited from other Romish theologians, e.g. Salmeron, Alcazar, Maldontaus.

B · Romish Authorities on History

(1.) Due de Broglie ("Histoire de L'Eglise," VI., 424-456): "The Bishop of Rome mounted the throne whence the Emperors fell, and took, little by little, the position rendered vacant by the desertion of the successor of Augustus."

(2.) The learned editor of the "Acta Sanctae Sedis" (V., 324) said of Pope Pius IX: "The Captain who gloriously fills the place of the ancient Caesars."

(3.) Pope Pius IX, in his "Discorsi" (I., p. 253), said: "The Caesar who now addresses you, and to whom alone are obedience and fidelity due."

(4.) Cardinal Manning, in his "Temporal Power" (Preface, pp. 42- 46), said: "From the abandonment of Rome (by Caesar) was the liberation of the Pontiffs." [He references 2 Thess. 2:7.] "He was elevated to be, in his Divine Master's Name King of Kings and Lord of Lords." "The abandonment of Rome … left them free to become independent sovereigns, and to take up the sovereignty the Emperor had just laid down" (p. 50).

(5.) Dr. Dollinger ("The Pope and the Council," p. 165): "The Popes called their acts by the same name as the Caesarean laws Rescripts and Decrees." "The notions about the plenary powers of the Caesars prevalent in the latter days of the Roman Empire had their influence here."

(6.) Just as Caesar had the power of making or unmaking sovereigns, assigning kingdoms, or taking them away, so the bishops of Rome claimed the right to degrade or depose sovereigns, and to deprive them of kingdoms (see Baronius, "Annals"; Foulis, "Roman Treasons", p. 115; Waddington, ch. xvi., p. 283; Daubuz, p. 585).

(7.) Pius VII, when he fulminated an "Excommunication against Napoleon," June 10th, 1809, claimed this very authority, saying, "Let them learn that they are subject to our Throne, and to our commands" (Abbe' de Pradt, "Quatre Concordats").

(8.) Of course, these popes claimed to possess this deposing power, in virtue of being successors of Peter and vicars of Christ not as successors of Caesar; but the claim was false, for no such power was bestowed on Peter, whereas this power was bestowed by the Roman Republic upon Caesar, as its mouthpiece and executive officer; and it was solely as successors of Caesar that the popes became imbued with the idea of temporal power. The Church of Rome, in its Breviary (May 25th) has a "Saint's Day" in honor of Pope Gregory VII, because he Deprived the Emperor Henry IV of his kingdom, and released his subjects from their oaths of allegiance to him." Innocent III, Honorius III, Gregory IX, Innocent IV, Paul III, Pius V, Gregory XIII, Urban VIII, all used this Caesarean power, enforcing it by the terrors of religious interdict, falsely claimed from Christ.

C - Romish Expositors of Prophecy

(1.) Cardinal Newman, in his *Treatise on Antichrist,* said, in 1840: There is an association which professes to take His place without warrant. It comes forward instead of Christ, and for Him; it speaks for Him, it develops His words, it suspends His appointments. It grants dispensations in matters of positive duty; it professes to minister grace; it absolves from sin, and all this on its own authority. Is it not, forthwith, according to the very force of the word, Antichrist? He who speaks for Christ must either be His true ambassador, or Antichrist. *There is no median between a Vice-Christ and Antichrist.*"

(2.) Cardinal Manning, in his "Caesarism and Ultramontanism" (1874, p. 36), said: *"It is Christ or Antichrist."*

(3.) The organ of the "Guild of Our Lady of Ransom," edited by Father Philip Fletcher, in the February, 1914, (p. 229), said: "The vicar of Christ or Antichrist ... If the Pope is not the vicar of Christ, he must be Antichrist; there is no middle view."

(4.) The Hon. G.A. Spencer, *alias* "Father Ignatius," in reply to Dr. Cumming, said: "If the Church of Rome be not the Church of Christ, it is the masterpiece of the Devil; it can be nothing between." (5.) Hortensius said: "The Pope and Christ make but one consistory, so that, sin excepted, to which the Pope is subject, the Pope, in a manner, can do all that God can do" (Extr. de Translat. Proccl. c. Quant Ab.; see Bishop Lowell's "Works," VI., 92, Oxford, 1787).

(6.) Pope Leo XIII, in his Apostolic Letter of June 20th, 1894, said of himself: *"We hold the place of Almighty God on earth."* His successor, Pius X, said: *"The Pope ... is Jesus Christ himself* hidden under the veil of flesh, *all must be subject to him."*

(7.) Cardinal Manning ("The Present Crisis of the Holy See," London, 1861, p. 73) said: "The Catholic Church … cannot cease to preach the doctrine of the sovereignty, both spiritual and temporal, of the Holy See"(where mark the word "See," and compare it with Daniel 7:8}. In his *"Caesarism and Ultramontanism"* (1874, pp. 35, 36), he said: "This is the doctrine of the Bull *Unam Sanctam,* and of the Syllabus, and of the Vatican Council. Any power which is independent, and can *alone fix the limits of its own jurisdiction, and can thereby fix the limits of all other jurisdictions, is (ipso facto) supreme.* But the Church of Jesus Christ (i.e., the Papal Church) … is all this, or nothing, or worse than nothing, *an impostor and a usurpation-that* is, *it is Christ or Antichrist."*

(8.) On the 30th of April, 1922, in the Vatican Throne Room, a throng of Cardinals, Bishops, Priests and Nuns, boys and girls, who all fell on their knees, were addressed from the Throne by Pope Pius XI, who, in a haughty tone, said: "You know that I am the Holy Father, the representative of God on the earth, the vicar of Christ, *which means that I am God on the earth"* ("The Bulwark," October, 1922, p. 104).

I believe that enough has been presented from some very preeminent Romish scholars. The blasphemies were plain to see, and well documented.

To Continue Forty And Two Months: Verse 5 went on to affirm the prophecy that this power was destined to remain all-powerful in temporal sovereignty for forty-two prophetical months (as already discussed in Revelation 11:2), or 42 X 30 = 1,260 years, using the day-for-a-year principal. I believe it will be reinforcing to once again examine the primary historic period of the papal beast's dominion and rampage.

In 533 A.D. the decree issued by the eastern Emperor, Justinian, elevated the bishop of Rome as "head of all the holy Churches, and of all the holy priests of God." Up to this time the bishops of all the various dioceses were looked upon as being on an equal footing in all parts of Christendom. However, the emperor decided that the Roman bishop should have preeminence. This decree by the Emperor Justinian was an important event for the Bishop of Rome because it paved the way for the first of the popes to rise, namely Boniface III, who is named as the first pope by Dr. Grattan Guinness in his well known book, *The Approaching End of the Age.*

When the 1,260 year period is applied to 533 A.D., we come to the year 1793, the time of the French Revolution, which marked the beginning of the end of papal temporal power, especially in France.

In the earlier centuries France had slaughtered or exiled all her Protestants, and was known as the Vatican's "eldest daughter." But now there was a complete change in the period of the French Revolution. France did just the reverse. Within 5 years 2 million people were slain. According to historians; 24,000 priests were murdered and 40,000 churches were turned into stables. Not only that, but the impact of the Revolution spread to all other Roman Catholic nations in Europe by means of the press and revolutionary agents. France never fully recovered from the effects of that terrible revolution and the power of the Roman Catholic Church was shattered in that country.

> *6 And he opened his mouth in blasphemy against God, to blaspheme his name, and his tabernacle, and them that dwelt in heaven.*
> *7 And it was given unto him to make war with the saints, and to overcome them: and power was given him over all kindreds, and tongues, and nations.*

History reveals to us that literally millions (some historians claim 50,000,000) lost their lives, either as martyrs, or those who fought in opposition to the Papal regime and its claims (see also Daniel 7:25).

To Make War With the Saints: In Fox's Book of Martyrs, and Dr. Grattan Guinness' *The Approaching End of the Age,* there are presented outlines and summaries of persecutions suffered by the true Church at the hands of this beast. Here are just a few of the conflicts:

1237-1342   Tens of thousands of Vaudois massacred in Northern Italy, by order of the Pope.

1300-1413   Terrible persecution of the Lollards in England, by order of the Pope.

1421   Thousands of Protestant Hussites in Bohemia killed, by order of the Pope.

1481-1808   The Spanish Inquisition "burnt alive" 31,912 Protestants, and tortured 300,000.

1488   In Piedmont 3,000 Vaudois burnt and suffocated to death in one cave.

1546   Emperor Charles V caused 50,000 Fleming Protestants to be hanged, burned, or buried alive.

1555   In England over 300 burned alive, under Catholic Queen "Bloody Mary."

1567   The Duke of Alva in the Netherlands executed 36,000 Protestants.

1572   Massacre of St. Bartholemew's Day in France-60,000 butchered in one day.

1631   Over 20,000 Protestants massacred in Magdeburg, Germany.

1641   In Ireland the Roman Catholics proclaimed a "war of religions" in which 40,000 Protestants were martyred without mercy.

1685   The French Dragoons butchered 400,000 Huguenot Protestants, while 500,000 escaped to Britain.

1686   Over 11,000 Protestant Vaudois put to death in Northern Italy.

No wonder the prophet Daniel contemplated in amazement, and inquired, *"How long shall it be to the end of these wonders? And I heard the man clothed in linen, which was upon the waters of the river, when he held up his right hand and his left hand unto heaven, and sware by him that liveth forever that it shall be for a time, times, and a half; and when he* [the beast, man of sin, wicked one, little horn, antichrist] *shall have accomplished to scatter the power of the holy people"* (Daniel 12:6,7).

> *8 And all that dwell upon the earth shall worship him, whose names are not written in the book of life of the Lamb slain from the foundation of the world.*
>
> *9 If any man have an ear, let him hear. He that leadeth into captivity shall be in captivity: he that killeth with the sword must be killed with the sword. Here is the patience and the faith of the saints.*

The popes of Rome led many into captivity, and they themselves were led into captivity as a result of the effects of the French Revolution. In 1798, Napoleon Bonaparte effected the conquest of Italy, and the Pope, a prisoner, was a supplicant at his feet. In 1804 he ordered the Pope, who was now his puppet, to come to France and crown him emperor of the French. In 1805, he assumed the title King of Italy. During his reign he ruled the papacy with an iron fist, broke up the old European system, emancipated the nations from the terror of Rome, and by the time Napoleon fell, the temporal authority of Rome had received a fatal wound. To this day the pope remains as *"The Prisoner of the Vatican."* There he will remain until his utter destruction from the face of the earth. The Scriptures assure us that this will happen (see 2 Thessalonians 2:8; Revelation 19:20). And the apostles and prophets cry, Amen! (Revelation 18:20)

> *11 And I beheld another beast coming up out of the earth: and he had two horns like a lamb, and he spake as a dragon.*
>
> *12 And he exerciseth all the power of the first beast before him* [literally 'in his presence'], *and causeth the earth and them which dwell therein to worship the first beast,* [paganism] *whose deadly wound was healed.*
>
> *13 And he doeth great wonders, so that he maketh fire come down from heaven on the earth in the sight of men,*
>
> *14 And deceived them that dwell on the earth by the means of those miracles which he had power to do in the sight of the beast; saying to them that dwell on the earth, that they should make an image to the beast, which had the wound by the sword and did live.*
>
> *15 And he had power to give life unto the image of the beast, that the image of the beast should both speak, and cause that as many as would not worship the image of the beast should be killed.*

This second wild beast was not the principle one on the theater of action, but, in a manner, subordinate. This lamb-like dragon raises the stakes of this dangerous deception.

I Beheld Another Beast Coming Up Out Of We Earth: John saw this second monster coming up out of the earth, a beast that had two horns like a lamb, and a voice like the voice of a dragon. There is a close connection existing between the ten-horned and the two-horned beast. The latter (1.) exercises the power of the first beast before him, (2.) causes the earth to worship the first beast, (3.) says to the earth that it should make an image of the first beast (verse 4), (4.) gives life unto the image of the first beast, and (5.) causes those who will not worship the image to be slain (verse 15). These statements show that there exists a close connection between the two, and that the last is the supporter and restorer of the first. I have found the first to be a symbolical representation of the temporal power of Rome. Most Protestant commentators see in the second beast the spiritual power of Rome the power which gave life to, and built up, the temporal dominion of the papacy. The papal claims are two-fold, both of spiritual and temporal dominion. St. Peter with the sword and the keys are always represented as the symbol of papal power; the sword of temporal sway and the keys of the Kingdom. The Pope not only claims to be the vicar of Christ, but the rightful ruler of the kings of the earth; and in this capacity, in the days of his greatness, had made and deposed kings, and granted kingdoms.

Two *Horns Like A Lamb … Spake Like A Dragon:* There is a similitude like the Lamb of God; a counterfeit representation; but a voice like the old dragon of Pagan Rome. Both features show themselves. It professes to be a Christian power. Sometimes its servants do a really lamb-like work, but then again we hear the dragon's voice. It can hardly be necessary to state that symbolism could choose no language more appropriate to represent the harsh, arrogant utterances of Rome when she puts forth her power, or asserts her authority. How appropriately this language describes the bulls of Popes, or the fulminations of anathemas and excommunications against their enemies.

He Makes The Earth… To Worship The First Beast: The spiritual power of Rome is exercised before, or in the presence of, the temporal power. They have dwelt together, and it is the spiritual power that has made those that dwell upon the earth regard and pay homage to the temporal. If an earthly ruler refused to heed the mandates of the Pope, his subjects were absolved from allegiance and bidden to depose him. If they refused, the whole kingdom was laid under interdict, the churches were closed, religious rites were suspended, the dead were not buried in the consecrated grounds, and a superstitious population would soon demand deliverance by submission. It was by the terrors of the spiritual power that the earth was brought into subjection to the imperial temporal sway of the Popes. The second beast has made men worship the first.

And He Doeth Great Wonders: The second beast did great wonders, pretended to perform miracles, and thus *"deceived them that dwell upon the earth."* Rome has claimed the possession of miraculous power in all ages, and no fact in history is better established than that she has continually resorted to lying miracles.

And Deceiveth … By Reason Of Those Miracles: The object of these false miracles was to rivet the chains of the spiritual dominion, so as to build up the temporal sway of the papacy. The dragon-lamb commanded men to make an image of the beast, and to offer it homage.[105]

THE MARK OF THE BEAST

16 And he causeth all, both small and great, rich and poor, free and bond, to receive a mark in their right hand, or in their foreheads:

---

105   The above discourse on the "lamb-like dragon" was the summation of B.W. Johnson's thoughts on the matter. Other historicists expound further on its interpretation. Pointing to the final destruction of the ten-horned beast in Rev. 19:20, "And the beast was taken, and with the false prophet that wrought miracles before him… These both were cast alive into the lake of fire… ", they reveal that another name for the lamb-like, two-horned beast is the "false prophet!" It is not speaking of atheism, it is speaking of a false religious prophetic ministry (see Matt. 7:15; 24:24). So they go on to divide this two horned beast into representing the Roman "priests" and "cardinals," which caused the Roman earth to worship the paganism of the first beast. It is interesting to note that since the time of Pope Gregory, A.D. 590, all bishops wore a pallium of specially blessed lamb's wool. The abbots also wore two pointed miters, and were known as the "Goruti" or the "horned ones."

17 And that no man might bay or sell, save he that had the mark, or the name of the beast, or the number of his name.

18 Here is wisdom, Let him that hath understanding count the number of the beast: for it is the number of a man; and his number is six hundred threescore and six.

Here are the clues for identification:

(1.) The "mark" is the "name of the beast."

(2.) The "name of the beast" is the "name of a man."

(3.) The numerical value of the "name of the beast" or the "name of the man" is 666.

What name did history give to the papal empire? The Eastern Roman Empire used Greek as their language, but for the western Empire of Rome it was *Latin.* It was a Latin world with a Latin liturgy for the Catholic Church. Their Bible was presented in Latin. Everything was Latinized in the Church, so that every inhabitant of Western Europe as a member of the Catholic Church used Latin and thus willingly received the characteristic "mark of the beast" of the Latin world.

Albert Barnes, in his notes on the Book of Revelation, presented the following analysis:

"This appellation, originally applied to the language only, was adopted by the Western kingdoms, and came to be that by which they were best designated. It was the Latin world, the Latin kingdom, the Latin church, the Latin patriarch, the Latin clergy, the Latin councils. To use Dr. More's words 'They *Latinize* everything: mass, prayers, hymns, litanies, canons, decretals, bulls, are conceived in Latin. The Papal councils speak in Latin. In short, all things are Latin.' With what propriety, then, might John, under the influence of inspiration, speak, in this enigmatical manner, of the new power that was symbolized by the beast is *Latin.*"[106]

It is interesting to note that Pope Vitallian issued a decree commanding the exclusive use of Latin in all services of the Catholic Church in the year A.D. 666.[107]

In verse 16, the words *"to receive a mark,"* are liberally translated in the Greek, *"to give themselves."*

The word "Latin" in the Latin language is *"Latinus"* (the Latin [Man]), which is a proper noun and the name of the father of the Latin race, hence the name of the papal empire, i.e., the Latin Empire, is also the name of a man.

As the New Testament, including the Book of Revelation, was written in Greek, it will be the Greek form of the word "Latin" which will supply the number 666. And the amazing fact is that this clue was suggested long before its fulfillment! In the second century, the famous Irenaeus, a disciple of the apostle John who wrote this Revelation, declared, "Then also *Lateinos* has the number six hundred and sixty-six; and it is a very probable [solution], this being the name of the last kingdom of the four seen by Daniel]. For the Latins *are* they who at present bear rule."[108]

---

106   Albert Barnes, *Notes on the New Testament,* "Revelation," page 337.

107   Robert Fleming, *Rise and Fall of the Papacy,* page 10.

108   Rev. Alexander Roberts, D.D., and Rev. W.H. Rambaut, A.B., *The Writings of Irenaeus,* page 137.

LATEINOS = $30+1+300+5+10+50+70+200 = 666$[109]

I am convinced that the multitude of Protestant scholars, who have identified the Latin man as Antichrist, are correct. This prophetic riddle was meant to be solved by the Body of Christ, and it has been. Please bear with me as I present another point of interest.

The Pope wears a crown at his coronation called the Triple Crowns or the "Triple Tiaras" [three crowns]. It bears the inscription, *"Vicarius Filii Dei."* In English this basically means, "Vicarious Son of God." A person who is vicarious is one who stands in the place of another (his substitute), and that is why the Pope claims to be the "vicar of Christ." By asserting this claim (vicar of Christ) he actually claims to be Antichrist, because the word "anti" means basically "in the place of" (substitute for). How many hundreds of times has the Pope of Rome claimed to stand in Christ's place here on earth? You tell me. Any Greek scholar will admit that the basic meaning of Antichrist is "one who stands in the place of Christ." You who dwell on the Tiber, I know who you are, and I will not look for another.

Now before we go on to verse 17, the buying and selling, let's look again at the mark of the beast. Surely by now you have come to understand the symbolic nature of the Book of Revelation. Why should we look for a literal mark? WITH THE MIND A MAN CONCEIVES HIS DOCTRINE, AND WITH THE RIGHT HAND HE BRINGS IT INTO FELLOWSHIP. I believe it is just that simple. I believe that this is exactly what the apostle John was trying to tell us here. When we briefly examine the "marking"

---

109   "As a matter of historical interest, it may be observed that the solution of the difficulty has been sought in numerous other words, and the friends of the papacy and the enemies of the Bible have endeavoured to show that such terms are so numerous that there can be no certainty in the application... It will be admitted that many of these, and others that might be named, are fanciful, and perhaps had their origin in a determination, on the one hand, to find *Rome* referred to somehow, or in a determination, on the other hand, equally strong, not to find this; but still it is remarkable how many of the most obvious solutions refer to Rome and the Papacy. But the mind need not be distracted, nor need doubt be thrown over the subject, by the number of the solutions proposed. They show the restless character of the human mind, and the ingenuity of men..." (Albert Barnes, *Notes on the New Testament,* "Revelation," pages 337,338.)

of the servants of God, we should see this clearly. However, be it know that many believe that the outward mark of the beast is revealed in the catholic sign of the cross!

In Chapter 7, the 144,000 are sealed. We must remember the symbolic language which was used. John wrote, *"Hurt not the earth, neither the sea, nor the trees, til we have sealed* [marked] *the servants of our God in their foreheads"* (Revelation 7:3). And in Chapter 22, John recorded that the servants of God *"shall see his face; and his name shall be in their foreheads"* (Revelation 22:4). Is it still a mystery? I think not.

That No Man Might Buy Or Sell: Many papal decrees, forbidding trading with the heretics or Protestants, could be quoted from history. For example, at the Third Lateran Council in 1178 A.D., Pope Alexander III issued an order that "no man presume to entertain or cherish them in his house, or land, to exercise traffic with them." This same pope passed a law against the Waldenses demanding that no man should presume to receive or assist them in selling or buying, that, being deprived of the comfort of humanity, they may be compelled to repent of the error of their way." And finally, Pope Martin V, in his decree issued after the Council of Constance (the council that burned Huss), commanded that "they permit not the heretics to have houses in their districts, or enter into contracts, or carry on commerce, or enjoy the comforts of humanity with (Catholic) Christians." Only the Lord knows how many perished because of this economic warfare waged by the papacy.

I hope you can begin to see this revealing picture that the Lord has painted for His Church. I must remind you that this is a great revelation, not a mystery.

REVELATION CHAPTER 14
THE TRIUMPH OF CHRIST

1 And I looked, and, lo, a Lamb stood on the mount Zion, and with Him a hundred forty and four thousand, having His Father's name written in their foreheads.

2 And I heard a voice from heaven, as the voice of many waters, and as the voice of a great thunder; and I heard the voice of harpers harping with their harps:

3 And they sang as it were a new song before the throne, and before the four beasts and the elders: and no man could learn that song, but the hundred and forty and four thousand, which were redeemed from the earth.

4 These are they which were not defiled with women; for they are virgins. These are they which follow the Lamb whithersoever He goeth. These were redeemed from among men, being the first-fruits unto God, and to the Lamb.

5 And in their mouth was found no guile: for they are without fault before the throne of God.

The terrible picture of the enemies of Christ's Church, given in Chapter 13, is understood to cause the saints to have a fearful foreboding. The picture painted by the artist, a picture of mighty enemies, their terrible power and fearsome struggles yet to come, could lead one to despair of our Lord's ultimate triumph so clearly revealed by other Scriptures (see Matthew 16:18). Hence, for the motivation and encouragement of the saints, their eyes are now turned, in the 14th chapter, to a much brighter vision. The storm clouds are dispersed, and the fruition of their struggle is revealed. The visions of this chapter have helped lead the Church forward through terrible centuries of persecution, knowing that ultimately, at the end of the age, righteousness will triumph.

And I Looked, And Behold: This is the usual language which introduces a new vision.

A Lamb Stood: Chapter 13 revealed to us a false and deadly lamb, one that had the voice of a dragon. Here, in great contrast, the Lamb of God is presented in appealing glory.

On Mount Zion: Here and in Hebrews 12:22 are the only places in the *New* Testament where this phrase appears. It is equivalent to the *"Jerusalem which is above"* of Galatians 4:26. Mount Zion, which we know to be the city of the great king, the seat of worship in Jerusalem,. was a type, and now could only be interpreted as a symbol of the true Christian Church. In Hebrews 12:22, the saints, who have entered into Christ's new covenant, are clearly said to have come to this mount, the heavenly Jerusalem.

A Hundred Forty And Four Thousand: In Revelation 7, I gave what I believe to be the interpretation of this symbolic number. It is not necessary that I write it again. But further notice, they are "redeemed". Christ came to redeem His people Israel! He died for the sins of the world, however redemption is exclusive to Israel.

They Sang ... A New Song: This admonition is a new feature pertaining to this elect company. The prophet Isaiah revealed the consolation of the *"new song"* in the midst of our Lord's indignation with the wicked: *"Ye shall have a song, as in the night when a holy solemnity is kept; and gladness of heart, as when one goeth with a pipe to come into the mountain of the Lord, to the mighty One of Israel"* (Isaiah 30:29; see also Psalm 28:7).

> *6 And I saw another angel fly in the midst of heaven, having the everlasting gospel to preach unto them that dwell on the earth,*

and to every nation, and kindred, and tongue, and people,

7 Saying with a loud voice, Fear God, and give glory to Him;

for the hour of His judgment is come:

and worship Him that made heaven, and earth, and the sea,

and the fountains of waters.

And I Saw Another Angel Fly: Angels in the Book of Revelation are symbolic of messengers or any agency that endeavors to promote the gospel of the Kingdom. The angel's flying alerts us that some great movement or change will take place rapidly. The fact that he possesses the *"everlasting gospel"* symbolizes the evangelization of the world. We know this will be worldwide because he is speaking to all races. His proclamation reveals glad tidings but also declares the consequences of their rejection (see Isaiah 60:12).

The Hour Of His Judgment Is Come: Here is some meat for thought. In Matthew 13 Jesus teaches about the judgment in the Parable of the Wheat and the Tares. The same metaphor of an "angel" is being used. In verse 41 they (the angels) are sent forth to separate and execute judgment. Jesus prefaced that statement by proclaiming that this event would take place at the *"end of this world"* (verse 40). It is interesting to take <u>careful note </u>of the words *"end"* and *"world"* used in this verse. In the Greek the word **"sun-teleia"** is interpreted as "end," and "aion" is interpreted as "world," however, meaning *the age.* It's remarkable that these same words *(sunteleia* and *aion)* are used in Hebrews 9:26, which speaks of Christ and states: *"... but now once in the end* [sunteleia] *of the world* [aion] *hath he appeared to put away sin by the sacrifice of himself."* Isn't that amazing? Scripture teaches that we have attained to the sunteleia of the aion![110] The harvest, therefore, must be

---

110   "Say not ye, There are yet four months, and then comes the harvest? behold, I say unto you, Lift up your eyes, and Jook on the fields; for they are white already to harvest" (John 4:35). "The last hour, you have heard that Antichrist is coming, even now many antichrists have arisen, by this you know that it is the last hour" (1 Jn. 2:18). "The end of all things" (1 Pet. 4:7).

a continual process throughout the new covenant period, thus rendering understanding to the proclamations of Revelation 14.

> *8 And there followed another angel, saying, Babylon is fallen, is fallen, that great city, because she made all nations drink of the wine of the wrath of her fornication.*
>
> *9 And the third angel followed them, saying with a loud voice, If any man worship the beast and his image, and receive his mark in his forehead, or in his hand,*
>
> *10 The same shall drink of the wine of the wrath of God, which is poured out without mixture into the cup of his indignation; and he shall be tormented with fire and brimstone in the presence of the holy angels, and in the presence of the Lamb:*
>
> *11 And the smoke of their torment ascendeth up for ever and ever; and they have not rest day nor night, who worship the beast and his image, and whosoever receiveth the mark of his name.*
>
> *12 Here is the patience of the saints: here are they that keep the commandments of God, and the faith of Jesus.*

Babylon Is Fallen: As a result of the gospel of the Kingdom presented in verses 6 and 7, the spiritual city of sin called Babylon, but also revealed as "spiritually Sodom, and Egypt, and where our Lord was crucified" (11:8), is destined to be destroyed. The rest of these verses magnify the intensity of anger displayed by our Lord at this terrible harlot system. The symbolic language used to depict the troubles and torments of her adherents is calculated to present ultimate and extreme consequences. The concept of being *"tormented with fire and brimstone"* is a symbolic concept, just as the wine and cup are symbols. If you forget the metaphorical nature of this prophecy you will misinterpret this furious judgmental language.

BABYLON

What is meant by this city Babylon? The dispensationalists have been guessing about the identity of Babylon for almost a century now. Their assumptions and theories are as ridiculous as allowed by the undisciplined and ignorant parameters of fanciful speculation. I won't waste your time and mine by reviewing them. However, for over a thousand years the Body of Christ knew of the identity of this apostate spiritual city. All the Reformation fathers saw it clearly and proved it in their writings.

The term "Babylon" only occurs in the New Testament in 1 Pet. 5:13, and in the Book of Revelation. It is shown in this passage that Babylon virtually signifies the same as the *"beast and his image,"* while in 17:5 Babylon is shown to be the mystical harlot who sat on the seven-headed and ten-horned beast. In Chapter 18 the fall of Babylon is again declared and it is said that all the kings of the earth have committed fornication with her. Of this spiritual Babylon the old Babylon on the Euphrates was a type. It was (1.) A wicked world power; (2.) It oppressed God's people and led them captive; (3.) **It was only when it was overthrown that Jerusalem was restored;** (4.) It was at or near Babylon that the confusion of tongues took place. This old Babylon in some way is a type of the Babylon meant by John. The facts stated about the spiritual Babylon are (1.) it was identified with the beast; (2.) it was a mighty oppressor of God's people; (3.) it led them into captivity; (4.) it ruled the earth; (5.) it was a harlot, or idolatrous church. It has been found in the preceding chapter that the beast and its image point to Rome; it will be found in Chapter 17, that the woman who is called *"Mystery, Babylon the Great,"* who sits on the beast, is the great apostate church which has ruled the nations. This passage shows the means by which this dominion shall be overthrown. It will be done by a pure and holy Church, filled with missionary zeal and the truth of His word. It is the preaching of the ancient gospel which shall bring Rome to destruction.[111] There is no divine time measure attached to the totality of this process. However, it is swiftly approaching.[112]

> 13 *And I heard a voice from heaven saying unto me, Write, Blessed are the dead which die in the Lord, from henceforth: Yea, saith the Spirit, that they may rest from their labors; and their works do follow them.*

Not all the dead are blessed, only those who die in the Lord; for it is they who shall rise unto the resurrection of life; and they that have done evil will rise to the resurrection of damnation (John 5:28,29).[113]

> 14 *And I looked, and behold a white cloud, and upon the cloud one sat like unto the Son of man, having on*
> *His head a golden crown, and in His hand a sharp sickle.*
> 15 *And another angel came out of the temple, crying with a loud voice to Him that sat on the cloud, Thrust in Thy sickle, and reap: for the time is come for Thee to reap: for the harvest of the earth is ripe.*
> 16 *And He that sat on the cloud thrust in His sickle on the earth; and the earth was reaped.*

---

111   "And then shall that Wicked be revealed, whom the Lord shall consume with the spirit of his mouth [The Bible], and shall destroy with the brightness of His coming" (2 Thess. 2:8).

112   The above discourse on "Babylon" is extracted, for the most part, from *The People's New Testament With Notes.*

113   See also Ecc. 7:1; Ps. 116:15.

Upon The Cloud One Sat: The prophecies point to a King coming on the clouds of heaven, and He is given dominion, glory, and a kingdom in these last days. Daniel 7:13 portrays the *"Son of man"* coming in the clouds of heaven. If you compare Exodus 19:18 and Revelation 1:6,7, you have references which hold the key to understanding our Lord manifesting Himself in the **cloud.**

Why did the disciples ask the question: "Are you the coming one *(he that should come)?"* (Matthew 11:3). And why did Jesus tell them in Mark 9:1, *"Verily I say unto you, That there be some of them that stand here, which shall not taste of death, till they have seen the kingdom of God come with power"* (cf. Luke 9:27). Some modernists try to teach that this only applies to the Transfiguration; however, this is not vindicated by the Word of God.

Let's mention four admonitions in Scripture to help clarify the picture. (1.) In Revelation 1:13, Jesus is pictured among the lampstands as the Son of man speaking things which must shortly (soon) come to pass. (2.) In Revelation 14:14, Jesus appears on the white cloud, crowned, and with the sickle (cf. Joel 2:28 to 3:18 which speaks of Pentecost) of power only manifested in the Holy Spirit. (3.) In Matthew 16:27,28, the Son of man proclaims a coming in glory the disciples die! It also speaks of a bright cloud overshadowing them. (4.) Matthew 24:27,30! The Son of man appears coming on clouds at the end of the age. The *sunteleia,* the harvest (Pentecost), is given as the time of his cloud coming (see again Hebrews 9:26). Now once in the end of the age (to which we have attained), the *sunteleia!* Why did the High Priest tear his robes during Jesus' trial when Jesus declared: *"… hereafter you* [the High Priests] *shall see the Son of man sitting on the right hand of* **power,** *and* **coming in the clouds** *of heaven?"* (Matthew 26:64) They understood that He had spoken against them. This prophecy was fulfilled in A.D. 70 when Christ came with the clouds of the Roman army and destroyed their nation. Jesus was the *"lord of the vineyard"* in the Parable of the Wicked Husbandman (Matthew 21:33-41).

It is interesting that in the historical context of this Revelation prophecy the Vials of wrath are being prepared to be emptied (beginning in the 18th century) on papal Europe at the same time the North American continent and England receive the great harvest of the Great Awakening. Europe was shattered with the French Revolution. However, America and England flourished under the preaching of the Wesleys, Whitfield, Edwards, and Finney, just to name a few.

> *17 And another angel came out of the temple which is in heaven, he also having a sharp sickle.*
> *18 And another angel came out from the altar, which had power over fire; and cried with a loud cry to him that had the sharp sickle, saying, Thrust in thy sharp sickle, and gather the clusters of the vine of the earth; for her grapes are fully ripe.*
> *19 And the angel thrust in his sickle into the earth, and gathered the vine of the earth, and cast it into the great wine press of the wrath of God.*
> *20 And the wine press was trodden without the city; and blood came out of the wine press, even unto the horse bridles, by the space of a thousand and six hundred furlongs.*

We must never forget that God harvests the wicked vine of the earth daily. This great winepress is outside the city of God and there the bloody grapes of wrath are pressed.

> *20 And the wine press was trodden without the city; and blood came out of the wine press, even unto the horse bridles, by the*

space of a thousand and six hundred furlongs.

There has been much discussion as to what this great distance (200 miles) signifies. Some say that it applies to the area of Palestine. Others note that Italy is about 200 miles wide. However, in attempting to interpret, through the code of metaphor, we must draw a different conclusion. In my opinion, this number continues in the symbolic pattern and is depicting, not only the terror of the continuing process of judgment, but implying its universality. The figures, 40x40, or 4x4, multiplied by 10x10, again imply totality. The *four* quarters, the *four* winds, the *four* corners of the earth are often mentioned, and *four* is understood to be the apocalyptical metaphor for the earth, while *ten*, like seven, is a perfect, or sacred, number.

REVELATION CHAPTER 15
ANOTHER GREAT AND MARVELOUS
SIGN IN HEAVEN

This chapter is introducing a detailed account of the final judgments upon the beast, its image, and those who have the mark of the beast. The overthrow of the "great city Babylon" was pictured in Chapter 14:8-10, but this chapter and Chapter 16 reveal the Seven last plagues which accelerate the process of Babylon's overthrow. Chapter 14 gave us a summary of the result of the future events; Chapters 15 through 19 present the same events in detail. These chapters are all relative to the fall of spiritual Babylon.

Let's briefly review the prophetic scenario. The opening of the sixth seal took us to the victory of Christianity over Roman paganism. The seven trumpets (which were released by the seventh seal) revealed the overthrow of the Western Roman Empire by the Goths, Vandals, Huns, and the Heruli Ruin of the Eastern Empire by the Saracens and Turks. The last trump of the seven extends to the close of secular history and the ultimate triumph of Christ. Revealed in that trumpet are the seven vials. These last plagues first weaken, then totally destroy the power of Papal Rome. Amen!

The mission of the seven seals was to overthrow Rome paganism. The seven trumpets were designed to overthrow the Roman Empire. Equally definite is the purpose for the seven vials. They will (and have already completed most of their mission) utterly overthrow this great blasphemous power variously described as the "city of fornication," "the great city Babylon," the scarlet adulteress, and the seven-headed and ten-horned beast.

1 And I saw another sign in heaven, great and marvelous, seven angels having the seven last plagues; for in them is filled up the wrath of God.

2 And I saw as it were a sea of glass mingled with fire; and them that had gotten the victory over the beast, and over his image, and over his mark, and over the number of his name, stand on the sea of glass, having the harps of Gold.

This heavenly scene is different from those which have just transpired. Its character is unique and a bit startling. The *seven last plagues* settle the issue once and for all with the beast and its image.

Sea Of Glass Mingled With Fire: This metaphor depicts the calmness and purity of Christ's Kingdom-its rule. Fire is now mingled within, signifying that it is time for judgments direct from God's throne. The righteous are rejoicing at the approaching overthrow of their great historic enemy.

3 And they sang the song of Moses the servant of God, and the song of the Lamb, saying, Great and marvelous are Thy works, Lord God Almighty; just and true are Thy ways, thou King of saints.

4 Who shall not fear Thee, 0 Lord, and glorify Thy name? for Thou only art holy: for all nations shall come and worship before Thee; for Thy judgments are made manifest.

The Song Of Moses ... The Song Of The Lamb: When Israel was delivered from the wickedness of Egypt, they sang the song of Moses on the banks of the Red Sea. Here, true Israel sings a great song of deliverance, a new song, a song that glorifies our true Redeemer, Jesus Christ.

Just And True Are Thy Ways: The salvation of the true Church and the destruction of the beast are a manifestation of the justice of God. The apostle Paul warned all in his epistle to the Romans. *"Behold therefore the goodness and severity of God: on them which fell, severity; but toward thee, goodness, if thou continue in his goodness: otherwise thou also shalt be cut* off (Romans 11:22).

All Nations Shall Come: When all enemies have been put under His feet (Romans 16:20; 1 Corinthians 15:24,25) the prophecy of Isaiah 2 will then be fulfilled in its totality. *"And it shall come to pass in the last days, that the mountain of the Lord's house shall be ... exalted above the hills; and all nations shall flow into it. And many people shall go and say, Come ye, and let us go up to the mountain of the Lord ..."* (Isaiah 2:2,3). Remember, the *last days* began at Pentecost. (See Acts 2:16,17.) Likewise, and yet to be discussed, the *"new Jerusalem"* is mentioned in Chapter 21: In it, *"the bride, the Lamb's wife,"* (Revelation 21:9) *"...the nations of them which are saved shall walk ..."* (Revelation 21:22).

> *5 And after that I looked, and, behold, the temple of the taber-nacle of the testimony in heaven was opened:*
> *6 And the seven angels came out of the temple, having the seven plagues, clothed in pure and white linen, and having their breasts girded with golden girdles.*
> *7 And one of the four beasts gave unto the seven angels seven golden vials full of the wrath of God, who liveth for ever and ever.*

The Temple Of The Tabernacle Of The Testimony: The *temple* of Solomon succeeded the *tabernacle* of Moses, in which there was the *testimony,* i.e., the two tables, Aaron's rod, the pot of manna and the holy anointing oil. All these sacred items bore *testimony* to the covenant that God had with Israel, and the continual miraculous interventions on their behalf.

> *8 And the temple was filled with smoke from the glory of God,*
> *and His power; and no man was able to enter into the temple*
> *till the seven plagues of the seven angels were fulfilled.*

Does this mean that heaven is closed until the fulfillment of this prophecy, as some have suggested? No, of course not. I believe the true meaning is plain. These verses have revealed, in symbolic language, the place of intercession in heaven. Christ is our mediator. In the midst of this vision the seven angels of *wrath* came forward and their mission was proclaimed. *The divine purpose has now been established.* The wrath angels will pour their vials; there is no longer any time for giving intercession to prevent the judgments of God from falling upon the deserving beast. No man can enter in and advert these judgments until the seven last plagues are fulfilled.

In Chapter 16 we will find our point in history relative to the sequence of vial judgments. This changes everything, doesn't it?

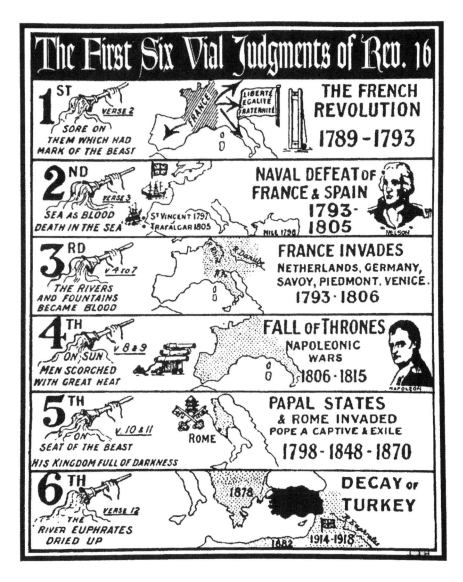

Illustration taken from: *The Pope, Communism and the Coming New World* by Thomas Foster

REVELATION CHAPTER 16
"POUR OUT THE VIALS"
THE UNFOLDING OF THE THIRD "WOE"

In Chapter 15 we saw the introduction of what is known as the seven last plagues; the completion of the wrath of Almighty God, in a series of calamitous events, against mystery Babylon, the papal power. These began to operate immediately after the close of her 1,260 years of spiritual, temporal, and persecuting domination. We know from Scripture (Revelation 13:5) that this time was given as time for repentance. What use did Rome make of these years? She filled up the cup of her iniquity by introducing all forms of false doctrines. She corrupted Christian truths with pagan traditions. She filled her churches with idols, and she persecuted and hounded to death every saint who dared raise a voice against her iniquities.

We will now discover that these series of judgments began in the year A.D. 1793.

FIRST VIAL (A.D. 1793)
THE FRENCH REVOLUTION

1 And I heard a great voice out of the temple saying to the seven angels, Go your ways, and pour out the vials of the wrath of God upon the earth.

2 And the first went, and poured out his vial upon the earth: and there fell a noisome and grievous sore upon the men which had the mark of the beast, and upon them which worshiped his image.

Upon The Earth: Let me remind you about the term "earth." It is still used by John to denote the Roman world. The Greek defines the term as a *region.*

We have already discussed a very important date and decree, the *Justinian Decree* of A.D. 533. Remember, he was the emperor of the Eastern Roman Empire. In A.D. 533 he decreed that the pope of Rome was the supreme bishop, of all the churches, and this is what brought the pope of Rome into absolute supremacy in the West. Many historicists have looked at this decree, and knew it was extremely important in the study of Bible prophecy. One man, Robert Flemming, displayed marvelous insight into the 1,260 years of papal dominion. Earlier in the book Flemming's insight was mentioned. It is worth another look.

The historicist Flemming wrote two vital works. They are called the *Apocalyptic Key* and *The Rise and Fall of the Papacy.* Both works were published in the first decade of the 18th century. These works were written almost a hundred years before the French Revolution. He showed his findings to King William III, who was then the Protestant King of Great Britain. It was William III who deposed James II, who was trying to bring the Roman Catholic religion back to England and make it the state religion. This was Prince William of Orange, who was then crowned King William III.

Flemming showed his findings to King William III around the year 1690. In his writings he looked at this date of A.D. 533, and said that exactly 1,260 years later we could expect to see God pouring out his "Vials" of judgment upon the Latin kingdom of Europe. He said it must begin in the year 1793-94. He went further and said that if the judgments didn't start in Italy, they would start in France, the *eldest daughter* of the papacy. And that was absolutely precise.

This first vial is the bursting forth of the French Revolution in A.D. 1793. France thought that she had entered into an age of reason. Reason became her god. She wanted to declare what was true to be true, and what was false, false. This was the time of the French poet, dramatist and historian *Voltaire,* the leader of the Enlightenment. He declared that the Bible was false. What had made it appear so false in France was the Latin church.

In A.D. 1793 France declared war on the ruling hierarchy in her own country and the surrounding nations of Europe. As a result, these nations of Europe were plunged into the bloodiest war recorded since the fall of Rome in the fifth century, the French Revolution. These were the worst horrors Europe had endured since the time of Pagan Rome. Over two million people were killed. Twenty five thousand priests were murdered and forty thousand churches were confiscated and turned into stables!

John likens this vial to a sore, ulcer, or boil on the papal peoples. When the human bloodstream is impure, such eruptions break out on the body. The prophet Isaiah used this metaphor to describe idolatrous Israel before she was punished. He stated, "*From the sole of the foot even unto the head there is no soundness in it; but wounds, and bruises, and putrifying sores: they have not been closed, neither bound up, neither mollified with ointment. Your country is desolate, your cities are burned with fire: your land, strangers devour it in your presence, and it is desolate, as overthrown by strangers.*" (Isaiah 1:6,7). As the result of the breaking forth of this painful ulcer, the mightiest Catholic nation was thrown into civil war, and every Catholic country in Europe was deluged in blood, and the papacy received a blow from which it would <u>never recover.</u>

SECOND VIAL (A.D. 1793-1805)
NAVAL WARFARE

3 And the second angel poured out his vial upon the sea: and it became as the blood of a dead man: and every living soul died in the sea.

The first calamity fell upon the Roman earth; the second is upon its oceans. Except to some blind futurist this must be highly symbolic language indeed. Nothing could destroy all life in the sea without at the same time destroying all life on earth.

So we must ask, in this series of calamities, is there one that transpires on the seas and weakens the Catholic powers? Under the second trumpet a burning mountain fell into the sea (Revelation 8:8,9). This was symbolic of the sea-going Vandal power that swept the Mediterranean and destroyed imperial Rome's navies. From the sea, spiritual Rome, under this second vial, is further weakened. This metaphor is prophesying the *greatest naval strife* ever recorded to this point in history. A.D. 1793 begins the deadly contest for mastery of the seas. Protestant England and Catholic Europe strive together upon the prophetic seas. Between the years A.D. 1793-1805, this terrible naval warfare cost Europe over 600 ships of the Line, the largest war vessels that then went to sea, besides thousands of ships of war of smaller size. Let me mention a few of those great Protestant victories:

1793   Lord Hood defeats the French at Toulon.

1794   Lord Howe also defeated the French at Ushant.

1797   Britain defeated the Spanish fleet off Cape St. Vincent.

1798   Lord Nelson defeated the French at the Nile.

1805   Lord Nelson defeated the Spanish and French at Trafalgar.

At Trafalgar the French fleet was annihilated. This fleet was created with the same intent as was the Spanish Armada (A.D. 1688). It was designed to destroy Protestant Britain.

In this way the maritime powers of the papal nations were swept off the seas by the British victories. A further result of the naval struggle was that Spain and Portugal lost their South American possessions which revolted and finally became independent. As a result of these disasters for Rome, it can be seen how the symbolism of the prophecy, *"every living soul died in the sea,"* came to pass; it was the decrease of the sea power and overseas colonies of the papal empire.

THIRD VIAL (AD. 1793-1806)
THE FRENCH INVASIONS

4 And the third angel poured out his vial upon the rivers and fountains of waters; and they became blood.

5 And I heard the angel of the waters say, You art righteous, 0 Lord, which art and wast, and shalt be, because Thou hast judged thus:

6 For they have shed the blood of saints and prophets, and Thou hast given them blood to drink; for they are worthy.

7 And I heard another out of the altar say, Even so, Lord God Almighty, true and righteous are Thy judgments.

Why was the Lord righteous in judging thus? This institution and its willing servants were responsible for the murders of over 50 million people, and God had not forgotten.

So we see that when France determined to force her philosophy on the other nations a war erupted with Germany. Her philosophies of atheism (agnosticism), her freedom of thought, her throwing off the yoke of tradition and radicalism were not going to be tolerated by her neighboring nations, so they took up arms. Beginning in A.D. 1793 the French fought against the Germans, the Austrians, the north Italian Sardinians and others.

The Rivers And Fountains … Became Blood: History graphically records that the rivers and fountains of the Rhine, Danube and Po had witnessed the cruel scenes of gallant Christian martyrs who perished because they would not take the *"mark of the beast"* by accepting the supremacy of the pope.

In the history of the whole of papal Europe, there had never been any one war in which the valleys of the Rhine, Danube, and Po rivers were so filled with blood. Remarkably, it was in these very same areas that multitudes of Lutherans, Moravians, Hussites, Albigenses, Waldenses, Vaudois, and Huguenots willingly laid down their lives for the true faith of Jesus Christ. Thus the days of judgment had come as symbolically described as the *"waters* [peoples] *became blood."*

This river system was also the focus of the third trumpet (Revelation 8:10,11). It was there that Attila the Hun, the "blazing star," the wormwood of these rivers, laid Pagan Rome prostrate at his feet. Now Christ is using the terrors of the French Revolution to do the same to papal Rome. For centuries Rome had dyed the rocks and streams of this region red with the blood of Christ's martyrs. For generations these righteous communities had to endure Rome's fanatical legions. Now the tide was turning, "true and righteous are Thy Judgments." [114]

---

[114]   "In the year 1796, a general, age 27, led a French army across the Alps. On the river system of Italy, on the Rhine, the Po and its tributaries, he battled with the Austrians and their allies. It is remarkable that every one of his great conflicts were fought upon the rivers" B. W. Johnson, *The People's New Testament With Notes.* See also Elliott's *Horae Apocalypticae,* "THE THIRD VIAL."

FOURTH VIAL (A.D. 1806-1815)
THE NAPOLEONIC WARS

8 And the fourth angel poured out his vial upon the sun; and power was given unto him to scorch men with fire.

9 And men were scorched with great heat, and blasphemed the name of God, which hath power over these plagues: and they repented not to give Him glory.

The *"sun"* as we have seen in the Book of Revelation, as well as the other prophets, is symbolic of a prominent ruling power-a king. Napoleon Bonaparte became the ruler of France, its "sun," and then scourged Europe. From 1796 to 1815 he was engaged in war on the European continent without a moment's cessation. His liberating armies are recorded by historians as the "scourge of Europe."[115]

How true is the Bible description for Napoleon that *"power was given unto him to scorch men with fire."* In 1798 the French Revolutionary army invaded the papal states, captured Rome, imprisoned the Pope (he died in captivity; Revelation 13:10), and spoiled his palaces and offices and confiscated his estates. The regalia robes of the pope and his cardinals were burnt to melt down the gold in them.

At last, Napoleon had shattered the blinding spell of Rome. He taught the world forever that the power of the popes could be successfully defied; a wonderful service to humanity. In spite of these recognizable judgments, Rome has not abated its blasphemous pretensions. *"They repented not to give Him glory."*

---

115   In the historian Dr. Keith's work, *The Signs of the Times,* on page 190 we read: "Napoleon performed the miracles of genius. His achievements still dazzle, while they amaze the world. Within the space of eight years he scorched every kingdom in Europe, from Naples to Berlin, and from Lisbon to Moscow. Ancient kingdoms withered before the intense blaze of his power ... Kingdoms were unsparingly rift like garments... **like the sun, there was nothing hid from his great heat.**"

FIFTH VIAL
THE THRONE OF THE "BEAST"

10 And the fifth angel poured out his vial upon the seat of the beast; and his kingdom was full of darkness: and they gnawed their tongues for pain,

11 And blasphemed the God of heaven because of their pains and their sores, and repented not of their deeds.

The *"seat* [throne] *of the beast"* must be interpreted as the seat of its power. With a voice of unanimity the greatest minds in Protestantism have proclaimed and proven that the throne of the beast resides in Rome, the very center of the papal power. Therefore, the scene of the calamities will be Italy and Rome.

With the loss of papal power and authority in Europe, Rome's kingdom was in *"darkness."* In the nation of Italy, the papal states were continually attacked until they disappeared. In 1798 the pope was removed from his residence in Rome. Basically, from 1798 to 1866 the authority of the papal system throughout Europe progressively disintegrated. Again in 1848 the pope had to flee Rome. In 1870 the Italian troops conquered Rome and incorporated it into the Kingdom of Italy.

The continual loss of power and the thought of its once mighty papal empire caused the papacy to *"gnaw their tongues for pain,"* but there was no repentance found in her. She continued to hurl her anathemas, but they had no power behind them. Also, instead of repenting of their idolatry which had brought this plague, the popes continued to blaspheme God by introducing new false doctrines which Paul, the apostle, called, *"doctrines of devils."* (See 1 Timothy 3:1-3.)

Among the most daring and defiant of Rome's historic whoredoms is the doctrine of the Immaculate Conception. This teaches that Mary was born without sin. They teach that all the rest of mankind was born with original sin, but Mary alone was exempted. The original decree was pronounced by Pope Pius IX on December 8, 1854, and reads as follows:

> We declare, pronounce and define that the Most Blessed Virgin Mary, at the first instant of her conception was preserved immaculate from all stain of original sin, by the singular grace and privilege of the Omnipotent God, in virtue of the merits of Jesus Christ, the Savior of mankind, and that this doctrine was revealed by God, and therefore must be believed firmly and constantly by all the faithful (From the papal bull, *Ineffabilus Deus*, quoted in *The Tablet*, December 12, 1953).[116]

This doctrine lacks any scriptural support. Quite the contrary, it attacks the accuracy of the Bible. Jesus said that the *"scriptures cannot be broken* [period!]." The Book of Romans has already pronounced that *"all fall short and come short of the glory of God"* (Rom. 3:23). Now who is right, the Bible or the blasphemous claims of Rome? Further, Mary clearly acknowledged her need of a Savior for she proclaimed, *"My soul doth magnify the Lord, And my spirit hath rejoiced in God my Savior"* (Luke 1:46,47).

To further the blasphemous surge of the fifth vial, Rome proclaims the doctrine of "ex cathedra" in 1870. This teaching states:

> The Roman Pontiff, when he speaks ex cathedra that is, when

---

116   The reader is highly encouraged to obtain a copy of Loraine Boettner's, *Roman Catholicism,* distributed by Baker Book House, Grand Rapids, Michigan. It powerfully unmasks the papal system, and should be in every true Protestant's library.

in the exercise of his office as pastor and teacher of all the Christians he defines … a doctrine of faith or morals to be held by the whole Church is, by reason of the Divine assistance promised to him in blessed Peter, possessed of the infallibility … and consequently such definitions of the Roman Pontiff are irreformable (*The Catholic Encyclopedia,* vol. 7, p. 796, art. "Infallibility.")

Only an institution void of truth and common sense could come up with that one. My Bible teaches me that only God is infallible and that all men, including and especially the pope, are human and therefore fallible [period!]. I say, these are anti-Christian proclamations.

On the day that they were to make this decree of infallibility, mirrors were positioned in the Vatican throne room, so as to have the sun's reflection upon the pope during this decree. However, a thunderstorm covered the city and no light was seen. How magnificently has Rome fulfilled the heavenly vision!

SIXTH VIAL
OUR PRESENT AGE
APPROACHING ARMAGEDDON!

12 And the sixth angel poured out his vial upon the great river Euphrates; and the water thereof was dried up, that the way of the kings of the East might be prepared.

13 And I saw three unclean spirits like frogs come out of the mouth of the dragon, and out of the mouth of the beast, and out of the mouth of the false prophet.

14 For they are the spirits of devils, working miracles, which go

forth unto the kings of the earth and of the whole world, to gather
them to the battle of that great day of God Almighty.
15 Behold, I come as a thief, Blessed is he that watcheth, and
keepeth his garments, lest he walk naked, and they see his shame.
16 And he gathered them together into a place called in the
Hebrew tongue Armageddon.

The Great River Euphrates … Was Dried Up: In Chapter 9, verses
13-19, under the *sixth trumpet* (the second woe) we saw how the river
Euphrates depicted the rise of the Turkish Empire. Now the sixth vial
reveals the end of its dominion and power. All great historicists knew
that the drying up of the great river Euphrates would mean the collapse
of the Turkish Empire. I quote from Cachemaille:

> It seems manifest that the same Turkish Power is here intended
> as was described under the Sixth Trumpet, and there said to be
> loosed from the Euphrates. Its water is its people (Revelation
> 17:15), and it is spoken of as "great" because of the multitude of
> people and nations therein. Like the Assyrian and other Powers
> of old, when providentially employed to desolate Judah (Isaiah
> 8:7,8; 17:12,13), it had overflowed from its Euphratean banks over
> Grecian Christendom (see also Jeremiah 46:7,8; 47:2). And now,
> as the next great event aft.er the outpouring of the Fifth Vial on
> the Seat of the Beast, that is, on Papal Rome, it was foreshown
> that the symbolic waterflood of that great river was to begin to
> be dried up; that is, that the population and area of the Turkish
> Empire were, from one cause or another, to begin to be dimin-
> ished. (E. P. Cachemaille, *The Visions of Daniel and the Reuelation*
> *Explained,* page 541).

In 1917-18 the once great Turkish Empire, which had its roots in the Euphrates River, was defeated by British Empire troops under General Edmund Allenby. In October 1917 he launched an attack on the Turkish forces controlling Palestine. This battle was fought in the Gaza-Beersheba sector with the result that Jerusalem surrendered to Allenby. Palestine was now freed from the heel of the Turks. The once mighty Turkish Empire was forever "dried up" and ceased to exist as a result of World War I.

It is vital to this prophecy to understand that the same year that the drying up of the Turkish Empire occurred, namely 1917, Russian communism appeared with the October Revolution! The exiled Bolshevik leaders—Lenin, Trotsky, Stalin, and others—had returned from abroad and the region of Siberia. With these men, came the ideology (later we'll understand that it's one of the three unclean spirits) which was to prepare and equip the kings of the east, namely *Russia* and *China,* the two great eastern nations which have arisen in this generation. Their ideology was communism. How wonderfully this prophecy has been fulfilled. In the very same year that the Euphrates dries up, the kings of the east receive their infusion of uncleanness. Their ideology, communism, will act as one of the gathering forces as we race towards Armageddon-the consuming of the arm age.[117] And believe it or not, we still have futurists waiting for the river Euphrates to literally dry up.

THREE UNCLEAN SPIRITS OR IDEOLOGIES

Today we still have the false ideology of the **Jews.**

Also, we have the false ideology of the **Communists.**

We also have the false ideology of the **Moslems.**

---

117   I am aware that communism has received a blow in Russia. However, what is emerging from her rubble is potentially more dangerous-nationalism; fueled by despair and economic chaos. Nevertheless, this "king" is being positioned by God for this hour, likewise China, where communism thrives! These kings have yet to fulfill their prophetic destinies.

From the chronology and the context of the prophecy we notice that these three unclean spirits are going to affect the nations of the earth in our time and our day. To better understand this we need to examine the term *"whole world."*

Up to this point in the chronology of the Seals, Trumpets and Vials, whenever the word "earth" appeared it was the Greek word *ghay* (Strong's #1093) meaning a "region." However, we now have the word *oikoumene* (Strong's #3625) translated, "world," prefaced by *holos* (Strong's #3650) translated, "whole." The Book of Revelation is now extending itself to the *whole inhabited world,* instead of just the dominant region of the beast, namely Europe. Now, the entire planet will be affected by the judgment pronounced in this sixth vial-Armageddon. The effect of Armageddon will be dramatic and end the arms age madness.

Great Day Of God Almighty: This term is a common metaphor for a day of judgment upon the wicked. There have been several days of judgment upon the wicked and also rebellious Israel. (See Isaiah 13:6,9; Joe12:1-2,11,31; Amos 5:18-20; Zephaniah 1:14-18.)

Now that we understand that this vial is applicable to the entire planet, our uncovering of the three unclean spirits should be relatively easy. These spirits must have the ability to affect the stability of the entire earth. Their mission is to gather the nations for an ultimate conflict, symbolically referred to as Armageddon. I believe that they are self-evident. I have already listed the three most deadly ideologies in existence—*Communism, Islam,* and *Judaism.* These are all hostile to Christianity and are **irreconcilable**; ultimately they will war each other into oblivion. This struggle will encompass all nations. I believe that World War I and World War II were only a prelude to this coming catastrophe. It is the next great event to transpire in the Book of Revelation's chronology. This is where we are. Can you think of more potentially volatile ideologies than these?

I Come As A Thief: It is interesting to notice that the first five words of verse 15 state: *"Behold, I come as a thief."* This most certainly does not refer to the second advent of the Lord to rapture an expectant Church. It clearly speaks of Christ moving in judgment as the *"Lord God, Almighty"* on sinful nations.

Furthermore, the dispensationalists try to teach us that in Revelation chapter 4, the so-called Rapture transpires. So, does Christ come again in Revelation Chapter 16 for another Rapture? A Rapture here, a Rapture there, Raptures everywhere. Will it ever end? Understand the rhetorical nature of the question.

ARMAGEDDON

And He Gathered Them Together Into ... Armageddon: I do not believe that this is in reference to just one battle. Surely by now we understand the *"symbolic"* nature of this great prophecy. The three unclean spirits are driving the whole world to the *"cross roads of conflict"* and the *"consummation of the arm age."*

If Armageddon is the last great battle that gathers all the armies of the world, and it occurs exclusively in the so called Valley of Megiddo, then we have a serious logistical problem. It has been calculated by scholars that you would have to stack men and their equipment *24 miles high* in order to gather all the world's armies in Megiddo. Sanctified common sense and consistent symbolic interpretation refuse to be entertained by the futurists' fanciful speculation.

Though I don't agree with David Chilton's (Alcazar's) preterist interpretation of the Revelation, I do however recognize his insight into the symbolic nature of the prophecies. He has concisely and scholarly presented his position on Armageddon, a position with which I agree.

The demons gather the kings of the earth together **to the place which in the Hebrew is called Armageddon.** Literally, this is spelled **Har-Magedon,** meaning **Mount Megiddo.** A problem for "literalists" arises here, for Megiddo is a city on a plain, not a mountain. There never was or will be a literal "Battle of Armageddon," for there is no such place. The mountain nearest to the plain of Megiddo is Mount Carmel [I have stood on both], and this is presumably what St. John had in mind. Why didn't he simply say "Mount Carmel"? Farrer answers: "One can only suppose that St. John wants to refer to Megiddo and to Carmel in one breath. Carmel because of its association with the defeat of Jezebel's false prophets, and Megiddo because it was the scene of several important military engagements in Biblical history. Megiddo is listed among the conquests of Joshua (Josh. 12:21), and it is especially important as the place where Deborah defeated the kings of Canaan (Jud. 5:19). King Ahaziah of Judah, the evil grandson of King Ahab of Israel, died at Megiddo (2 Kings 9:29). Perhaps the most significant event that took place there, in terms of St. John's imagery, was the confrontation between Judah's King Josiah and the Egyptian Pharaoh Neco … "Megiddo" thus was for St. John a symbol of defeat and desolation, a "Waterloo" signifying the defeat of those who set themselves against God, as Farrer explains: "In sum, Mt. Megiddo stands in his mind for a place where lying prophecy and its dupes go to meet their doom; where kings and their armies are misled to their destruction; and where all the tribes of the earth mourn, to see Him in power, Whom in weakness they had pierced" [see also Zech. 12:9-11].[118]

---

118   David Chilton, *The Days of Vengeance,* pages 411,412.

Another error made by most futurists is to suggest that Armageddon is this age's last conflict. How can it be when it comes under the sixth vial, with still further calamity clearly predicted under the seventh vial? It is the seventh vial which proclaims to us that the greatest symbolic political earthquake in history is yet to occur.

SEVENTH VIAL
THE "GREAT CITY" DESTROYED

17 And the seventh angel poured out his vial into the air; and there came a great voice out of the temple of heaven, from the throne, saying, It is done.

A great proclamation of triumph pronounced when God says, *"It is done."* This is to encompass all the cities of the papal nations. They are all destined to fall. In a parallel vision of the consummation recorded in Ezekiel 39:8, we read the same prophetic utterance: *"Behold it is come and IT IS DONE, saith the Lord God. This is the day whereof I have spoken."*

Important point: This seventh vial is poured into the air. Remember that Satan is called *"the prince of the power of the air"* (Ephesians 2:2). His final realm of authority will be shattered forever.

18 And there were voices, and thunders, and lightnings; and there was a GREAT EARTHQUAKE, such as was not since men were upon the earth, so mighty an earthquake, and so great.
19 And the great city was divided into three parts, and the cities of the nations fell: and great Babylon came in remembrance before God, to give unto her the cup of the wine of the fierceness of His wrath.

THE TRI-PART JUDGEMENT

Spiritually, politically and economically, Babylon is judged. Many (Protestant ministers) may have forgotten, but God has not, *"great Babylon came in remembrance before"* Him. Furthermore, true apostles and prophets (see Ephesians 4:11; Corinthians 12:28,29) will be the ministers of remembrance. They will have the anointing and courage to expose the great whore and bring Babylon down (Revelation 18:20).[119]

> *20 And every Island fled away, and the mountains were not found.*
> *21 And there fell upon men a great hail out of heaven, every stone about the weight of a talent: and men blasphemed God because of the plague of the hail; or the plague thereof was exceeding great.*

Many scholars believe that this speaks metaphorically of the curse and devastation wrought by aerial bombardment. This form of warfare is unique to this century and appears in the Book of Revelation at the proper time in history. Could this judgment be even more devastating than Armageddon? You decide. It is future, therefore we can only see in part. We must not become speculators. What I believe is clearly presented by these vials in the process which will ultimately bring down all illegitimate governments.

---

119   The reader is referenced to the prophets Isaiah 47:5,7-10; and Jeremiah 51:610, for further insight as to the origin of this prophetic language against Babylon. These prophets spoke against ancient Babylon of which modern Babylon imitates. Therefore, the "type and shadow" was easily understood and extracted by John the Revelator. For those of you with a weak theological stomach, please notice that John doesn't water the language down. He truly reflects Christ's intense hatred for this wicked "system."

Then was the iron, the clay, the brass, the silver,

and the gold, broken to pieces together, and became like the

chaff of the summer threshing floors; and the wind carried

them away, that no place was found for them: and the stone

that smote the image became a great mountain, and filled the

whole earth (Daniel 2:35).

This is the end of man's unrighteous governments. It is spoken of Christ, "Of the increase of his government and peace there shall be no end" (Isaiah 9:7). How can you have a rapture take the Church out for seven years, and still have an increase of Christ's government? It is a government which will never end, according to Isaiah.

REVELATION CHAPTER 17
THE JUDGMENT OF THE "GREAT WHORE"
(GOD HAS NOT FORGOTTEN!)

The 16th chapter of the Book of Revelation presents to us a series of great historical events which ultimately will lead to the complete annihilation of spiritual Babylon. The facts of history have given us a clear interpretation of the events which have already transpired. The sixth vial brings us to our present generation. Attempting to interpret the events presented in Chapter 17 puts us on a course which will demand diligent use of sanctified common sense and consistent application of the established metaphors.

We will see that in this chapter the great harlot church is finally judged and burned with symbolic fire in Europe. This calamity will occur at the hands of the very kingdoms which had given her their allegiance for centuries. They are destined to unite one more time for the purpose of destroying this most horrendous institution. Christ has thus judged.

1 And there came one of the seven angels which had the seven vials, and talked with me, saying unto me, Come hither; I will shew unto thee the judgment of the great whore that sitteth upon many waters;

2 With whom the kings of the earth have committed fornication, and the inhabitants of the earth have been made drunk with the wine of her fornication.

3 So he carried me away in the spirit into the wilderness: and I saw a woman sit upon a scarlet colored beast, full of names of blasphemy, having seven heads and ten horns.

4 And the woman was arrayed in purple and scarlet color, and decked with gold, and precious stones, and pearls, having a golden cup in her hand, full of abominations and filthiness of her fornication.

5 And upon her forehead was a name written, MYSTERY, BABYLON, THE GREAT, THE MOTHER OF HARLOTS AND ABOMINATIONS OF THE EARTH.

I believe the quotes from the following Protestant historicists— Walter Scott, Bishop Wordsworth, John Wesley, Adam Clarke and Bishop Thomas Newton—will suffice in interpreting the meaning of the above verses. Their quotes, along with a comment from David Campbell, will be extracted from Campbell's book, *Signs Are for Strangers.*

Walter Scott in his *Exposition of the Revelation of Jesus Christ,* says on pages 340,341, when comparing what he calls the HARLOT OF SATAN and THE BRIDE OF THE LAMB, "In every point of view these two women are set in sharp contrast. The harlot is subject to Satan. The Bride is subject to Christ. It is one of the Vial angels which shows both to the wondering Seer. A WILDERNESS (17:3) and a GREAT AND HIGH MOUNTAIN (21:10) are the respective points of observation. Great Babylon comes OUT OF THE EARTH; its historical origin is human (Genesis 11:1-9), its latter-day development satanic, as shown in the apocalypse. The New Jerusalem descends OUT OF HEAVEN, its native sphere, and FROM GOD, its blessed source. Satan decks the one (17:4); God adorns the other (19:8). Eternal ruin is the portion of the harlot; eternal glory the happy lot of the bride."

Wordsworth, writing on the apocalypse, said, "It cannot be doubted that our most eminent divines have commonly held and taught that the apocalyptic prophecies concerning Babylon were designed by the Holy Spirit to describe the Church of Rome. Not only they who flourished at the period of the Reformation such as Archbishop Cranmer, Bishop Ridley and Jewel ... but they also which followed them in the next ... I mean the end of the sixteenth and the beginning of the seventeenth century ... proclaimed openly the same doctrine. And it was maintained by those in that learned age who were most eminent for sober moderation and Christian charity, as well as profound erudition [learning]."

Is it Pagan Rome or Papal Rome who inherits the character and features of the apocalyptic Babylon? Surely Papal Rome. Each time that the Book of Revelation speaks about a woman in particular it is speaking about a Church, either true or false, the real or the counterfeit Church. The "woman Jezebel" in Revelation 2:20 is the church of Rome. Search it out and you will see that this is true. And in so far as popery has corrupted the truth, persecuted the children of God, advanced arrogant and blasphemous claims, assumed universal dominion, and otherwise has drunk into the spirit, and adopted the principles and practices of the great harlot, she is dead center in the character of the Babylon of the Apocalypse.

John Wesley, in his *Notes on the New Testament* commenting on Revelation 17:5 remarked, "And on her forehead a name written whereas the saints have the name of God and the Lamb on their foreheads. 'MYSTERY'-this very word was inscribed on the front of the pope's mitre, till some of the Reformers took PUBLIC notice of it. 'Babylon, THE GREAT'-Benedict 13th, in his proclamation of the jubilee, A.D. 1725, explains this sufficiently. His words are, 'Hasten to the place which the Lord hath chosen. Ascend to this New Jerusalem ... the city most rightfully called THE PALACE, placed for the pride of all ages, the city of the Lord, the Zion of the Holy One of Israel. This catholic and apostolic ROMAN church is the head of the worlds, the MOTHER of all believers, the FAITHFUL INTERPRETER of God, and MISTRESS of all churches."

Wesley then added these pungent words, "But God somewhat VARIES the style (i.e. from Pope Benedict 13th), 'THE MOTHER OF HARLOTS' the parent, ringleader, patroness, and nourisher of many daughters, that closely copy after her. 'And abominations' of every kind, spiritual and fleshly. 'Of the earth'—in all lands. In this respect she is indeed catholic or universal." John Wesley was therefore under no delusion as to who spiritual Babylon was. He steered clear of the Roman communion.

Adam Clarke commented on verses 4 and 5 of Revelation 17 with these words in pages 945 and 946 of his commentary, verse 4, 'And the woman was arrayed in purple and scarlet color, and decked with gold and precious stones and pearls, having a golden cup in her hand full of abominations and filthiness of her fornications.' This strikingly represents the most pompous and costly manner in which the Latin church has held forth to the nations, the rites and ceremonies of its idolatrous and corrupt worship.

"Verse 5, 'And upon her FOREHEAD was a name written, Mystery, Babylon the Great, the Mother of Harlots and Abominations of the Earth.' This inscription being written upon her forehead is intended to show that she is not ashamed of her doctrines, but publicly professes and glories in them before the nations; she has indeed a whore's forehead, she has refused to be ashamed. The inscription upon her forehead is exactly the portraiture of the Latin church. This church is, as Bishop Newton well expressed it, 'A mystery of iniquity.' This woman is also called 'Babylon the Great'; she is the exact antitype of the ancient Babylon in her idolatry and cruelty, but the ancient city called Babylon is only a drawing of her in miniature. This is indeed BABYLON THE GREAT. She affects the style and title of our Holy Mother, the Church; but she is, in truth, the mother of harlots and abominations of the earth."[120]

---

120   Here we see Adam Clarke quoting from Newton's *Dissertations on the Prophecies*, which were completed in 1754.

So this chapter opens with the woman still in control of the ten horns (kingdoms) in Europe, and God is taking careful note to bring us into remembrance. The papacy has had miraculous sway over these nations for centuries. However, the period of time given her has run out. It was a time (1,260 years) given for repentance, but she repented not. Suddenly, in this very same chapter, the picture drastically changes and the scene becomes deadly for Rome. The nations which she has ridden will suddenly destroy her. My friends, this could very well happen in our lifetime.

> *6 And I saw the woman drunken with the blood of the saints,*
> *and with the blood of the martyrs of Jesus: and when I saw her,*
> *I wondered with great admiration.*

There is only one body claiming to be the Christian church to whom this will apply. To deny this is to throw centuries of history away. God has not forgotten. Only the fearful and unbelieving have deserted this great testimony of martyrdom in Europe.

Summing up these glorious pages of history, the Rev. H. Grattan Guinness stated in his book, *The Approaching End of the Age* (5th ed. p. 212): "It has been calculated that the popes of Rome have, directly or indirectly, slain on account of their faith FIFTY MILLIONS OF MARTYRS." No wonder John looked at this vision in great amazement.

7 And the angel said unto me, Wherefore didst thou marvel? I will tell thee the mystery of the woman, and of the beast that carrieth her, which hath seven heads and ten horns.

Mystery Of The Woman:	**The false religion**
And Of The Beast:	**The government**
The Seven Heads And Ten Horns	**Europe**

8 The beast that thou sawest was, and is not; and shall ascend out of the bottomless pit, and go into perdition: and they that dwell on the earth shall wonder, whose names were not written in the book of life from the foundation of the world, when they behold the beast that was, and is not, and yet is.

Beast That Was:	**Pagan Rome**
And Is Not:	**Fall of Pagan Rome**
And Yet Is:	**Papal Rome**

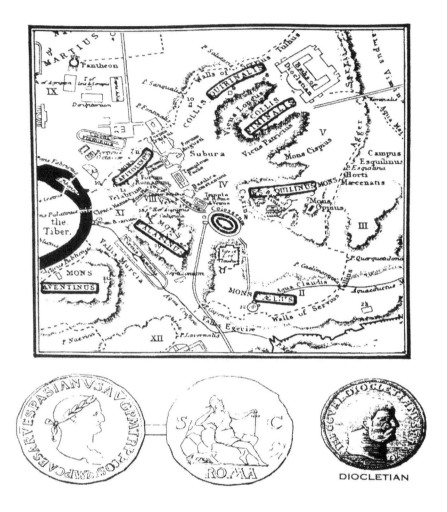

DIOCLETIAN

Above: A map of ancient Rome showing the sites and names of the famous "seven hills." Below is shown a coin of Vespasian, 79 A.D., with Imperial Rome symbolized as a woman sitting on the seven hills.

Illustion taken from: *The Pope, Communism and the Coming New World* by Thomas Foster

9 And here is the mind which hath wisdom. The seven heads are seven mountains [Palatine, Quirinal, Aventine, Caelian, Viminal, Esquiline, and the Janiculan], *on which the woman sitteth.* [Strongs indicates that the Greek word used here for mountain is "oros" and that it means "a mountain (as lifting itself above the plain), hill, mount[ain]."]

10 And there are seven kings [Basileus-foundations of power]: *five are fallen, and one is, and the other is not yet come; and when he cometh, he must continue a short space.*

11 And the beast that was, and is not, even he is eight, and is of the seven, and goeth into perdition.

The apostle John is given a great revelation as to the identity of the *"beast, that was and is not, and yet is."* In the Book of Revelation, this is the third appearance of the ten-horned beast. Historically, remember, it first appeared as Rome Pagan, then transitioned into Rome Papal. Its third appearance is for our time, manifesting itself in the European Economic Community (EEC), embracing a socialist mentality.

John told us that we must look toward the seven-hilled city to properly recognize this beast. This city could only be Rome.

In St. John's time Rome was called (as it is to this very day) the seven-hilled city. I have already identified the historic names of the seven hills. The seven-hilled city of Rome also had an annual national festival called *Septimontiun,* "The Festival of Seven Mountains *(septem montes)."*

On the coins and imperial medals of John's day, which are still located in various museums, we find Rome proudly displayed as a woman sitting on seven hills, the unchallenged matron of the world as it was then, even as she is represented in the Book of Revelation.

This "BABYLON" of Revelation was still in the future in John's day and although it would be located in the seven-hilled city it was to be different from the pagan empire. In fact it would be spiritual. Cardinal Bellarmine was one of Rome's greatest thinkers and controversialists, and he declared, "John, in the Apocalypse calls Rome Babylon." Another great Roman writer, Cardinal Baronius, said, "Rome is signified by Babylon; it is confessed of all." Bishop Bossuet, another of their thinkers, said, "All the Fathers taught that the Babylon of the Apocalypse is Rome." In like manner Bishop Walmsley, Alcazar and numerous other Roman Catholic theologians have admitted the same.[121]

In order to answer this perplexity (actually, it's a revelation), we must look at the history of Rome. It is not well known that she had seven forms of government (or foundations of power) before the eighth appeared. In his great work, *The Approaching End of the Age,* p. 162, H. Grattan Guinness identified these distinct forms of sovereignty:

> The great Roman power did actually exist under seven distinct ... forms of government, enumerated by Livy, Tacitus, and historians in general, as such. Rome was ruled successively by KINGS, CONSULS, DICTATORS, DECEMVIRS, MILITARY TRIBUNES, MILITARY EMPERORS [Caesars], AND DESPOTIC EMPERORS,
> [emphasis mine].

---

121   David Campbell, *Signs Are for Strangers,* page 42.

Guinness went on to say on page 170:

> Seven kings formed the first head, and lasted 220 years; consuls, tribunes, decemvirs [a council of 10 magistrates which lasted from B.C. 451-499 and drew up the law code of the Twelve Tables], and dictators, were the next four heads, and governed Rome in turn for nearly 500 years; sixty-five emperors followed, and ruled the Roman world for 500 years more. Now the man of sin, Antichrist, is to be the last [eighth], and the most important "head" of this same Roman beast.

We must understand that John wrote the Revelation during the time of the Caesars. The prophecy stated, *"five are fallen."* The kings, consuls, dictators, decemvirs, and military tribunals had all passed away (fallen). *"And one is,"* the sixth or present form, the Caesars. *"And the other is not yet come."* These were the emperors, the seventh form.

John said that after the first seven forms of government passed away, another (the eighth) would arise and go into perdition. After the last emperor was toppled in A.D. 476, the eighth form of Roman government, the papacy, ascended into power. Who dares deny that it was *"of the seven"* before it? Does the pope, to this very day, claim the title *Pontifex Maximus,* which was held by all the Roman emperors? Simple to understand, isn't it? This is no mystery, it's a revelation.

And Goeth Into Perdition: The Greek translation of the word perdition is *apolia.* This is the same word that Christ applied to his betrayer Judas. He called him the *"son of perdition (apolia)"* (John 17:12). This condemnation is apostolic in its connotation. It denotes wicked and rebellious apostolic authority. How marvelously has the Book of Revelation applied this term to the "eighth" form of Roman government-the papacy. It claims to be apostolic, therefore it justly receives this condemnation.

> *12 And the ten horns, which thou sawest are ten kings, which*
> *have received no kingdom as yet; but receive power as kings one*
> *hour with the beast.*
> *13 These have one mind, and shall give their power and strength*
> *unto the beast.*

The angel is reminding John about the historic cycle and transition of Rome Pagan to the ten-horned kingdom of Rome Papal. The ten horns were presented in Chapter 12, verse 3, and the transition in Chapter 13, verses 1-5. These ten kings or kingdoms did not exist in the time of John, but should later receive authority in the "same hour" to do the will of the resurrected beast.

For One Hour: The Greek words for "one hour" are *mia hara,* translated "one season." We have already seen the carnage produced by these ten horns and the papal beast which governed them (was their mind). Millions fell prey to this most horrific scenario.

> *14 These shall make war against the Lamb, and the Lamb shall*
> *overcome them: for He is Lord of lords, and King of kings; and*
> *they that are with Him are called chosen, and faithful.*

Who can deny the aid that was given to the papacy by the medieval nations in Europe? Aid that was used by the false church in its war on the saints. By the confirmation of history and the glory of the written prophetic, we know that this war lasted for 1,260 years. Christ truly has overcome these horns, for the gospel is now being preached more than at any time in recorded history. It will continue to accelerate until the *"stone"* becomes a *"great mountain"* and fills the whole earth.

> 15 And he said unto me, The waters which thou sawest, where
> the whore sitteth, are peoples, and multitudes, and nations and
> tongues.

See verse 2 and Revelation 13:7. This is another wonderful example of the use of **metaphors.** The *"waters"* are not literal rivers, lakes or oceans. They are symbolic; they are metaphors. This pattern never changes in the Book of Revelation, no matter what the silly futurists say.

> 16 And the ten horns which thou sawest upon the beast, these
> shall hate the whore, and shall make her desolate, and naked,
> and shall eat her flesh, and burn her with fire.
> 17 For God hath put in their hearts to fulfill His will, and to
> agree, and give their kingdom unto the beast, until the words
> of God shall be fulfilled.

THE REBELLION OF EUROPE AND
THE DESTRUCTION OF THE PAPACY

Verse 3 of this chapter informs us that the *"woman"* (Catholicism) is now sitting on a *"scarlet-colored beast."* The beast now receives the metaphor of being "red." Its nature is changing. Something has transpired which produced this change of complexion. The change began with the French Revolution (review the Vials). This was the introduction of *communism* to the world. Fueled with the ideology of the Revolution, the nations which once so willingly served the woman, began to hate the whore and burn her with the fire of their fury. The effects of the French Revolution are still manifesting themselves according to the Book of Revelation.

In the year 1957 the European Economic Community (Common Market) was created under the TREATY OF ROME! This should open the eyes of true prophetic students. I believe that this is the final revival of the ten KINGDOMS and they will unite because God has put it in their hearts to destroy the church of Rome, though they understand it not. Rome is pictured trying to ride the red beast; however, it will turn on her and make her desolate.

Therefore, I believe that the stage is set for the greatest political earthquake of all time, the fall of Babylon (see Revelation 16:18,19). Europe will be consumed with the RED BEAST of Euro socialism/communism, and this ideology is dangerously hostile towards the Vatican.

To quote Campbell, "The pseudo-rock (THE POPE) will be smashed in Europe by these forces, and the pseudo-church (CATHOLICISM) will be smashed, because it will be the time of God's judgment." This is exactly what verses 16-18 tell us. There is no getting around it. Rome can court this fury all she wants, but it will not stay the hand of God. She is destined to fall, and how great a fall it will be!

> *18 And the woman which thou sawest is that great city, which reigneth over the kings of the earth.*

If you will look at Revelation 16:19, you will see that this *"great city"* is called *"Babylon."* And this chapter has made it clear that Babylon is synonymous with Rome (her spiritual city). Yet some of the futurists try to convince us that America is the Babylon of the Book of Revelation. God help us.

REVELATION CHAPTER 18
BABYLON THE GREAT IS FALLEN
"REJOICE OVER HER"

Having looked at the opening of the Seventh Vial (Chapter 16:17-21), we now see a further clarification of the effects on the great and deadly anti-Christian power—Rome papal, to include Babylon corporate. There is a Babylon spiritual, Babylon politic, and Babylon economic, and the whole lot is going to come crumbling down when *"the saints of the most High … take the kingdom, and possess the kingdom…"* (Daniel 7:18).

Rev. R. H. Harms expressed what I believe to be the proper attitude for approaching this magnificent chapter of victory over these vile institutions. He stated:

> The idea here is that this "Mystical Babylon"—papal Rome, will be reduced to a state of utter desolation resembling that of ancient Babylon. The prediction is not against Rome as a city merely, but Rome as the Seat of the "Beast" or Papacy, and the home of the "Harlot" (chapter 17:9).
> Let me say here that it is the Roman Catholic System that God hates, and that we are to hate, and not the Roman Catholic people. We are to love those unfortunate victims of deception and delusion, doing all in our power to rescue them from the predicted ruin of the System (v. 4).[122]

With great anticipation, let's see what lies just ahead for our great enemy.

---

122   R.H. Harms, *Protestant Page. ,* page 201. Christian Evangelistic Assemblies, Long Beach, California.

1 After these things, I saw another Angel come down from heaven, having great power, and the earth was lightened with his glory.

2 And he cried rightly with a strong voice saying, Babylon the great is fallen, is fallen, and is become the habitation of devils, and the hold of every foul spirit, and a cage of every unclean and hateful bird.

3 For all nations have drunk of the wine of the wrath of her fornication, and the kings of the earth have committed fornication with her, and the merchants of the earth are waxed rich through the abundance of her delicacies ["the power of her luxury" R. V. margin].

This vision reveals to us that just prior to the destruction of Babylon there will be a great illumination upon her history, character, and age-old deceptions. These strong appeals are clearly founded upon centuries of wickedness, which have ultimately revealed her thoughts and intents. God, in His mercy, will make this judgment plain for all to see, and in this forewarning He sheds forth His mercy. E. P. Cachemaille noted:

> At the time corresponding with the opening of this chapter, the actual sudden destruction of Babylon has not yet taken place. There is first (v. 2, 3) some awful change in her for the worse, some great moral downfall, now recognized and proclaimed far and wide over the earth. Then (v. 4-7) a warning voice to any of God's people who may still be in her, at their peril; together with a declaration of the retributive character of the judgment now imminent. After which (v. 8-21), the long delayed destruction come upon her all in a moment, and she disappears like a millstone flung into the sea.[123]

---

123   E.P Cachemaille, *The Visions of Daniel and the Revelation Explained*, page 616.

I don't need to say much more about these first three verses, because it has been covered in Chapter 17. But it is profitable to our understanding if we take notice in verse 3 of the first mention of "merchants." The Moffat translation calls them "traders." The Amplified New Testament translates it "the businessmen of the earth." It will help us if we remember that when the Book of Revelation speaks of the "earth" it means the Roman earth, or the part of the globe which lay in its ancient parameters.

> *4 And I heard another voice from heaven, saying, Come out of*
> *her, MY PEOPLE, that ye be not partakers of her sins, and that*
> *ye receive not of her plagues.*

This commandment to God's people is very clear. The Spirit of God is pleading, "Get out and stay out!" This is not optional. Furthermore, it is a direct rebuke to the concept of ecumenism.

This institution is in imminent peril; she has committed undescribable spiritual whoredom, and her judgment will not be delayed. Dear reader, please take further note of the fact that this verse devastates the rapture doctrine. The futurists teach that it transpired in chapter four; however, here in Chapter 18 Christians *("my people")* are still struggling with Babylon.

> *5 For her sins have reached unto heaven, and God hath remem-*
> *bered her iniquities.*
> *6 Reward her even as she rewarded you, and double unto her*
> *double according to her works: in the cup which she hath filled,*
> *fill to her double.*
> *7 How much she hath glorified herself and lived deliciously, so*
> *much torment and sorrow give her, for she saith in her heart,*

I sit a Queen, [This is where we are now!] *and am no widow, and shall see no sorrow.*

8 Therefore, shall her plagues come in one [prophetic] *day; and mourning, and famine, and she shall be utterly burned with fire* [Revelation 17:16], *for strong is the Lord God, who judgeth her.*

This great prophetic language needs little interpretation. I believe it speaks loud and clear about the Catholic church, which throughout 13 centuries ruthlessly crushed MILLIONS of voices that rose up to protest her sins. The late great historicist and church historian David Campbell expressed:

It is estimated that about 100,000 French Protestants were slain during the St. Bartholomew Day Massacre. Ten thousand alone in Paris (see *The Approaching End of the Age* by Grattan Guinness, pp. 202-212). Men and women of devout and pious conviction, from the days of the Waldensians and the Wycliffites onwards, who refused to accept, and protested against her many heretical teachings, these men, with their women and children, were openly massacred, and the papacy struck medals to commemorate the fact that, as they put it, God had used them as His instrument to wipe out the heretical Protestants. The blood of these pious people flowed freely over the centuries, but God has not forgotten, and He is going to mete out to spiritual Babylon (who has been drunk with the blood of the saints) DOUBLE JUDGMENT in one prophetic hour.

Friends, midnight hour is about to strike.[124]

---

124   David Campbell, *Signs Are for Strangers,* pages 50,51.

With the mixture of future and past combined with the present, John continues to paint the picture of this swiftly approaching catastrophe.[125] Now, from verses 9-24 we are swept into the chaos of the nations which are directly and drastically affected by the disintegration of Babylon, these being the nations of the European Economic Community. The economic ramifications of the prophetic utterances are plain to see.

> 9 *And the kings of the earth, who have committed fornication* [i.e. spiritual idolatry, etc.] *and lived deliciously with her, shall bewail her and lament for her, when they shall see the smoke of her burning* [see again Revelation 17:16].
>
> 10 *Standing afar off for the fear of her torment, saying, Alas, alas, that great city Babylon, that mighty city: for in one hour is thy judgment come* [see Revelation 17:12].
>
> 11 *And the merchants of the earth shall weep and mourn over her, for no man buyeth their merchandise any more.*

The Amplified New Testament expounds verse 11 as follows: "And earth's businessmen weep and grieve over her, because no one buys their freight [cargo] any more." We must remember that the European Economic Community was formed with the Treaty of Rome, 1957. Roman Catholicism is totally intertwined with the heartbeat of Europe's economic system. It is estimated by some scholars that the Vatican owns one-third of Europe's real estate.

The following verses, 12 and 13, reveal a list of merchandising articles which help clarify the economic implications presented in the prophecy. Beyond all reasonable doubt, the Bible is revealing the breakdown of a

---

125   The reader is strongly encouraged to read Jeremiah's dirge over the Babylon of the Old Testament in Chapters 50 and 51, and Isaiah's predicted doom of ancient Babylon in Chapter 47. It is there that the foundation for this vision was laid.

great economic system which is dependent upon the prosperity of spiritual Babylon.

> *12 The merchandise of gold, and silver, and precious stones, and*
> *of pearls, and fine linen, and purple, and silk, and scarlet, and*
> *all thyme* [sweet or scented] *wood, and all manner vessels of*
> *ivory, and all manner vessels* [articles] *of most precious wood,*
> *and of brass, and iron, and marble,*
> *13 And cinnamon, and odours* [spices] *and ointments* [and
> perfume], *and frankincense, and wine, and oil, and fine fiour,*
> *and wheat, and beasts, and sheep, and horses, and chariots*
> [conveyances1 *and slaves and* **SOULS** *of men.*

The prophecy clearly associates the fall of Rome papal with economic chaos in Europe's markets; certainly to create a shock wave and produce worldwide ramifications. Verse 14 continues with words which should spike terror into the hearts of unregenerate men and women.

> *14 And the fruits that thy soul lusted after* **ARE DEPARTED**
> *from thee, and all things which were dainty, and goodly, are*
> **DEPARTED** *from thee, and thou shalt find them no more at all.*

Once again, from verses 15-19, the great merchants, traders and businessmen are brought into focus, and by doing so all those who are determined to profit from the corruptions of economic Babylon are implicated .

> *15 The merchants of these things, which were made rich by her,*
> *shalt stand afar off for the fear of her torment, weeping and wailing,*

16 And saying, Alas, alas, that great city which was clothed in fine linen, and purple, and scarlet, and decked with gold, and precious stones, and pearls!

17 For in one hour so great riches is come to nought. And every shipmaster, and all the company in ships, and sailors, and as many as trade by sea, stood afar off,

18 And cried when they saw the smoke of her burning, saying, What city is like unto this great city!

19 And they cast dust on their heads, and cried, weeping and wailing, saying, Alas, alas, that great city, wherein were made rich all that had ships in the sea by reason of her costliness! for in one hour is she made desolate. [See Revelation 17:16.]

What a sad and painful commentary this is on Papal Rome and the nations which became drunk with the wine of her spiritual fornication and economic idolatry. The prophet Hosea stated: *"For they have sown the wind, and they shall reap the whirlwind"* (Hosea 8:7). Rome sowed the wind of greed, idolatry, and corruption; now she is destined to reap the whirlwind of Christ's righteous anger.[126] Likewise, the prophet Ezekiel is concerned that "with their idols have they committed adultery" (Ezekiel 23:37).

*20 Rejoice over her thou heaven, and ye holy **apostles and prophets;** for God hath avenged you on her.*

Notice carefully that apostles and prophets are still on the scene. If you don't believe that, you have a *serious theological problem.* Your mind-

---

126   Isaiah had something to say about this in Chapter 2 of his prophecy, verses 19-22. The reader is encouraged to read these verses for further insight into God's attitude concerning economic injustice and idolatry.

set was given to you by man's perverted teachings, not the Scriptures. For they clearly state that these offices will continue in the church until the consummation of all things. (See Ephesians 4:11; 1 Corinthians 12:28.)

The Englishman Campbell observed:

> The early Church was built on the teaching of the Apostles and Prophets (Eph. 2:20) and the Church of Rome with her heresies, superstitions, Mariolatry, saint worship and sacrifice of the mass, transubstantiation, indulgences, relics and idolatry, has torn that simple yet profound apostolic foundation of the early Church to shreds, and erected instead a counterfeit church, with a counterfeit system and counterfeit form of worship. God will judge her.[127]

The remaining verses continue to pronounce Babylon's epitaph.

> *21 And a mighty angel took up a stone like a great millstone, and cast it into the sea, saying, Thus WITH VIOLENCE shall that great city Babylon be thrown down, and shall be found no more at all.*
>
> *22 And the voice of harpers and musicians, and of pipers and trumpeters* [the Vatican] *shall be heard no more at all in thee: and no craftsman, of whatsoever craft he be, shall be found any more in thee and the sound of a millstone shall be heard no more at all in thee;*
>
> *23 And the light of a candle shall shine no more at all in thee: and the voice of the bridegroom and of the bride shall be heard no more at all in thee: for thy merchants were the great men of the earth:* ***FOR BY THY SORCERIES WERE ALL NATIONS DECEIVED.***

---

127   David Campbell, *Signs Are for Strangers,* page 53.

24 And IN HER was found the blood of prophets [men like Savanorola, John Huss, Jerome of Prague, Tyndale and thousands of others], *and of saints, and of all that were slain upon the earth.*

And A Strong Angel Took Up A Millstone: Please see Jeremiah 51:61-64. This symbolic act implies a complete destruction. In Jeremiah's prophecy the stone is cast into the Euphrates. Now it is cast into the sea, because another Babylon is implied.

In Her Was Found The Blood Of The Prophets: This is one reason the Most High is judging her, because she has slain His saints. As Jerusalem in the time of our Lord filled up the cup of the sins of Israel (see Matthew 23:29,35,36; Luke 11:51; 13:33), so this spiritual Babylon fills the measure of the sins of the beast and the false prophet, and therefore is required to give account of all which have fallen in the epic struggle.

REASONS FOR THE JUDGEMENT

I have chosen to conclude this chapter with an excerpt from Cachemaille's recorded testimony of a traveler in Spain. One of the reasons for the judgment of Babylon was that *"in her was found the blood of prophets and of saints, and all that have been slain upon the earth."* This naturally implies that a thorough inquiry is made and relevant history investigated. I believe that (in measure) has been produced in this work. However, this Spanish traveler helps us see the great whore as Christ sees and understands it. Here is the testimony of a traveler:

"In the early part of 1870 I crossed the Pyrenees, and on reaching Madrid went with a friend to see the newly opened Quemadero. Some workmen employed in cutting a road across the summit of a low hill close to the city had inadvertently dug into a broad bank of ashes, which had been buried for one or two centuries. Mingled with the ashes they had found a large quantity of charred human bones, together with fragments of rusted iron and melted lead. The spot was speedily verified as the famous Quemadero, or place of burning, one of twelve places where so-called 'heretics' were annually burned in Spain, during the reign of the Inquisition. I found the road had been cut through the centre of this bank of blackened bones and ashes. The strange stratum displayed seemed about six feet in depth, and covered quite a large area. There, then, exposed to the light of day, were the ashes of Spanish martyrs. I stood in silence, and looked at the ghastly monument. I had seen before not a little of Romanism on the continent and in other countries, and had read of the multitude of martyrs who had suffered cruel deaths in past centuries at the hands of Spanish priests and inquisitors, on account of their faith in the pure Gospel of the grace of God, and their opposition to Popish superstitions and idolatries. Now, for the first time, I found myself face to face with a terrible demonstration of the truth of these histories. There, lying before me, were the bones and ashes of Spanish confessors and martyrs who had suffered death at the stake. I could examine them and satisfy myself of their character. I could handle them, and did. Reverently, I removed some burnt bones from the general masse and wrapped them, together with a quantity of ashes, in a Spanish newspaper which I still possess, bearing the date of the day...

"The reluctance to shed blood, which had so honorably distinguished the Fathers, completely passed away [in the twelfth century], or, if we find any trace of it, is only in the quibble by which the Church referred the execution of her mandates to the civil magistrate. Who, as we have seen, was not permitted to delay that execution for more than six days, under pain of excommunication. Almost all Europe, for many centuries, was inundated with blood, which was shed at the direct instigation or with the full approval of the ecclesiastical authorities, and under the pressure of a public opinion that was directed by the Catholic clergy, and was the exact measure of their influence.

"That the Church of Rome has shed more innocent blood than any other institution that has ever existed among mankind, will be questioned by no Protestant that has a competent knowledge of history [emphasis mine]. The memorials, indeed, of many of her persecutions are now so scanty, that it is impossible to form a complete conception of the multitude of her victims, and it is certain that no powers of imagination can adequately realize their sufferings … These atrocities were not perpetrated in the brief paroxysms of a reign of terror, or by the hands of obscure sectaries, but were inflicted by a triumphant Church, with every circumstance of solemnity and deliberation."[128]

"Rejoice aver her, thou heaven, and ye holy apostles and prophets: for **God** *hath avenged you* **on** *her."*

(Revelation 18:20)

OUR LORD JESUS CHRIST ALLOCATE'S CHAPTERS, 17 & 18, IN HIS GLORIOUS REVEALING TO THE JUDGMENT OF THE GREAT WHORE!

Significance:

Judgment of Rome Pagan in the West (Gothic)	7 verses
Judgment at the hands of the Mohamadins, Rev. 9	12 verses
Judgment at the hands of the Turks, Rev. 9	9 verses
TOTAL	28 verses

---

128   E.P. Cachemaille, *The Visions of Daniel and of the Revelation Explained,* pages 620-622. (This testimony and commentary was extracted from Lecky's *Rationalism in Europe,* Ch. IV)

Verses allotted in Rev. 17 & 18 to the judgment of the harlot church during the 7th vial:

TOTAL   42 verses

REVELATION CHAPTER 19
THE KINGDOM OF CHRIST CONQUERS
THAT OF THE BEAST BY GOD'S WORD

B. W. Johnson concisely and accurately introduced this chapter in his notes. He observed:

> The 19th chapter of Revelation describes some of the events that precede the full acknowledgment of the reign of Christ among the children of men. These have been partly described in preceding chapters. In chapter 14:6 the apostle points out the mighty strides of the gospel of Christ. In succeeding verses he announces the fall of Babylon, a mighty event which is more fully described in succeeding chapters. In chapter 16:13 the gathering of the united hosts of the dragon, the beast, and the false prophet, to the battle of Armageddon is pointed out. This is the battle in which shall take place the final overthrow of the allied powers which have exerted so malign an influence on the earth. But before this catastrophe is fully explained the apostle brings in a delineation of the great spiritual apostasy under the form of a harlot, then changes the symbol to a city, alludes to its fate, and in an episode, pictures the mourning over its destruction. In chapter 19, the opening part is a picture of heavenly rejoicings over the great victory about to be won, and then the events that lead up to the great battle are introduced.[129]

---

129   B.W. Johnson, *The People's New Testament With Notes,* page 491.

Please keep in mind that Chapters 19 and 20 are PARALLEL chapters.

> *1 And after these things I heard a great voice of much people in heaven, saying, Alleluia; Salvation, and glory, and honor, and power, unto the Lord our God:*
>
> *2 For true and righteous are His judgments; for He hath judged the great whore, which did corrupt the earth with her fornication, and hath avenged the blood of his servants at her hand.*
>
> *3 And again they said, Alleluia. And her smoke rose up for .ever and ever.*
>
> *4 And the four and twenty elders and the four beasts fell down and worshipped God that sat on the throne, saying,. Amen; Alleluia.*
>
> *5 And a voice came out of the throne, saying, Praise our God, all ye servants, and ye that fear Him, both small and great.*

These songs of praise, rejoicing, and thanksgiving are experienced in the Book of Revelation whenever a great triumph or blessing is about to occur. (See 5:13; 7:12; 11:15; 12:19.) Here Christ is receiving great adoration for what He has accomplished by delivering the Church from its persecutions and causing it to triumph in spectacular proportions over its enemies. The repetition of the word *"Alleluia"* shows the magnitude of the joy expressed by the hosts of heaven in clear view of this victory.

> *6 And I heard as it were the voice of a great multitude, and as the voice of many waters, and as the voice of mighty thunderings, saying, Alleluia; for the Lord God omnipotent reigneth.*
>
> *7 Let us be glad and rejoice, and give honor to Him: for the marriage of the Lamb is come, and His wife hath made herself ready.*

The Marriage Of The Lamb Is Come: It would seem as if this event was yet in the future, but the parable of the marriage feast recorded in Matthew 22:1-14, is all that is needed to explain this prophetic language. In Christ, we have already attained to this event. Yet the prophecy signifies that the True Israel, at this point of triumph, attains to permanent union with her husband.

The Parable of the Marriage Feast is a Kingdom parable. Jesus compared the marriage to the *"kingdom of heaven,"* (v.1). He then goes on and states that, *"all things are ready: come unto the marriage,"* {v.4}. And in verse 8 he exclaimed, *"The wedding is ready!"* It is evident that the marriage feast was not postponed for thousands of years. That's dispensational thinking. Christ proclaimed it ready during his ministry. The Jews rejected this affair, and the king [Jesus] destroyed those *"murderers,"* (v.7). So his servants went to the nations ("James a servant of God and to the Lord Jesus Christ, to the twelve tribes which are scattered abroad, greeting." James 1:1) and gathered them in. This process has not ceased.

His Wife Hath Made Herself Ready: What a great testimony to the growth principle of the Kingdom. The "bride" has now matured into a full functioning *"wife."* She grew into maturity, and is now prepared to rule. It's just that simple.[130]

> *8 And to her it was granted that she should be arrayed in fine linen, clean and white: for the fine linen is the righteousness of the saints.*
> *9 And he saith unto me, Write, Blessed are they which are called unto the marriage-supper of the Lamb. And he saith unto me, These are the true sayings of God.*

---

130   Truth In History – www.truthinhistory.org – "The Bride of Christ" by Karl Tester

We must understand that it is not the saint's perfection, it is God's righteousness in which we are clothed. There is "old Adam" in the most perfect Christian. (See I Corinthians 15:22.) This is why Isaiah stated: *"I will greatly rejoice in the Lord … for **He hath clothed me with the garments of salvation, He hath covered me with the** robe **of righteousness**, as a bridegroom decketh himself with ornaments, and as a bride adorneth herself with her jewels … So the Lord God will cause righteousness and praise to spring forth before all the nations"* (Isaiah 61:10,11).

> *10 And I fell at his feet to worship him. And he said unto me, See thou do it not; I am thy fellow-servant, and of thy brethren, that have the testimony of Jesus: worship God: for the testimony of Jesus is the spirit of prophecy.*

And I Fell At His Feet: In this verse, and in 22:7,8, John offered worship to a fellow creature, here being an angel. In each occurrence the prohibition is immediate. This seems to be introduced to show us the sinfulness of any creature worship-something the great apostate church failed to learn. Man, who is created in God's image, is to worship Christ only-not popes, saints, angels, relics, Mary…

It is interesting that this angel declares himself *"of thy brethren."* [Israel] In 22:9, he added, *"of thy brethren, the prophets."* Then the explanation is added that the testimony of Jesus is the spirit of prophecy. In testifying of Jesus, the angel became one of the prophets. The rest of this prophecy, verses 11-21, entails warfare between godly spiritual powers and satanic powers. We have seen this struggle in Chapter 13, verses 4-10, and Chapter 17, verses 13-14. True interpretation of the prophetic language has established the fact that this conflict was to be *long in duration* but of certain outcome.[131]

> *11 And I saw heaven opened, and behold a white horse; and He that sat upon him was called Faithful*
> *and True; and in righteousness He doth judge and make war.*
> *12 His eyes were as a flame of fire, and on His head were many crowns; and He had a name written that no man knew but He Himself:*
> *13 And He was clothed with a vesture dipped in blood, and His name is called The Word of God.*
> *14 And the armies which were in heaven followed Him upon white horses, clothed in fine linen, white and clean.*
> *15 And out of His mouth goeth a sharp sword, that with it He should smite the nations: and He shall rule them with a rod of iron: and He treaded the wine press of the fierceness and wrath of Almighty God.*
> *16 And He had on His vesture and on His thigh a name written, KING OF KINGS, AND LORD OF LORDS.*

And I Saw The Heaven Open: Again, this implies the unveiling of a new vision. (See 4:1; 11:19.) This is not the continuation of a former vision. That formula was accompanied by the phrase, *"After these things."* However, this series of pictures prepares us to grasp the intensity of the events which will destroy the governments of man and establish the eternal authority of the Kingdom of God. Concerning the illegitimate governments of man Daniel prophesied that they *"became like the chaff of the summer threshing floors; and the wind carried them away, that no place was found for them..."* (Daniel 2:35).

---

131   For further insight, cross reference Dan. 7:25-27; Isa. 11:1-10; Eph. 6:11-17; 2 Cor. 10:3-6; 11:23-33; 12:1-10.

Behold A White Horse: This is always the metaphor for conquest and triumph. (See notes on 6:2.) And this is not the fulfillment of Acts 1:11, the Ascension scene. Jesus did not go to heaven on a white horse. This verse is informing us that the Word of God will ride prosperously. Please compare Psalms 45:4 with Acts 6:7; 12:23, 24; 19:20. The militant Church is determined to wage spiritual warfare until we attain a final victory and all Christ's enemies are conquered, but our warfare is not with carnal weapons, 2 Corinthians 10:4, 5. It was the Jews who thought that Messiah would come back to physically conquer their hated enemies with the literal sword. This misinterpretation cost them their inheritance and their nation![132]

Verses 12 and 13 present to us symbolic language consistent with the Revelation. From Chapter 1, verse 14 we acquire this burning picture of authority and confrontation, and the name which distinguishes him from all other beings is revealed to us in John's gospel Chapter 1, verse 1. The vesture dipped in blood is always before the throne—for our sakes.

And The Armies Which Were In Heaven: The Bible clearly teaches us that we are in heaven with Jesus, though our bodies are here. Paul emphasized this several times. For example he stated that God has presently blessed us in *"heavenly places in Christ"* (Ephesians 1:3). He went on in the Ephesian epistle and emphasized that God, *"hath raised us up together, and made us sit together in heavenly places in Christ Jesus"* (Ephesians 2:6). In the light of this apostolic teaching we must interpret the vision. The Biblical commentator, Albert Barnes, forces us to think soberly about this vision. He observed: "Doubtless the original of this picture is Isaiah 63:3: *'I have trodden the wine press alone, and of the people there was none with me.'* These hosts of the redeemed on white horses accompany him to be witnesses of his victory, and to participate in the joy of triumph, *not to engage in the work of blood* [emphasis mine]."[133]

132　　The following Scriptures elaborate further: Heb. 4:12-13; 12:25-28; ICor. 15:25; Rev. 1:16; 11:15-17; Ps. 110:1; Dan. 7:25-27.

133　　Albert Barnes, *Notes on the New Testament,* "Revelation," page 413.

A Sharp Sword: This could only be the Word of God as it penetrates the hearts of men to the point of redemption, or creates a work of destruction upon his foes. (See 2 Thessalonians 2:8; Isaiah 60:12.) The *"rod of iron"* likewise is His Word. The prophet Isaiah revealed that *"with righteousness shall He judge the poor, and reprove with equity for the meek of the earth: and He* **shall smite the earth with the rod of his mouth, and with the breath of His lips shall He slay the wicked"** (Isaiah 11:4).

In the process of revealing this surge of the Kingdom, the vision presented to us three glorious titles of our Lord, *"Faithful and True* (11); *"The Word of God"* (13); and *"KING OF KINGS, AND LORD OF LORDS* (16).

If you are still waiting for this white horse rider to lead the armies of heaven, I encourage you to consider very carefully the understanding of Paul. He claimed that Christ was on the white horse at the time he wrote to Timothy. First Timothy 6:15 states: *"Which in his times he shall show, who is the blessed and only Potentate, the King of kings, and Lord of lords."*

> *17 And I saw an angel standing in the sun; and he cried with a loud voice, saying to all the fowls that fly in the midst of heaven, Come and gather yourselves together unto the supper of the great God; That ye may eat the flesh of kings, and the flesh of captains, and the flesh of mighty men, and the flesh of horses, and of them that sit on them, and the flesh of all men, both free and bond, both small and great.*

Well, as the humorous proverb states, "You're either going to a supper, or you'll be the supper!" Silly, yet profound. We either participate in the marriage supper of the Lamb, or we become the feast of the fowls. Of course, this is highly symbolic. (Compare Isaiah 18:6; 56:9; see also Jeremiah 7:33; 12:9; Ezekiel 39:4-20.)

19 And I saw the beast, and the kings of the earth, and their
armies, gathered together, to make war
against him that sat on the horse, and against his army.
20 And the beast was taken, and with him the
false prophet that wrought miracles before him, with which he
deceived them that had received the mark of the beast, and them
that worshipped his image. These both were cast alive into a lake
of fire burning with brimstone.
21 And the remnant were slain with the sword of
Him that sat upon the horse, which sword proceeded out of His
mouth: and all the fowls were filled with their flesh.

I Saw The Beast: My notes on Chapter 13, verses 1-10, do not need to be repeated here. In summation, this beast represents the focal world power opposed to true Christianity under its changing forms. The two primary forms were the Roman Pagan Empire and the Roman Papal Empire. The Revelation has revealed to us that it even continues after the primary duration of these two forms have passed away. The final form is yet for history to record.

And The Beast Was Taken: He is now finally overthrown. These wicked entities, the false prophet, the beast, and the dragon were previously identified in Chapter 16 as calling the rulers of the earth together for the battle of Armageddon. Please refer to those notes. This is the same conflict. The difference is that in this verse the results of that conflict are revealed.

Cast Alive Into The Lake Of Fire: The symbolism is clear. What is cast into that lake is seen no more. This metaphor speaks of her utter destruction.

Remnant Were Slain With The Sword: Again, vindication of the teaching that all of Christ's enemies will ultimately be conquered by the Word!

THE COMING OF CHRIST

A challenging and thought provoking summation by B. W. Johnson:

"The coming of Christ, pictured in this chapter, has been seized upon by the advocates of His visible coming before the millennial period which is described in the next chapter. They insist that the passage embraced in verses 11-16 describes a personal coming which shall be visible to the eyes of all men, and which is the coming so often referred to in the Scriptures. To this it might be objected: (1) That the language of this description is all the language of symbolism. None expect that when the Lord comes, He will be seen riding on a white horse with an army following Him riding on white horses, and having a name 'written on His vesture and on His thigh.' The language is undoubtedly symbolic. (2) If this be His coming to judgment of which He spoke in Matt. 24:30, Luke 21:27, Matt. 25:31 and described by Paul in 1 Thess. 4:16, Revelation does not rightly describe it. He declares that He shall come on the clouds of heaven preceded and heralded by the trump of the archangel. The coming described in Revelation is evidently not the one meant by our Lord. (3) This personal, visible coming of the Lord is always associated with the Last Judgment. See Matt 25:31-34; I Cor. 15:23; 2 Thess. 2:8, etc. The Scriptures only recognize *one visible* Return or Coming of Christ. Now, the Last Judgment is not reached in Revelation until we come to chapt. 20:11. Here it is placed after the metaphor of the thousand year period. Hence, we must conclude that the *Visible* Return of the Lord does not take place before the symbolic thousand years, and that chapt. 19:11-16 describes a coming in power, the power of His Word, but not a visible coming. (4) It is objected that in 20:11 nothing is said of the coming of Christ. It is said (Matt 25:31) that when the Lord comes He shall be seated on the throne of judgment, and in

Rev. 20:11 John sees this throne and the Lord sitting on the throne. He does not describe here His coming, but shows Him already come and engaged in judgment."[134].

---

134   **B.W.** Johnson, *The People's Notes on the New Testament,* page 494

REVELATION CHAPTER 20
THE SYMBOLIC MILLENNIUM

It is imperative that this chapter be prefaced with an awareness of just how foreign the teaching of a *literal Millennium* was, not only to Christ, His apostles, and the epistles they produced, but to the vast majority of Christian scholars over the last 15 centuries.

Emma Weston, wife of the late Charles Gilbert Weston, who gave us the *Weston Study Bible,* in an article entitled, "Is Dispensational Teaching 'Another Gospel?' " addressed the biblical and historical perspective around this issue. She stated:

"Did you know that the modern teaching of a secret rapture of the church, a seven-year tribulation, and a literal thousand-year reign of Christ on earth are not found in the Bible?

"The current popular millennial teaching is found in some Bible notes and writings of teachers who practice private interpretation and quote from writings of some early church fathers who believed in it. However, this teaching was not part of the belief of the church after A.D. 431. The Reformers, Luther, Calvin, and Knox, and the fathers of the Great Awakening, such as Wesley, Whitfield, and Finney, did not believe in it. But, even if they had accepted it, that bears no real weight. The important issue is, what did Jesus say about it? Nothing! Absolutely nothing!

"What did the Apostle Paul say about it? Nothing! Absolutely nothing!

"What did the other Epistle writers say about it? Nothing! Not one word!

"What does the Apostles' Creed say about it? Nothing at all. This centuries-old statement of faith of the church declares [abridged]: 'I believe in God the Father Almighty, maker of heaven and earth, and in Jesus Christ, His only Son, our Lord… He ascended into heaven, and sitteth on the right hand of God... From thence He shall come to judge the quick and the dead...' (In one coming.)

"Some teachers insert a line after **FROM THENCE**. They would have it read, 'From thence He shall come to set up an earthly kingdom for a thousand years,' and then He shall come to judge the quick and the dead.

"The Scripture does not bear this out. Where, then, did it come from?[135]

"The earthly kingdom doctrine was taught by the Pharisees. The Messiah would come, conquer their enemies, and set up a literal kingdom. This is what the disciples had in mind when they asked Jesus, 'Wilt thou at this time restore the kingdom to Israel?' They did not understand why Jesus did not set about doing this very thing. However, after Pentecost they never mention again this 'doctrine of the Pharisees' that Jesus had warned them about.

"The whole contrived millennial theory of a thousand-year reign of Christ on earth, depends on a literal and incorrect interpretation of one portion of Scripture, Rev. 20:1-7. A thorough search of all the Bible and history brings this whole house of cards tumbling down.

"The word 'millennium' is not in the Bible. This Rev. 20:1-7, is a symbolic portion that can not be taken literally. Even if it did mean a literal one thousand years, Jesus said, as He quoted in Mt. 18:16b words from Deut 17:6, '...In the mouth of two or three witnesses every word may be established.' This Rev. 20 is the only witness, and it is not safe to build a whole doctrine on one Scripture portion, especially since the teaching is not backed up by the Gospel writers. It says, 'The *souls* of them that were beheaded ... lived and reigned with Christ a thousand years...' There is nothing about a Second Coming, Jerusalem, a temple, animal sacrifices

---

135   The scholar is urged to obtain the *Weston Study Bible* and examine the excerpt on Millennarianism from the *History of Christian Doctrine,* by W.T. Shedd, D.D., 1892, Chapter I, "Second Advent of Christ," page 389. Also, from Eusebius' *Ecclesiastical History,* Book 3, ch. 28, Popular Edition, the essay entitled "Cerinthus the Heresiarch." Thirdly, the essay entitled "Acharith and Eschaton."

or a literal kingdom. Modern teachers have read into this, words that are not there...

"In Bible usage, one thousand is a round, indefinite number. Psalm 50:10 states, 'Every beast of the forest is mine and the cattle on a thousand hills.' Does that mean only a thousand? Or are all the cattle and all the hills His? 'God keeps covenant and mercy to a thousand generations,' Deut. 7:9. Does His mercy stop there? 'He commanded His word to a thousand generations.' Psalm 105:8. The thousand is not literal in any of these."

Emma Weston brought to light several of the main issues presented by the prophecy and took a look at them based on Scripture and sanctified common sense. This I will continue to do as we unveil the prophecy of Revelation 20.

There are basically three major schools of thought on the millennial topic. The word "Millennium," as Weston pointed out, is not in your Bible. It's the Latin word for "thousand years," an expression which appears six times in the first seven verses of Chapter 20.

One of the views to emerge in the study of this chapter is called "Post-Millennialism." The Evangelist and author John L. Brays presents very concise and accurate abstracts of these major views. Bray summarizes the views starting with Post-Millennialism:

> This view says that this passage in Revelation refers to part of this gospel age, with the effects of the gospel message increasing sufficiently during this age that by the time Christ comes we will have a relatively converted and Christian world order. It says that Christ will come AFTER the thousand years [literal] of such blessed world conditions, hence the prefix "Post" meaning "after."

Another view is called, "Pre-Millennialism." This view says that the passage in Revelation refers to a thousand year period between the second coming of Christ and the final great white throne judgment, during which time Christ will reign on earth from David's throne in Jerusalem. The prefix "Pre" means "before."

Another view is called "A-Millennialism," and the prefix: *"A:"* (meaning "No") signifies a view that does not hold to a literal thousand year period at all, either before or after the second coming of Christ. Rather, it looks on the expression "thousand years" as symbolic of a long period of time, mainly during the gospel age, during which time saints in Heaven [heavenly places] reign with Christ and during which time the Devil's power is limited on earth.[136]

The above author accomplished a very difficult task, because there are several variations to these positions and it would not be expedient to address them all. What I propose is that we let the Scriptures teach us the meaning of the thousand years. I believe that by thoroughly examining the context of the symbolic language we will come to the same conclusion that J. Marcellus Kik did in his excellent book *An Eschatology of Victory.* I encourage every reader to obtain it. Kik stated:

An individual Christian may ask himself this question: "What more could the popular conception of the millennium give me than I already possess? I have a Savior who is my Prophet, Priest, and King. God the Father is my covenant God. I have the forgiveness of sin. I have the promise of eternal life in heaven.

136   John L. Bray, *The Millennium: the big ?,* page 1. (P.O. Box 1778, Lakeland, Florida 33802)

I belong to the Church which is the Lamb's Bride.[Nope—His Body] I have the Holy Spirit. as my Teacher, Sanctifier, and Comforter. I have security against my greatest enemies: Death, Hell, and the Devil. I am standing on Mt. Zion and am a citizen of the Holy City. I belong to the commonwealth of Israel and am not a stranger from the covenants of promise."

"What more does a Christian desire? More material prosperity? Is not the Lord wealth enough? Perhaps we desire less "tribulation, or distress, or persecution, or famine, or nakedness, or peril, or sword?" But are we not in all these things more than conquerors through Him who loves us?[137]

Therefore, let us take the time and effort necessary to unveil the prophetic scenario which Christ presents to us. We will fix ourselves a boundary for our interpretive study. This boundary is Christ's warning, *"The Scriptures cannot be broken!"*

> *1 I saw an angel come down from heaven, having the key of the bottomless pit and a great chain in his hand.*
> *2 And he laid hold on the dragon, that old serpent, which is the Devil and Satan, and bound him a thousand years.*
> *3 And cast him into the bottomless pit, and shut him up, and set a seal upon him, that he should deceive the nations no more, till the thousand years should be fullfilled: and after that he must be loosed a little season.*

The abyss mentioned in verse 1 is named three other times in the Book of Revelation (9:1,11; also 11:7, and 17:8). It symbolizes the pres-

---

137   J. Marcellus Kik, *An Eschatology of Victory,* page 206. Presbyterian and Reformed Publishing Co. Phillipsburg, New Jersey.

ent habitation of Satan and his army of demons. The "chain" is clearly symbolic and signifies a restraining power upon the devil. His power is restricted by a great chain of circumstance.

And Bound Him: Jesus came first to bind Satan, then destroy him. This binding was for the purpose of restricting his power to totally throw entire nations into complete idolatry. (I am not saying that this stops individual temptation.) History records nation after nation, civilization after civilization which existed under one form or another under Satan's complete deception, i.e., Egypt, Assyria, Babylon, Medo-Persia, Greece and finally the Romans. However, the Scriptures and history reveal that Christ turned the tables. Will Durant observed:

> There is no greater drama in human record than the sight of a few Christians, scorned or oppressed by a succession of emperors, bearing all trials with a fierce tenacity, multiplying quietly, building order while their enemies generated chaos, fighting the sword with the Word, brutality with hope, and at last defeating the strongest state that history has known. Caesar and Christ had met in the arena, and Christ had won.[138]

Jesus came and demonstrated His commission by signs and wonders, especially displaying His authority over demons. He said, "But if I cast out devils by the Spirit of God, then the kingdom of God is come unto you" (Matthew 12:28). Jesus proved His Kingdom authority by casting out devils. However, the people reacted and accused Him of doing these wonders by the authority of the Devil. Immediately Jesus responded, "… how can one enter into a strong man's house, and spoil his goods, except he first bind the strong man? and then he will spoil his house" (Matthew 12:29). The message is clear, first "bind" then "spoil" the other's domin-

---

138   Will Durant, *The Story of Civilization III,* "Caesar and Christ," page 652.

ion. This Jesus did. Please note: The word "bind" here is the same word which appears in Revelation 20:2. Christ, in this present age, has bound the devil. It's just that simple.[139]

The Church today needs to awaken to the realization that she has the power to do a better job than she's doing. Our power has been drastically limited by dispensationalism's "other gospel." Marcellus Kik observed:

> Unfortunately the Church of today does not realize the power that Christ has given her. Christ has placed in her hands the chain by which she can bind Satan. She can restrain his influence over the nations. But today the Church bemoans the fact that evil is becoming stronger and stronger. She bemoans the fact that the world is coming more and more under the control of the Devil. Whose fault is that? It is the Church's fault. She has the chain and does not have the faith to bind Satan even more firmly. Satan is bound and the Church knows it not! Satan can be bound more firmly and the Church does it not![140]

A Thousand Years: This symbolic phrase denotes an indefinite period of time (again see Deuteronomy 7:9; Psalm 105:8; 50:10). God is not revealing all the secrets of the times and seasons. Jesus stated emphatically, *"But of that day and that hour knoweth no man, no, not the angels which are in heaven, neither the Son, but the Father"* (Mark 13:32).

And After That He Must Be Loosed A Little Season: Oh, wonderful fulfilled prophecy! And to think about how many who have let this phraseology confuse the interpretation. All that is needed to interpret this statement is an examination of the word *"after."* This word in the

---

139   Other verses which vindicate this understanding are, Lk. 10:17-19; Jn. 12:31; Col. 2:15; Heb. 2:14; Eph. 4:8 and 1 Jn. 3:8.

140   J. Marcellus Kik, *An Eschatology of Victory,* page 196.

Greek is "meta," meaning, *"accompaniment* or *amid."* All John is saying is that accompanying the thousand years, Satan will be allowed a little season of testing. This was fulfilled during his 1,260 years, which we have examined already. Remember in Chapter 12 John stated, *"Woe to the inhabiters of the earth … for the devil is come down to you, having great wrath, because he knoweth that he hath but a short time* [little season!]" (Revelation 12:12). Twice in that chapter the *"short time"* or *"season"* is defined symbolically as the 1,260 years of papal terror; verses 6 and 14. It is no mystery. It's a revelation.

> *4 And I saw thrones, and they that sat upon them, and judgment was given unto them: and I saw the souls of them that were beheaded for the witness of Jesus, and for the word of God, and which had not worshipped the beast, neither his image, neither had received his mark upon their foreheads, or in their hands: and they lived and reigned with Christ a thousand years.*
> *5 But the rest of the dead lived not again until the thousand years were finished. This is the first resurrection.*
> *6 Blessed and holy is he that hath part in the first resurrection: on such the second death hath no power; but they shall be priests of God and of Christ, and shall reign with Him a thousand years.*

We must never forget that we, who are presently in Christ, have entered into the Holy of Holies with Him (see Ephesians 2:4-6; Hebrews 10:19-22; Matthew 12:22-28). Christ is at the right hand of the Father, and He will not leave His throne **UNTIL** He shall come (once) to judge the living and the dead. His commission demands that He rule from the throne until all His enemies are put under His feet Psalm 110:1-4. He cannot and will not leave and sit some where else! He doesn't need to. All power and authority is His **NOW** (Matthew 28:18; 25:31-46).

This Is The First Resurrection: I believe that the key to unlock the interpretation of this chapter was presented to us in the expression: *"This is the first resurrection."* Common sense dictates that if we can determine when the first resurrection occurred we will progress greatly in our understanding of this entire chapter. Therefore, let's go back further and discover when the "first death" occurred.

The revelation of death was first presented to Adam in the garden. God said, *"But of the tree of the knowledge of good and evil, thou shalt not eat of it: for in the day that thou eatest thereof thou shalt surely die"* (Genesis 2:17). This is the death of the soul, because Adam did not immediately die physically. The death of the body came later.

The New Testament vindicates this position. Paul addressed the state of the Ephesians before their salvation. He stated that they were, *"dead in trespasses and sins"* (Ephesians 2:1). Even our Lord said, *"Let the dead bury the dead"* (Matthew 8:22). These dead are dead souls.

It stands to reason that since the Bible presents to us the "first death" as that being of the soul, then it is this dead soul which must be resurrected first. Paul went on and informed the Ephesians: *"Even when we were dead in sins, hath quickened us together with Christ, (by grace ye are saved;) and hath raised us up together, and made us sit together in heavenly places in Christ Jesus"* (Eph. 2:5,6). Take careful note that the word *"quickened"* is translated *"made alive"* (A.R.V.). It is the dead soul which is first made alive. This is God's divine order of events.

I believe the context of these verses (Revelation 20:4-6) is enhanced by Jesus' teaching on the resurrection. He stated, *"But as touching the resurrection of the dead, have ye not read that which was spoken unto you by God, saying, I am the God of Abraham, and the God of Isaac, and the God of Jacob? God is not the God of the dead, but of the living"* (Matthew 22:31,32). The Christian's first resurrectional experience is spiritual; the second is the physical body being raised not only the bodies of the righteous, but also the bodies of the wicked. They are raised **TOGETHER** at the last day, not in a segmented rapture scenario. (See John 5:24,25,28,29; 11:25,26; Job 19:26; Isaiah 26:19; Daniel 12:2.) One is spared from the sad doom of the second death only through the power of the first resurrection. Only the redeemed can live and reign with Christ in this present age.[141]

I Saw The Souls Of Them: Of the martyrs. It could not be plainer. John saw **SOULS,** not bodies.

> *7 And when the thousand years are expired, Satan shall be loosed out of his prison,*
>
> *8 And shall go out to deceive the nations which are in the four quarters of the earth, Gog and Magog, to gather them together to battle; the number of whom is as the sand of the sea.*
>
> *9 And they went up on the breadth of the earth, and compassed the camp of the saints about, and the beloved city: and fire came down out of heaven, and devoured them.*
>
> *10 And the devil that deceived them was cast into the lake of fire and brimstone, where the beast and the false prophet are, and shall be tormented day and night for ever and ever.*

The struggle and warfare shown in these verses **CANNOT** occur after Christ's return. We have already examined the fact that when Christ

---

141   "If any should think such an interpretation of symbolical language far fetched, let him compare Scripture. This explanation is not forced nor the interpretation of the language unusual. It was predicted by the prophets that Elias must come again before the Messiah. He did come in spirit and power, not in person, but as the stern, fearless, upright reformer of the wilderness of Jordan. In the same sense Ezekiel speaks (chap. 37:12-14) of the return of the captive Jews to their own land: 'I *will open your graves,* oh my peoples, and cause you *to come up out of your graves,* and bring you into the land of Israel.' When Martin Luther was engaged in deadly struggle with the Papacy, Pope Adrian sent a brief to the German Diet at Nuremburg, which contained these words: *'The heretics Huss and Jerome are now alive again in the person of Martin Luther'"* (B.W. Johnson, *The People's New Testament With Notes,* page 496.)

leaves His throne in the heavens and returns, all enemies will have been conquered. Never again will they rise in rebellion. (See Psalm 110:1; Acts 2:34,35; 1 Corinthians 15:24-26, for a threefold cord is not easily broken.) What we have here is the start of Satan's final apostasy. I don't pretend to be able to define it for you. The ages to come will record these events with great accuracy, just as we are able to record the events of the Seals, Trumpets, and first five Vials. However, other prophets have given us some insight.

Gog And Magog: This is the same struggle seen by the prophet Ezekiel in Chapter 38 of his prophecy just prior to his vision of the temple. However, here in the Book of Revelation, John sees this struggle just prior to his vision of New Jerusalem! Both visions reveal the devastation wrought by this final assault and the resulting victory of Christ *through His People!* (See 2 Thessalonians 1:7-10.) It is not my desire to try to explain who Gog and Magog are in this work. I don't believe it is necessary.

The Lake Of Fire And Brimstone: A seething metaphor for the final abode of Satan and his fallen angels. Jude declared, *"And the angels which kept not their first estate, but left their own habitation, he hath reserved in everlasting chains under darkness unto the judgment of the great day"* (v.6).

THE JUDGEMENT OF THE WICKED

11 And I saw a great white throne, and Him that sat on it, from whose face the earth and the heaven fled away; and there was found no place for them.

12 And I saw the dead, small and great, stand before God; and the books were opened: and another book was opened, which is the book of life: and the dead were judged out of those things which were written in the books, according to their works.

13 And the sea gave up the dead which were in it; and death
and hell delivered up the dead which were in them: and they
were judged every man according to their works.
14 And death and hell were cast into the lake of fire This is the
second death.
15 And whosoever was not found written in the book of life was
cast into the lake of fire.

Be not deceived, my friend, the day will come when Christ will gather all the nations and judge them according to how they have dealt with Israel, the true Israel and its Church. Jesus Himself taught concerning this coming great and terrible day. He warned that *"When the Son of man shall come in His glory and all the holy angels with Him, then shall He sit upon the throne of His glory: And before Him shall be gathered all nations: and He shall separate them one from another, as a shepherd divideth his sheep from the goats"* (Matthew 25:31,32).[142]

With the gratefully acknowledged help of the late Charles Weston, and his insights on this subject in the *Weston Study Bible,* let's attempt to summarize these powerful five verses.

Evil is destined to persist through the present age in which we live, and then go no further. Jesus made this plain in the Parable of the Wheat and the Tares. He revealed that when this struggle climaxes in a great consummation yet to come, the wicked would be cast into a *"furnace of fire,"* and the righteous would shine forth forever. (See Matthew 13:37-43; 25:31-46.) The fullness of reward will then be manifested. It is hard to presently grasp this event.

---

142   Verses 33-46 of Matthew reveal the context of this judgment. For further insight see, Ro. 14:1-12; Jn. 5:22; Ac. 10:42; 17:31; 2 Pe. 3; Heb. 1:10-12; 12:26-27; 2 Ti. 4:1.

God has clearly revealed the scenario of the Millennium by symbols—an angel, a key, a pit, a great chain and a dragon. For a comprehensive summation examine the content of verses 1-4 closely and compare 6:9-11 (souls) and 12:11 (victory over the dragon). For the thousand years metaphor—compare Deuteronomy 7:9 in a literal context and see what you get. And remember the short time of Chapter 12:12 compared with the little season of verse 3, resulting in an unidentifiable scenario which had already been revealed and interpreted. What am I saying? This entire chapter is portraying a VERY TRYING AGE! An age which ultimately ends in judgment.

Our Lord was enthroned because he overcame Satan. This fact is witnessed in Hebrews 2:14 and in Matthew 12:28-29.[143] Furthermore, Psalm 110:1-4 shows Christ's session which has been overlooked by so many prophetic students. My friend, as surely as God lives, our sovereign Lord, Jesus Christ, will come again only after death is forever destroyed; hence, this millennial passage must be fulfilled in this age before He comes. The Scriptures allow no other interpretation.

Never must any symbol be interpreted so as to alter, transgress, or go beyond the clear teaching of Christ or the apostles as developed in the Gospels, the Acts, or the Epistles. The Bible sternly warns about such practice.

Some of our brethren have been just so indoctrinated and cannot grasp the truth of the present growing spiritual Kingdom of Christ. Unfortunately, great schisms have arisen from whether we take Revelation 20 literally or not. The context cannot be literal.

Nevertheless, the divine inspiration sheds its light upon those whose sad lot it is to be consigned to the *"lake of fire."* Theirs is a terrible fate. There is a second death.

---

143   Compare with Rev. 3:21; Ac. 2:22-36; Eph. 1:19-23. Clear victory and enthronement.

REVELATION CHAPTER 21
THE NEW JERUSALEM

*"But ye are come unto mount Zion, and unto the city of the living God, the **heavenly Jerusalem**, and to an innumerable company of angels."*

Hebrews 12:22

*"But the **Jerusalem which is from above** is free, which is the mother of us all."*

Galatians 4:26

The vision of Chapter 21 is beautifully poetic and emblematic; it is elevating and an appropriate conclusion to the Book of Revelation and the entire canon of Scripture. In its context, the Church is admonished to grasp what lies ahead as a result of this glorious redemption we have part in. It reveals the wonderful termination of all the heartbreaking struggles which have ensued the redeemed of Israel and the saved all over the world over the centuries. It promises to bring us to a bliss more encompassing than Eden. When understood, this vision should calm down all anxiety and instill confidence in our Lord's plan of salvation. As a result of the vision, John cried, "Come, Lord Jesus!"

> *1 And I saw a new heaven and a new earth: for the first heaven and the first earth were passed away; and there was no more sea.*

Just as we have become a new creation in Christ, yet we remain in the same body, so likewise is the metaphor for the removal of the curse and the total restoration of all things. The earth will appear as new. John did not witness total annihilation, but as we will see, Christ Himself stated that He*"makes all things new"* (v.5). Notice that He did not mention anything about recreation, instead, the intent is *regeneration.* A simple look at the word "new" and the picture is clarified. The word selected by John was not *neos* (sequential newness) but *kainos* (of superior quality).[144]

No More Sea: What could this mean? I really don't know. Some suggest that the vast areas of the earth which are presently occupied by the oceans will one day become inhabitable. Others allude to the metaphorical intent and see, in context with the future blessedness of the righteous, no more wasted areas, a totally redeemed and occupied earth.

> *2 And I John saw the holy city, new Jerusalem, coming down from God out of heaven, prepared as a bride adorned for her husband.*

Ephesians Chapter 2

> *19 Now therefore ye are no more strangers and foreigners, but fellowcitizens with the saints, and of the household of God;*
> *20 And are built upon the foundation of the apostles and prophets, Jesus Christ himself being the chief corner stone;*
> *21 In whom all the building fitly framed together groweth unto an holy temple in the Lord:*

There is no other *"new Jerusalem"* than that which we have already attained to in Christ (proof texts: Galatians 4:26; Hebrews 12:22). What John is metaphorically describing is the Bride of Christ true Israel in her ultimate authority and maturity. Albert Barnes commented:

---

144   The reader is urged to read Isaiah's discourse, Chapter 65, verses 17-25, to further grasp the Biblical concept of regeneration.

This, of course, does not mean that this great city was literally to descend upon the earth, and to occupy any one part of the renovated world; but it is a symbolical or figurative representation, designed to show that the abode of the righteous will be splendid and glorious. The idea of a city literally descending from heaven, and being set upon the earth with such proportions—three hundred and seventy miles high (v. 16), made of gold, and with single pearls for gates, and single gems for the foundations—**is absurd. No man can suppose that this is literally true** [emphasis mine]...[145]

Our friend fortunately didn't live to see present day dispensationalism's ignorance gone to seed. Oh, what error is upon our fellow brethren who have been so deceived![146]

I once attended a conference on Bible prophecy, and I am going to give you an example of just how ridiculous futuristic interpretation has become. By the time the teachers had gotten to the subject of the new Jerusalem, my blood was already boiling. Even so, what I was about to witness topped it all. An esteemed and aged minister began to expound. He said words to this effect: "I see the Book of Revelation picturing for us new Jerusalem hovering over the earth, and not descending all the way down." Now he was promptly questioned by one of the attending ministers. "Brother, how then will Christ and the redeemed communicate with the inhabitants of the earth?" Our esteemed, but yet confused brother responded, "Well you see, they will com-

---

145   AJbert Barnes, *Barnes' Notes,* "Revelation," page 443.

146   Chilton observed: "Unfortunately, the almost exclusively futuristic interpretation of such passages in the recent past-and the accompanying neoplatonic outlook, as if to say that it is useless and even sinful to work for the 'heavenization' of this world-has meant that a proper emphasis on the present reality of the Kingdom appears to reverse the movement of the New Testament. Where the Bible says: 'Not in this age only, but also in the age to come,' our zeal to recover the biblical perspective sometimes leads us to say: 'Not in the age to come only, but also in this age.' The danger in this, obviously, is that it can produce contempt for a truly biblical eschatology." David Chilton, *The Days of Vengeance,* page 645.

municate through telepathic communication!" Need I say more. This was a typical example of the fruit of literalist prophetic interpretation.

> *3 And I heard a great voice out of heaven saying, Behold, the tabernacle of God is with men, and He will dwell with them, and they shall be His people, and God Himself shall be with them, and be their God.*
>
> *4 And God shall wipe away all tears from their eyes; and there shall be no more death, neither sorrow, nor crying, neither shall there be any more pain: for the former things are passed away.*
>
> *5 And He that sat upon the throne said, Behold, I make all things new. And He said unto me, Write: for these words are true and faithful.*
>
> *6 And He said unto me, It is done. I am Alpha and Omega, the beginning and the end: I will give unto him that is athirst of the fountain of water of life freely.*
>
> *7 He that overcometh shall inherit all things: and I will be his God, and he shall be My son.*
>
> *8 But the fearful, and unbelieving, and the abominable, and murderers, and whoremongers, and sorcerers, and idolaters, and all liars, shall have their part in the lake which burneth with fire and brimstone; which is the second death.*

The preceding language gives room for an infinite number of revelations and applications. The command to *"write"* is given only three times in this book, in addition to the messages to the seven churches in Chapters 2 and 3. It denotes a capsulating emphasis upon the credibility of the pronouncement. Our God demands we understand that His promises are *"true and faithful."*

I feel that it is important to elaborate on one point - "the *fearful.*" The Scriptures reveal a fear that has a torment. This type of fear is being addressed. The use of the word *"fearful"* by John has caused some to be highly troubled by their own experiences of fear. I'm talking about the fear a Christian experiences. Don't tell me you haven't experienced fear. Therefore, I believe it is good to inquire as to what type of fear is meant.

Many fear their own weakness, or the power of strong temptation, or of falling aside and coming short of the mark. Interestingly enough, this type of fear can cause one to run to the Lord. But I believe that it is the fear associated with unbelief, a fear of the opinions and opposition of the world, a fear to put your trust in God and walk by faith according to His promises, a fear that He will not be able to perform as He did in the Scriptures. This attitude is most dishonoring to Christ. Isaiah stated, *"Hearken unto me, ye that know righteousness, the people in whose heart is My law; fear ye not the reproach of men, neither be ye afraid of their revilings"* (Isaiah 51:7). This is the fear which will be judged in the resurrection of the dead. This is the fear which will have a part in the lake of fire and taste of the second death.

> *9 And there came unto me one of the seven angels which had the seven vials full of the seven last plagues, and talked with me, saying, Come hither, I will show thee the bride, the Lamb's wife.*
> *10 And he carried me away in the spirit to a great and high mountain, and showed me that great city, the holy Jerusalem, descending out of heaven from God,*
> *11 Having the glory of God: and her light was like unto a stone most precious, even like a jasper stone, clear as crystal;*

Now, the angel shows John Zion in a state of glorification. The stones which are used are symbolic of Israel "reflecting" the glory of God. It's just that simple. For example, in Revelation 4:3 we saw a vision of Christ upon His throne, *"and He that sat was to look upon like a jasper…"* Here we have the Kingdom seen as a jasper stone resplendent with His majesty.

A Great And High Mountain: The prophecy of Daniel 2:35 is now fulfilled. *"THE STONE [KINGDOM] THAT SMOTE THE IMAGE BECAME A GREAT MOUNTAIN, AND FILLED THE WHOLE EARTH!"*

> *12 And had a wall great and high, and had twelve gates, and at the gates twelve angels, and names written thereon, which are the names of the **twelve tribes of the children of Israel.***
> *13 On the east, three gates; on the north, three gates; on the south, three gates; and on the west, three gates.*
> *14 And the wall of the city had twelve foundations and in them the names of the twelve apostles of the Lamb.*

These verses need little expounding. The Gospels reveal that Christ laid the foundation of His Kingdom upon His twelve apostles (see Ephesians 2:20). This structure is to grow until the building is *"fitly framed together [and] groweth into a holy temple in the Lord"* (v.21). When it stands perfected, its *"gates"* will always be open to those who are willing to pass through.

> *15 And he that talked with me had a golden reed to measure the city, and the gates thereof and the wall thereof*
> *16 And the city lieth foursquare, and the length is as large as the breadth: and he measured the city with the reed, twelve thousand, furlongs. The length and the breadth and the height of it are equal.*
> *17 And he measured the wall thereof, a hundred and forty and four cubits, according to the measure of a man, that is, of the angel.*

God showed the prophet Amos a vision of a plumbline and inquired of him *"Amos, what seest thou?"* Amos responded, *"A plumbline."* Then the Lord said, *"Behold, I will set a plumbline in the midst of My people Israel"* (Amos 7:8). The purpose of this plumbline was to test or, "measure" the faith of Israel. In Revelation 11:2 we saw an angel bring forth a measuring reed, but was restricted from measuring the "Court of the Gentiles," or the false Roman church. Now the golden reed appears again to measure the true Israel, the true Kingdom. It has been fully calibrated and is now a perfect structure (Ezekiel's temple, Chapters 40-48). Its dimensions are symbolized by the number "twelve," the number of *completion* and *government*. The House of Israel has matured so that *"the nations of them which are saved"* (NOTICE: THERE ARE STILL NATIONS AFTER THE **MILLENNIUM!**), and the *"kings of the earth"* (v.24) can be guided in righteousness-forever! (See Daniel 7:18.)

> *18 And the building of the wall of it was of jasper: and the city was pure gold, like unto clear glass.*
>
> *19 And the foundations of the wall of the city were garnished with all manner of precious stones. The first foundation was jasper; the second, sapphire; the third, a chalcedony; the fourth, an emerald;*
>
> *20 The fifth, sardonyx; the sixth, sardius; the seventh, chrysolyte; the eighth, beryl; the ninth, a topaz; the tenth, a chrysoprasus; the eleventh, a jacinth; the twelfth, an amethyst.*
>
> *21 And the twelve gates were twelve pearls; every several gate was of one pearl: and the street of the city was pure gold, as it were transparent glass.*

These verses further complement those of the prophet Isaiah, who like John, saw the ultimate glorification of the Kingdom of God, and likened it to precious stones. He stated: *"I will lay thy stones with fair colors, and lay thy foundations with sapphires, and I will make thy windows of agates, and thy gates of carbuncles, and all thy borders of pleasant stones. And all thy children shall be taught of the Lord; and great shall be the peace of thy children"* (Isaiah 54:11-14).

This is also a picture of the Old Testament High Priest's breastplate. Upon it were twelve precious stones which represented the twelve tribes of Israel. Now they are represented by the glorious stones of this strong and high city.

> *22 And I saw no temple therein: for the Lord God Almighty and the Lamb are the temple of it.*
> *23 And the city had no need of the sun, neither of the moon, to shine in it: for the glory of God did lighten it, and the Lamb is the Light thereof.*

I Saw No Temple Therein: Reconcile that statement with dispensationalist "literal rebuilt temple" theology!

Let's don't miss something special here. Notice that the end of governmental authority (sun and moon) of verse 23 relates to the city, *not to the nations.* John informed us that there will be no need of the five-fold ministry in this city because the saints are now fully equipped. (Reference "till" or "until" in Eph. 4:13.) Furthermore, the nations *yet to be guided* by this city still have their kings (v. 24). This is not a mystery; it's a revelation.

THE NATIONS ARE BLESSED

24 And the nations of them which are saved shall walk in the light of it: and the kings of the earth do bring their glory and honor into it.

25 And the gates of it shall not be shut at all by day: for there shall be no night there.

26 And they shall bring the glory and honor of the nations into it.

I have already brought to your attention that there are still *"nations"* or various peoples functioning on this earth at this point in the Book of Revelation. God enjoys the diversity of nations. These great symbolic prophecies are not for the ethereal beyond, but rather for the ages to come on this earth in which we live.

The prophet Micah gave us a foretelling of this time yet to come in the Kingdom when *"many nations shall come, and shall say, Come, and let us, go up to the mountain of the Lord and to the house of the* **God of Jacob;** *and He will teach us of His ways, and we will walk in His paths"* (Micah 4:2).

This vision was also revealed to Isaiah, in which the Holy Spirit wrote, saying: *"Lift up thine eyes round about, and behold: all these gather themselves together, and come to thee. As I live, saith the Lord, thou shalt surely clothe thee with them all, as with an ornament, and bind them on thee as a bride doeth"* (Isaiah 49:18; see also Isaiah 60:5,6,9,11).

Chilton, in quoting William Symington, raises a serious question about present day attitudes concerning the separation of church and state. Symington stated:

The prophecy [see Isa. 49:22,23) refers to New Testament times, when the Gentiles are to be gathered unto the Redeemer. A prominent feature of these times shall be the subserviency of civil rulers to the Church, which surely supposes their subjection to Christ her Head. *Kings shall be thy nursing fathers* is a similitude which imparts the most tender care, the most enduring solicitude; not mere protection, but active and unwearied nourishment and support. If, according to the opinions of some, the best thing the state can do for the Church is to let her alone, to leave her to herself, to take no interest in her concerns, it is difficult to see how this view can be reconciled with the figure of a nurse, the duties of whose office would certainly be ill discharged by such a treatment of her feeble charge.[147]

The point raised by Chilton and Symington are critical issues that the Body of Christ presently wrestles with. I am sure the struggle will intensify; however, the Book of Revelation, coupled with th visions of the other prophets, assures us that the struggle will consummate in the proper structure and relationship between Church and state, which will endure forever. Our present insanity is temporal. Take courage.

> *27 And there shall in no wise enter into it any thing that defileth, neither whatsoever worketh abomination, or maketh a lie: but they which are written in the Lamb's book of life.*

The wheat and the tares have forever been separated.

---

147   David Chilton, *The Days if Vengeance*, page 563.

REVELATION CHAPTER 22
NEW JERUSALEM (CONTINUED)
EPILOGUE

1 And he showed me a pure river of water of life, clear as crystal, proceeding out of the throne of God and of the Lamb.

2 In the midst of the street of it, and on either side of the river, was there the tree of life, which bare twelve manner of fruits, and yielded her fruit every month: and the leaves of the tree were for the healing of the nations.

3 And there shall be no more curse: but the throne of God and of the Lamb shall be in it; and His servants shall serve Him.

4 And they shall see His face; and His name shall be in their foreheads.

5 And there shall be no night there: and they need no candle, neither light of the sun; for the Lord God giveth them light: and they shall reign for ever and ever.

The Bible was divided into chapters by Stephen Langton about A.D. 1288. In the 15th and 16th centuries the Scriptures were divided into verses.[148] This has been both a blessing and a curse. What Stephen Langton was thinking about when he separated the 21st and the 22nd chapters of the Book of Revelation is beyond me. It should again warn us about having textual teachings distorted by the inaccurate separation of chapters and verses. It is evident that the first five verses of Chapter 22 are the continuing vision and description of new Jerusalem.

---

148   1 The Old Testament was divided into verses by R. Nathan in A.D. 1448 and the New Testament by Robert Stephanus in A.D. 1551. The first Bible divided into chapters and verses was the Geneva Bible which appeared in 1560.

A Pure River Of Water Of Life: We are reminded of the Garden of Eden (Genesis 2:6) and its river which ascended from the midst of beautiful springs and parted in four directions for the purpose of watering the rest of the earth (Genesis 2:10-14). Likewise, Ezekiel revealed this great river which proceeds forth from this new covenant temple. It was measured to perfection, and its purpose was to see that *"everything will live where the river goes."* (See Ezekiel 47:1-9.)

On Either Side Of The River, Was There The Tree Of Life: John told us that this tree was not limited to seasons, but yields its fruit *"every month."* Furthermore, Ezekiel revealed to us that there are more than two symbolic trees; he stated that *"at the banks of the river were very many trees on the one side and on the other!"* (Ezekiel 47:7)

Healing Of The Nations: Again, John informed us that "nations" are still active and relevant before God. There will always be nations upon this earth—according to the Scriptures.

There Shall Be No More Curse: The curse came to those in the Garden of Eden because of sin. There will be no sin present in New Jerusalem, therefore the curse and its pain will never enter. It is because of transgression that the human heart anguishes; that the human body travails; and that the human mind fears. These terrible things will have no part of that great celestial city.

His Name Shall Be In Their Foreheads: It never ceases to amaze me how the futurists demand a literal fulfillment of the mark of the beast (Revelation 13:16), yet they admit that this is symbolic. All that the angel is saying is that it will always be known that these are Christ's people.

No Night...No Candle, Neither Light: At last, Isaiah's vision of the Church militant transformed into the church triumphant has come to pass:

Arise, shine; for thy light is come, and the glory of the Lord is risen upon thee. For behold, the darkness shall cover the earth, and gross darkness the people: but the Lord shall arise upon thee, and His glory shall be seen upon thee. And the Gentiles shall come to thy light, and the kings to the brightness of thy risings (Isaiah 60:1-3).

They Shall Reign For Ever And For Ever: There is no end to the reign of the righteous upon this earth. This is what the prophet Daniel revealed. (See Daniel 2:44; 7:14,18.)

THE EPILOGE

6 And he said unto me, These sayings are faithful and true. And the Lord God of the holy prophets sent His angel to show unto His servants the things which must shortly be done.

7 Behold, I come quickly: blessed is he that keepeth the sayings of the prophecy of this book.

8 And I John saw these things, and heard them. And when I had heard and seen, I fell down to worship before the feet of the angel which shewed me these things.

9 Then saith he unto me, See thou do it not: for I am thy fellow-servant, and of thy brethren the prophets, and of them which keep the sayings of this book: worship God.

10 And he saith unto me, Seal not the sayings of this prophecy of this book; for the time is at hand.

11 He that is unjust, let him be unjust still: and he which is filthy, let him be filthy still: and he that is righteous, let him be righteous still: and he that is holy, let him be holy still.

12 And, behold, I come quickly; and My reward is with me, to give every man according as his work shall be.

13 I am Alpha and Omega, the beginning and the end, the first and the last.

14 Blessed are they that do His commandments, that they may have right to the tree of life, and may enter in through the gates into the city.

15 For without are dogs, and sorcerers, and whoremongers, and murderers, and idolaters, and whosoever loveth and maketh a lie.

16 I, Jesus, have sent Mine angel to testify unto you these things in the churches. I am the root and the offspring of David, and the bright and morning star.

17 And the Spirit and the bride say, Come. And let him that heareth say, Come. And let him that is a thirst come. And whosoever will, let him take the water of life freely.

18 For I testify unto every man that heareth the words of the prophecy of this book, If any man shall add unto these things, God shall add unto him the plagues that are written in this book:

19 And if any man shall take away from the words of the book of this prophecy, God shall take away his part out of the hook of life, and out of the holy city, and from the things which are written in this book.

20 He which testifieth these things saith, Surely I come quickly. Amen. Even so, come, Lord Jesus.

21 The grace of our Lord Jesus Christ be with you all. Amen

What a magnificent prophesied conclusion to the eternal affairs of man.

MODERN "PATHETIC" INTERPRETATIONS
(A SAMPLING OF LEARNED RESPONSES TO THE DECEPTIONS OF RIBERA AND ALCAZAR)

What a journey we have taken together. I realize that if this was your initial introduction to the **historicist interpretation** of Bible prophecy, you are probably in a mild state of shock. I don't need to systematically expound to you the implications of what has been written because they are too numerous to define. Others, I'm sure, will undertake that task from various perspectives. I have simply challenged several empires of superstition and presented the truth not I, but Christ in me. So be it.

I would encourage you to go back and again read **"Fox's Overview."** It will help the information presented become an outline in your heart. Don't worry, your head will catch up in due season. Reformations are destined to hurt the brain, but yet make the heart leap. So be it.

The judgments of the following learned theologians and historical scholars provide a sample of the fury which will again bring the Body of Christ into remembrance. Simply stated, the **futuristic** interpretation of Bible prophecy was birthed by the **Jesuit Ribera** for the purpose of countering the Protestant Reformation and protecting the papacy. It was designed to destroy what true Christianity stands for. It is the foundation of the modern absurdity called **dispensationalism.** (I know several ministers who enjoy refuting dispensationalism, but yet when it comes to Rome's futurism, they remain silent. In the Marine Corps we had various terms to describe such men. Frankly, I'm not impressed with their limited tactics. Peace if possible, but truth at all costs!)

About 30 years later the **preterist** interpretation of Bible prophecy was birthed by the **Jesuit Alcazar.** He sought to relieve the papacy of the stigma of Antichrist by perverting the interpretation of the Book of Revelation. Let's examine the weighty and courageous judgments put upon Rome's eschatology by true scholars in Christ's militant and violent kingdom. Much of this information will be extracted from Baron Porcelli's powerful book, *The Antichrist:*

"The learned Rev. C.H.H. Wright, D.D., in his *Daniel and his Prophecies* (Williams and Norgate, 1906, p. 14) says: 'The Futuristic School of prophetical interpretation has been, to no small degree, responsible for the success which has attended the modem onslaught on the credibility of the prophecies of the Old and New Testament Scriptures. The interpreters of that narrow school of thought, however, imagine themselves to be the only real defenders of Holy Scripture. The origin of that school, in its modem phase, may be traced back to Ribera, a distinguished Jesuit expositor (1585), and to the other remarkable Jesuit interpreters of the seventeenth century. Futurist views of prophecy, as was natural, were soon accepted by the theologians of the High Church School, and were also caught up by many popular preachers of the Evangelical party in the National Church. The interest, however, in prophetical studies, did not long continue to be a general characteristic of the High Church party, but their prophetical views spread among writers of the so-called "Plymouth Brethren." Most of their leaders wrote on prophecy, and all more or less in support of Futuristic views. *A craving after sensationalism* is a marked characteristic of many of the writers of the Futuristic school. The book of Daniel itself ought to have acted as a warning against their fantastic views of the imaginary Antichrist of the latter days...*these are idle dreams of men imperfectly acquainted with the prophecies.*' "

Porcelli notes, "That it must be remembered that Dr. Wright was a great scholar, learned in Hebrew and Greek, and therefore competent to pass judgment on such uncautious and wild writers as those he criticises..."

Dr. Wright went on to state: " 'The Antichrist' and, 'the deceiver' has been working in the Church since St. John's days (2 Jn. 7). The outward and visible Church very soon began to wrap earthwoven robes around her, and to dream of 'infallibility', all the while that she abounded with false doctrines, and had departed widely from the *faith once for all delivered to the Saints.*' Outside the Church there is no Antichrist, in the biblical sense of the term; inside the Church that evil power has sat for nearly 2,000 years as 'God in the temple of God.'

"The attempt to interpret Old and New Testament prophecies *literally,* as these writers term it, led the Futurists into conclusions which, as Professor Birks of Cambridge, long ago stated, **tended to undermine the foundations of all Christian evidences.** [emphasis mine]. That learned writer noted that their reasonings and principles were more incredulous than those of the infidel, and asserted that, when such opinions gained general currency and approval in the Church, the reign of open infidelity would be at hand."[149]

Dr. Wright went on to firmly criticize the modern Futurists by calling them "ultra liberals" who were *"doing as much damage to God's Word* as the critics whom they regard as the precursors of Antichrist."

And finally, on page 239 of his work, he says: "The mistakes ... may be traced up to the false schools of exegesis, in which they were trained, and have been mainly due to their desire to predict a future quite outside the horizon of the prophecy. There is not a line in the prophecy [seventy weeks of Daniel 9) concerning the 'Antichrist,' of whom the Fathers wrote so fantastically."

Another eminent and scholarly author, the Rev. E.B. Elliott, who gave us the massive *Horae Apocalypticae,* the most able examination and commentary on the Apocalypse written, has added a "Critical Examina-

---

149   This statement was made about 1841, in Dr. Wright's book on the *First Elements of Sacred Prophecy.*

tion and Refutation of the Three Chief Counter-Schemes of Apocalyptic Interpretation"-the German Praeterist, the Futurist, and the "Church Scheme." Of the second, (futurism) he states: "The Futurists' is the *Second* grand Anti-Protestant Apocalyptic scheme. I might perhaps have thought it sufficient to refer to Mr. Birk's masterly work in refutation of it, but for the consideration that my own would be incomplete without some such examination of this Futurist scheme... The Futurist scheme was first, or nearly first, propounded about 1590 by the Jesuit Ribera, as the fittest one whereby to turn aside the Protestant application of the Apocalyptic prophecy from the Church of Rome. In England and Ireland, of late years, it has been brought into vogue chiefly by Mr. Maitland and Mr. Burgh; followed by Mr. Newman, in some of the Oxford Tracts on Antichrist. Its general characteristic is to view the whole Apocalypse... as a representation of the events of the consummation and Second Advent all still future; literal Israel; literal days; and the Antichrist.... a personal infidel to reign for just three and a half years." ... "A great advantage that they have over the Praeterists" is "that instead of being in any measure chained down by the facts of history, *they can draw on the unlimited powers of fancy, wherewith to devise in the dreaming future whatever may seem to them to fit the sacred prophecy.*"[150]

Mr. Elliott's work triumphantly shows the absurdity of every facet of Ribera's theology. He shows "the insuperable difficulties attending the Futurist scheme," how it "sets language, grammar and context at defiance"; how "inconsistency" marks it from beginning to end; how erroneous is their conception of Antichrist; how self contradictory and illogical; how opposed to History, Scripture and the Ancient Fathers is the Futurist view of the religion of Antichrist; and "that it is not merely unaccordant with the Apocalyptic and the other cognate prophecies of Antichrist but that it is, even intellectually speaking, a mere rude and commonplace concep-

---

150   *Horae Apocalypticae*, Vol. IV., page 506.

tion of Satan's predicted masterpiece of opposition to Christ, compared with what has been actually realised and established in the Papacy." "The Papal system is beyond anything that the Futurists have imagined, or ever can imagine, the very perfection of Anti-Christianism."

Professor T. R. Birks, who is often referenced by the great scholars, commented on the dangers of Futurism in his "First Elements of Sacred Prophecy," after enumerating the "maxims in the interpretation of the sacred prophecies generally received hy the Protestant Churches, ever since the time of the Reformation," adds "all of these maxims, however, without distinction, have been rejected by several late [Futurist] writers ... Burgh, Maitland, Todd, Dodsworth, Tyso... etc. [Today the list would include, Lindsey, Jeffery, Sutton, Van Impe, Pentecost, Taylor, Walvoord, Kirban, LaHaye,...] They agree in few points, except in rejecting the conclusions of all previous expositors and maintain that nearly the whole of Daniel's prophecies and of the Apocalypse are *unfulfilled. Now, if the theories of these writers are entirely groundless, the responsibility which they have incurred is very great, and the effects of their error may prove extremely fatal to the Church.* The strongest bulwark against the revived zeal of the Romish Church will have been taken away when it is most needed; and the danger of a renewed apostasy will have been fearfully increased... A spirit of feverish and sceptical doubt... will have been injected, without warrant, into the minds of thousands; **the light which the Word of God has thrown on half the whole period of the Church's history, will have been quenched in darkness;** and her hopes for the future, by a perplexed and fallacious application of irrelevant prophecies, be involved in a *chaos of fanciful conjectures* and *inextricable confusion.*"

Porcelli further expounded on Mr. Birks' analysis of the Futurist system: "Mr. Birks, by a careful analysis of the statements of the above-mentioned Futurists, demonstrates incontrovertibly their 'rashness,' 'emptiness,' their 'groundless,' 'untrue' attacks upon Protestant expositors of note, their 'gross absurdity,' which 'directly contradict the early writers'; their 'irrelevance,' 'inconsistency' 'self contradictions,' 'illogicality'; their 'bold inversion of facts,' 'willful perversions of Scripture;' and, finally, 'the view of the Futurists brings down the servants of God in every age to the level of the unbelievers... and, by a wretched alchemy, turns all their most patient and prayerful researches into one pile oflaborious blunders. This reason alone, with every thoughtful Christian, should be enough to convict their [Futurist] system, as a system of utter falsehood.' "

The late Dr. H. Grattan Guinness, in his *Approaching End of the Age* said: "The Futurist view is that which teaches that the prophetic visions of Revelation, from chapters iv to xix, prefigure events still wholly future, and not to take place till just at the close of this dispensation. It supposes 'an instant plunge of the Apocalyptic prophecy into the distant future of the consummation.' This view gives the literal Israel a large place in the Apocalypse, and expects a solitary infidel Antichrist, who shall bitterly oppress the saints for three and a half years, near the date of the Second Advent, thus interpreting time as well as much else in the Apocalypse, *literally.* In its present form it may be said to have originated at the end of the sixteenth century with the Jesuit Ribera, who, moved like Alcazar to relieve the Papacy from the terrible stigma cast upon it by the Protestant interpretation, and tried to do so by referring these prophecies to the distant *future*, instead of, like Alcazar, to the distant past. It is held under a great variety of modifications, no two writers agreeing as to what the symbols do prefigure ... The Futurist view denies progressive revelation..."

Dr. Guinness replies to various Futurist attacks upon his work: "The critic who undertakes to reply to a work of this character should at least be accurate in his statements of the views he opposes. The author... spends most of his strength in commenting on confusions which he has himself created… Futurist critics are an enigma… They cannot deny or be blind to certain grand historical facts … yet they deny that the symbols foretell the facts… though Futurists admit how exactly the symbols of prophecy answer to these facts… and they *assert—what, of course, can neither be proved nor disproved—"that* they foretell other future events!"

"Not only by this writer, but by all writers of the Futurist School, are these supposed future acts of the supposed future Antichrist largely discussed and gravely insisted on. Few would surmise how frail the foundation on which this cardinal doctrine that Antichrist is to make a covenant with the Jews rests. Few would suppose that the notion has really *no solid ground at all in Scripture,* but is derived from an erroneous interpretation of one single clause of one single text … Daniel 9:27 … *one of the gravest evils of Futurism is the terrible way in which it tampers with this great fundamental prophecy, applying to … Antichrist its Divine description of… Christ.*"

Referring to another futurist critic, sir Robert Anderson, and his work *The Coming Prince, the Last Great Monarch of Christendom,* Dr. Guinness remarked: "The title is a combination of error and assumption … 'The Coming Prince'—intended as it is for a quotation from Daniel 9:26—is an erroneous citation, for there is no definite article in the Hebrew. The book…is marred by error and assumption, as well as by rash statements and wild speculations… So close and accurate is the correspondence of history with prophecy (in the division of the Roman earth into ten kingdoms) that … this writer himself perceives it, while he denies it…"

"The monstrous 'gap' theory of the Futurist School is maintained in the most dogmatic way by Dr. Anderson, who makes the strangely false assertion that 'all Christian interpreters are agreed in it' … 'the entire Historic School of Protestant interpreters … would utterly and unhesitatingly reject such an interpretation as offensive to common sense, and doing violence to the oracles of God.'" "The Futurist Theory, which confines the evil career … of Antichrist to a period *subsequent* to the destruction of Babylon by the ten horns must be erroneous…" "Futurists are obliged to admit that the Babylon of Revelation 17 is the Apostate Church of Rome. They cannot, moreover, question that the Church of Rome has endured for twelve or thirteen centuries. The great Anti-Christian persecution takes place during the reign of Babylon, not after her destruction. That destruction is followed, not by that great Anti-Christian persecution, but by the Marriage of the Lamb (Rev. 19)." "If the ten kingdoms have existed for the last thirteen or fourteen centuries, so has the Antichrist, for he is their contemporary; and Futurism falls to the ground."

"To conclude: The Futurist conception of Antichrist as an openly-avowed Atheist, and infidel King, who will oppose all religion and morality, and set himself in direct and daring opposition to Christ, is, to say the best of it, an unutterably poor and low conception, even intellectually, compared to the great and terrible reality!"

"The last authority to be cited is the late Dr. M. O'Sullivan, whose, *Of the Apostasy Predicted by St. Paul,* published in 1842, is by far the most cautious, careful and erudite analysis of Scriptures known to me [Porcelli]. It possesses also the merit of critically examining the Futurist theories of Dr. Todd and other writers of that school. Its extensive knowledge of Greek, of Scripture, and of prophecy, establishes it as a monument of learning, and fidelity to the test. Now what is the view of this elaborate commentary? It simply annihilates, though most courteously, the Futurist perversions of Scripture, which do duty for interpretations of prophecy. With great patience, and infinite care, it shows how 'conjecture as to the interpretation of a prophecy' is miscalled 'consideration of the true meaning' of such terms as 'apostasy'; how mere 'opinions' are twisted into *'authority'* to determine the meaning of terms. Take, for instance, the phrase, 'Temple of God,' which Dr. Todd and other Futurists—in spite of admissions that 'a modem Christian might very well understand the Church of Christ'—persist in regarding literally of some still future earthly building, in which a solitary Antichrist is to sit. Dr. O'Sullivan patiently investigates past solutions and Futurist assumptions, pointing out objections, difficulties, inconsistencies fallacies, contradictions, and confusion between 'literal' and 'material,' between apostolic usage of terms and Futurist misuse of them. He cites McKnight on the Epistles: 'It is an observation of Bochart, that after the death of Christ, the Apostles never called the temple of Jerusalem the temple of God, but as often as they used that phrase they meant the Christian Church (I Tim. 3:15; I Cor. 3:16; 6:19; II Cor. 6:16; Eph. 2:19,24). Besides, in the Revelation of St. John, which was written some years after the destruction of Jerusalem, there is mention made of men's 'becoming pillars in the Temple of God' (Rev. 3:12). "Hence, it is evident that the 'sitting of the man of sin in the Temple of God' *by no means implies that he was to show himself in Judea.*"

This has been but a sampling of scholastic Protestant fury towards the abominations of the futurist and preterist counter schemes. If men would once again open their history books they would see immediately the origins of these calculated deceptions. Yet, today, prophecy teachers are, for the most part, totally ignorant of the origins of their doctrines. And look at how much damage has been done. We were warned, and we heeded it not. Therefore, we are eating the bitter fruit of dispensationalist theology. But my friends, these counter schemes are food for us indeed.

We do not need an army to defeat this terrible enemy of the gospel of the Kingdom. No, my friend, all we need is for a few men and women with the courage of Luther to arise and challenge these illegitimate theologies. They will come down. In doing so, we will wrap ourselves in the mantle of spiritual violence, a mantle that Christ said would be necessary to establish the truth of his kingdom.

"I HAVE SWORN ETERNAL HOSTILITY TO THAT WHICH HOLDS THE MINDS OF MEN CAPTIVE!" In doing so, I walk the path that Christ and his apostles took. I invite you to join me.

"Peace if possible, but truth at all costs."[151]

---

151   For further qualified reactions to the writings of Ribera and Alcazar, I refer you to my book, *Seventy Weeks: The Historical Alternative,* chapter entitled "The Jesuits."

23538150R00192

Printed in Poland
by Amazon Fulfillment
Poland Sp. z o.o., Wrocław